CARSTAIRS

CARSTAIRS
HOSPITAL FOR HORRORS

DAVID LESLIE

BLACK & WHITE PUBLISHING

First published 2015
by Black & White Publishing Ltd
29 Ocean Drive, Edinburgh EH6 6JL

1 3 5 7 9 10 8 6 4 2   15 16 17 18

ISBN   978 1 84502 998 2

Copyright © David Leslie 2015

The right of David Leslie to be identified as the author of this work has been asserted by him in accordance with the Copyright, Designs and Patents Act 1988.

All rights reserved. No part of this publication may be reproduced, stored in a retrieval system, or transmitted in any form, or by any means, electronic, mechanical, photocopying, recording or otherwise, without permission in writing from the publisher.

The publisher has made every reasonable effort to contact copyright holders of images in this book. Any errors are inadvertent and anyone who for any reason has not been contacted is invited to write to the publisher so that a full acknowledgment can be made in subsequent editions of this work.

A CIP catalogue record for this book is available from the British Library.

Typeset by RefineCatch Limited, Bungay, Suffolk
Printed and bound by Gutenberg Press, Malta

Though this be madness, yet there is method in't.

William Shakespeare, *Hamlet*, **Act II**

CONTENTS

ACKNOWLEDGEMENTS		ix
TIMELINE		x
PREFACE		xiii
1	MAD MONEY	1
2	BUYING FREEDOM	11
3	DISAPPOINTMENT IN MARRIAGE	21
4	ESCAPE TO KILL	30
5	SUFFER LITTLE CHILDREN	43
6	ON THE WORD OF THE DEVIL	56
7	GOOD SAMARITAN SLAYER	64
8	BODY IN THE SUITCASE	74
9	CAIN AND ABEL	84
10	THE BOX MAN	89
11	CHILDREN YET UNBORN	96
12	SLIPPING AWAY	104
13	THE PHANTOM	111
14	THE JANITOR'S SECRET	119
15	THE CRACKED MIRROR	125
16	PLAYING TRUANT	134
17	TILL DEATH US DO PART	141
18	VOICES IN MY HEAD	149
19	A MEETING OF DEVILS	157
20	THE SANDWICH MAN	167
21	ANGEL OF DEATH	174
22	MURDERBALL	181

23	THE BIRTH OF HELL	189
24	PERDITION	192
25	AFTERMATH	201
26	A GENTLE MAN	206
27	THE FAMILY MAN	213
28	FREED TO KILL	222
29	FREED TO DIE	231
30	SEX, DRUGS AND BLU-TACK	239
31	ONCE IN, NEVER OUT	248
32	A LOVER OF NUDES	257
33	SMOKING MAD	263

ACKNOWLEDGEMENTS

I am indebted to the staff of the superb Highland Archive Centre in Inverness, in particular Colin Waller, for their help and their courtesy in allowing me access to records of Craig Dunain Hospital.

The *British Journal of Psychiatry* kindly granted me permission to use material from 'A Fifteen-Year Review of Female Admissions to Carstairs State Hospital' by Patrick W. Brooks and Geoffrey Mitchell, which appeared on pages 445–7 in the issue of November 1975 (No. 127).

My sincere thanks go to those former patients of the State Hospital who kindly told me of their experiences at and memories of Carstairs, while requesting anonymity and in one case overcoming great distress at certain recollections.

I am grateful also to Robert Mone, still in the custody of the Scottish Prison Service, for providing a series of statements relating to the incident in 1968 that resulted in his becoming a Carstairs patient, his knowledge of Thomas McCulloch and the events surrounding their escape in 1976. This is the first time that either man has voluntarily made public a precise account of the escape.

TIMELINE

1800   Criminal Lunatics Act gives the sovereign power to order the safe custody of criminal lunatics but makes no provision for the cost of their upkeep.

1855   Doctor David Skae, physician at the Royal Edinburgh Hospital, calls for a single institution to detain criminal lunatics.

1865   Scotland's first criminal lunatic department opens at Perth prison.

1877   A prison service report complains of a lack of accommodation in the lunatic department at Perth.

1933   The first escape from the Perth criminal lunatic department by a female.

1935   The government admits Perth is unsatisfactory and says the question of building a new place to hold criminal lunatics is getting 'active consideration'.

1935   Details are revealed of a Bill authorising the building of the new proposed lunatic asylum at Carstairs.

1937   The government decides it needs Carstairs accommodation for military use, and the facility is used as an army hospital throughout the Second World War.

1941   Seven men escape from Perth criminal lunatic department.

1948   The army no longer require the facility at Carstairs, and it finally opens as the State Institution for Mental Defectives.

1950   Thomas Howie drowns in the River Tay after escaping from Perth criminal lunatic unit.

TIMELINE

1957   Ninety criminally insane prisoners are transferred from Perth prison to Carstairs. This combined unit becomes the State Mental Hospital. In the same year, John McGhee and John McDade escape from the facility.

1959   The first female patients are transferred to Carstairs.

1962   Iain Simpson is sent to Carstairs for murdering two hitchhikers.

1963   The government announces plans for enlarging Carstairs.

1967   Robert Mone shoots dead schoolteacher Nanette Hanson at Dundee and is sent to Carstairs.

1968   Carstairs nurses giving evidence to an inquiry into bullying and staff safety tell of being subjected to Belsen and Gestapo taunts.

1970   Thomas McCulloch is sent to Carstairs after a shooting incident at the Clydebank Hotel.

1972   The escape from Carstairs of Alexander Reid and Malcolm McDougall sparks fury. Three nurses are suspended.

1973   Robert Mone and Thomas McCulloch begin a relationship at Carstairs.

1973   A sheriff rules that natural justice rules don't apply in mental cases.

1976   Mone and McCulloch escape, murdering three men, patient Iain Simpson, nurse Neil McLellan and policeman George Taylor.

1977   Carstairs management is severely criticised in an official report on the formal inquiry into the escape of Mone and McCulloch.

1978   Former Carstairs patient Robert Gemmill gets life imprisonment for murdering a teenage schoolgirl.

1994   Patient Noel Ruddle is disciplined after a Christmas party at Carstairs leads to the discovery of drugs and drink.

1998   Patients make legal moves to be released from Carstairs, arguing they are sufficiently cured to be transferred to prison.

2012   The major rebuilding of Carstairs is completed at cost of almost £90 million.

PREFACE

It is officially termed the 'State Hospital' but to most it is simply 'Carstairs'. That word alone is sufficient to send a shiver down the spine, because Carstairs is no ordinary hospital. It is effectively a prison holding the most seriously demented and dangerous men in our society, among them the perpetrators of hideous crimes. Some have psychiatric illnesses so deep-rooted that they are untreatable. All are there to protect them from us; and we from them. In short, it is a hospital for horrors.

The common image of Carstairs – as a terrifying pit of evil where patients are subjected to torture and humiliation – is one largely resulting from the refusal of successive managements to illustrate to the public who fund it precisely what goes on behind its barbed wire and bars. Secrecy is paramount. Officially, staff must never discuss their work. Some former patients believed that should it become known they had discussed their experiences, they would be hauled back inside, never to re-emerge. In compiling this story of Carstairs and the how and why it came into being, the State Hospital was invited to become the major contributor. It refused. Carstairs is akin to the very thing that it seeks to treat: the human brain – an organ locked within a fortress refusing to give up the secrets of its working.

Carstairs: Hospital for Horrors tells the story of Scotland's State Hospital through the stories of the people that have been incarcerated there over the years. This book concentrates on the crimes which led to them being committed there, the challenges they pose for the State Hospital, the problems with security and the (often misguided) decisions to release them from the facility. The lack of cooperation from Carstairs in writing this book has meant that it is not possible to explore the treatments that are used at the facility or the security measures in as much detail as necessary. This secretive approach from Carstairs' administrators discourages sympathy for its patients. And yet, tragically, sympathy and understanding are what patients need and deserve. For centuries, madness has been a condition largely regarded with sympathy even though the care of sufferers has lacked support. There was little or no discrimination between the varying degrees of severity of psychiatric illness, often simply the product of poverty, with the result that the afflicted were frequently simply left to mingle with the sane, void of treatment or help. Records held at the Highland Archive Centre in Inverness show how often seriously disturbed men and women were thrown together to sink in their despair or swim back to sanity.

As our story will reveal, doctors in Scotland were among the first in Britain to recognise the need for the dangerously afflicted to be kept apart from the merely mentally ill. The first dedicated criminal lunatic asylum was opened in ramshackle buildings at Perth prison, where escapes were frequent and, in at least one case, tragic. Although it was evident the asylum was neither big nor secure enough, it was not until the mid 1930s that plans for a specially developed centre at Carstairs in rural Lanarkshire to hold dangerous male and female lunatics received formal government approval. Yet the intervention of the Second World War and other delays meant it would be twenty years before the first patients were transferred to what would eventually become the State Hospital. In recent years females have been transferred away to other psychiatric hospitals where security is more relaxed and Carstairs, now part of the National Health Service, has undergone a major redevelopment. Sadly the policy of secrecy binding the State Hospital has meant its reputation is built not on the achievements of dedicated and brave staff but on a tragic escape by two patients in 1976 that left three men dead.

Robert Mone and Thomas McCulloch had met while both were

PREFACE

patients in Carstairs. Staff failed to recognise their friendship had deepened into a close sexual relationship and appalling security lapses allowed the men to stockpile a terrible array of weapons secretly made in the State Hospital workshops and elsewhere. How and why they escaped is told in graphic detail by Mone himself in a remarkable and candid series of letters to the author. He has never forgotten the events for which the State Hospital is even now, sadly, best remembered. The terrible memory of their flight to freedom is one Carstairs will never shake off.

1

MAD MONEY

Treating mental illness is an expensive business. It costs the British taxpayer more than £14 billion a year, but medical staff and politicians frequently argue that that is not enough, that facilities and treatment lack quality while research resources are inadequate. Many with problems of the mind or brain are simply treated in the community. For others there are hospitals with varying grades of security. Those regarded as the most dangerous – a major proportion of whom have committed serious crimes and from whom the public at large must be protected – are held in four high-security establishments. Those among these most difficult patients living in England and Wales are detained at three specialist institutions – Broadmoor in Berkshire, Rampton in Nottinghamshire and Ashworth on Merseyside, whose most infamous occupant is the Glasgow-born Moors murderer Ian Brady. Carstairs in Lanarkshire is home to seriously disturbed and dangerous patients from Scotland and Northern Ireland.

Carstairs uses National Health Service funds amounting to around £36 million each year, but those running it appear to be paranoid at the thought of the public discovering how that money is spent and refuse to justify such a huge outlay. Patient numbers vary. The establishment is intended to hold up to 140 men – the last female patient was removed to another psychiatric hospital in 2009 – in conditions supposed to be of the highest possible security. According to the 2013/14 annual report from the State Hospital, inmates actually number around 125. How many men and women are paid to look after them? The fact is, nobody is sure.

CARSTAIRS

The hospital in its annual report says it has 695 employees. The NHS was reluctant to give a figure, finally coming up with 652 and admitting it could not explain the discrepancy. Regardless of the confusion at Carstairs, there is an astonishing ratio of more than five and a half employees for each inmate. Even more staggering is the annual cost of keeping each patient in the hospital – £288,000 – which is seven times that of holding an average prisoner and three times the cost of caring for a regular hospital patient. The institution was invited to take a major role in compiling and writing this book, guaranteed any requested confidentiality, offered the unique opportunity to explain to taxpayers how its patients are treated, promised anonymity wherever required and given the chance to gain public understanding of its work. But after a wait of several months it declined. Carstairs is determined to keep its secrets. It has also refused to give any information about the various jobs performed by its huge workforce.

The story of Carstairs is littered with incidences of carelessness: glaring and, in one case, fatal security bungling; patients held there for years and racking up huge bills before being told they are untreatable; and a general terror from the mentally ill of once being inside never getting out. Carstairs is virtually a state within a state – a real-life Hammer House of Horrors. The word of its psychiatrists is law.

In our regular hospitals, overworked nurses and doctors struggle to cope in often antiquated conditions while the mad and bad, murderers, rapists, killers of mothers and children, perpetrators of the most hideous crimes are, according to former inmates of Carstairs, treated in comfort and live in comparative luxury enjoying satellite television and the latest electronic games. Carstairs arguably exists to protect not the public, but its inmates.

Just as Carstairs is a closed book, mental illness is a mystery that has baffled the medical profession for over 7,000 years. The brain, which dictates human actions and emotions, is a sealed unit; we can look at it from the outside but not access its innermost workings and thus those who specialise in its study can never be sure whether their tinkering has repaired its damaged workings. Nowadays expensive drugs and simple counselling are the tools mostly used in the treatment of the mentally ill. In the distant past, methods were less refined.

Early man believed madness was the result of evil spirits infiltrating the brain and a cure was only possible by evicting these. That was achieved by hacking a hole through the skull with sharpened stone instruments. Amazingly, some patients survived. Mesopotamians treated mental illness by holding religious rituals generally ending in the sacrifice of an animal. Ancient Egyptians carried out operations using metal saws and knives and encouraged the afflicted to dance and party their way back to normality. Roman doctors practised their surgery on criminals and captives, a routine that would be followed 2,000 years later in Nazi concentration camps by the likes of Drs Josef Mengele at Gross-Rosen and Eduard Wirths at Auschwitz.

In the past, mental illness was often taken as a sign that the afflicted person or their family had offended the gods and so victims were frequently hidden away. The first known asylum was established in the Middle East, but because of the social stigma attached to the condition it was mostly left to the family to care for anyone believed to be mad. Attitudes varied hugely. On the European mainland during the Middle Ages, mad people were often abused and beaten, sometimes flogged on the grounds they were a nuisance. In England a madman might find himself in the stocks, a woman ducked in the village pond, or those of either sex driven away to wander and live as paupers and tramps.

During a scene in *The Searchers*, the 1956 cowboy film, one of the characters, old-timer Mose Harper, played by Hank Worden, recalls how he was able to escape unharmed after being captured by hostile American Indians. 'Made out I was crazy. Ate dirt. Chewed grass. I fooled 'em,' he says. The movie itself was fiction, but this tiny segment had a ring of truth. Native Americans were among many tribes that were largely sympathetic to those showing signs of madness. Sadly, all too often such tolerance was not demonstrated by civilisations that, while considering themselves superior in intellect and sophistication, regarded lunatics as misfits who needed to be locked out of sight, an embarrassment to their families, and largely approached them with fear and loathing. It was therefore often left to members of religious orders to give the mentally ill at least some of the sympathy and support that was denied by the majority of the community.

In London's Bishopsgate in 1247, during the reign of King Henry III, the Priory of the New Order of Saint Mary of Bethlehem was established to collect alms with which to help finance the Crusades, but as the years passed both its location and purpose would change. Gradually it became known as an asylum where the insane could seek refuge. At first numbers were small – in 1400 it had six male patients – but the population increased, particularly as it offered free care while elsewhere the custom was for the families of mad people to pay for their upkeep in homes where conditions were sometimes close to barbaric. Establishments like the Bethlem Royal Hospital, as the Priory of the New Order of Saint Mary of Bethlehem became known – later it would be nicknamed the more familiar 'Bedlam' – began offering better facilities as sympathetic merchants and wealthy families donated money towards their upkeep.

Looking after the mad was slowly becoming a business on which some unscrupulous landlords cashed in, taking money from the relatives of patients while simply dumping them in cold, bare rooms, leaving them lonely and frightened. Eventually, in 1774, the government stepped in and ruled that, in future, private madhouses had to be licensed.

In Scotland, the insane tended to be treated more kindly, but there was still a crying need for hospitals specialising in their care, and in 1781 Susan Carnegie, a staunch advocate of setting up a formal countrywide programme of mental care, established the Montrose Lunatic Asylum, Infirmary and Dispensary on the town's links, which would later be known as Sunnyside Royal Hospital. It was the first asylum in Scotland and word of its achievements, particularly those of its first medical superintendent Dr William A. F. Browne, reached the ears of wealthy Dumfries widow Elizabeth Crichton whose views on the insane matched those of Susan Carnegie. Crichton set up the Crichton Royal in Dumfries and persuaded Browne, largely thanks to her offer to increase his salary from £150 a year to a staggering £350, to run the institution. Now more and more towns and cities in Scotland began giving thought to opening asylums.

In Edinburgh, leading citizens had been embarrassed by the fact that it lagged behind Montrose and, a year after Susan Carnegie's act of generosity, an appeal was opened in the capital for money to set up an asylum. Much of the impetus behind the appeal resulted from the death in Edinburgh's Darien House hospital at the age of just twenty-four of the highly acclaimed poet Robert Fergusson, whose work deeply influenced the likes of Robert Burns and Robert Louis Stevenson. The sad fate of Fergusson, who had been suffering from depression, prompted his doctor Andrew Duncan to determine to assist other victims of mental illness. The appeal was boosted thanks to a government donation of £2,000. That figure sounds generous, but it was actually money taken from the estate of supporters of Bonnie Prince Charlie, whose attempt in 1745 to take over the throne of Britain ended on the bloody field of Culloden. His failure left many Jacobite families penniless when their homes and lands were confiscated as punishment.

Other donations trickled in. The Earl of Glasgow handed over £50; Her Grace the Duchess of Buccleuch and Mr Adam Anderson on behalf of the Incorporation of Hammermen each gave twenty-five guineas (£26.25); the Earl of Leven and Melville and the Incorporation of Goldsmiths each coughed up twenty guineas (£21); Thomas Miles, described as the 'proprietor of the wild beasts', gave £9 and Mr George Pickard of South Bridge donated three guineas (£3.15).

On 18 January 1808, the *Caledonian Mercury* newspaper commented:

> It has long been a matter of deep regret, that, among the number of Charitable Institutions in this city, there has been no suitable public provision for the reception and care of the Insane – from the want of which, both the safety of the public, and the safety of the unhappy persons themselves, have been often endangered. To remedy this culpable defect in the system of our charities, a plan has been formed for the establishment of a lunatic hospital at Edinburgh. The

establishment is intended for the reception of patients from the opulent ranks of life, as well as from the indigent; and the benefits of it are not to be confined to any particular district of the country, as patients will be received from all quarters. To country parishes, where there are no means of confining maniacs, the utility of such an establishment will be much felt; - to those of a higher rank, who may have the misfortune to labour under this unhappy malady, the asylum will afford a safe and advantageous place of seclusion.

The Edinburgh Lunatic Asylum in Morningside opened its wards only to paying customers in 1813 but was later expanded to take in the poor mad, who supported themselves and the asylum by keeping pigs, farming, gardening and carrying out tailoring and carpentry work. It would later become the Edinburgh Royal Hospital. One of the early physician superintendents was Dr David Skae, a man of considerable foresight who advocated setting up a national criminal lunatic asylum to be provided and maintained by the government. His calls fell largely on deaf ears, principally due to the cost issue, but eventually the wisdom of his idea would be appreciated. In fact money to care for the insane was always a problem. The Criminal Lunatics Act of 1800 gave the sovereign power to order the safe custody of criminal lunatics but made no allowance for the cost of their upkeep. Eight years later the County Asylums Act made magistrates responsible for building institutions to house pauper lunatics.

In the west, Glasgow was determined not to be left behind in the welfare of the insane. In 1804 a management committee for an asylum was established and wealthy merchants and businessmen were canvassed for cash help. Newspapers reported that in 1806 Glasgow's bakers had 'generously' raised £50. Building started in Cowcaddens in 1810 and the Glasgow Lunatic Asylum opened four years later. A fund started to build an asylum in Dundee was given a welcome boost, according to the *Aberdeen Journal* in December 1812, when the newspaper reported that 'Mr Erskine of Linlathen has subscribed one hundred guineas for the benefit of the Dundee Lunatic Asylum.'

MAD MONEY

The institution welcomed its first three patients in 1820, but like virtually every asylum it was forever begging for money and reliant on charity. Sometimes the source of cash was unusual. The *Caledonian Mercury* told its readers in April 1813, 'The Secretary to the Glasgow Lunatic Asylum has lately received the sum of L8 [£8] sterling, being a fine imposed by the Commissary of Hamilton and Campsie, upon a person for defaming the character of a respectable tradesman in Glasgow.' Nine years later the same paper reported:

> Wednesday, The Rev Andrew Thomson, minister of St George's Church, Edinburgh, preached a sermon of great force and beauty to a crowded audience, in the East Church, Dundee, for the benefit of the Dundee Lunatic Asylum, from Ephesians ii 12. The church was crowded: and the collection for the charity amounted to L53 12s 6d.

Gradually those running institutions taking in the insane were forced to improve conditions. In 1828 Commissioners in Lunacy were appointed to supervise and license private asylums. Concerns about the treatment of mad people continued, and at the same time the problem of what to do with insane criminals was becoming more of an issue. In 1830 when he gave evidence to a House of Commons select committee, Sir William Rae, the MP for Buteshire and Lord Advocate, was asked, 'Is there any provision in Scotland for the maintenance of lunatics convicted as criminals for their safe custody other than the confinement of a common gaol?' His reply left the door open to campaigners for change such as David Skae, who complained the state was passing the buck. 'There is not,' admitted Sir William, who added, 'but the courts of law are in the habit of allowing the liberation of criminal lunatics upon their relations finding security to keep them in confinement.' He was then asked, 'Are there any instances of them being kept for years in common gaols?' to which he simply told the committee, without any attempt at excuses, 'There are.' He was asked, 'Has not that been accompanied with the greatest possible annoyance to others as well as in many instances hardship to the individual himself?' The Lord Advocate had to concede this was indeed the case.

When a committee member put the question, 'What in your opinion would be the best mode of remedying that evil?' his answer set off a train of thought that, more than a century later, would lead to the opening of the State Hospital at Carstairs. 'I conceive that there ought to be one asylum or compartment in Scotland for the custody of all criminal lunatics,' he said, adding that he believed one state asylum for criminals would be adequate, that it should be sited in Edinburgh and ought to be separate from normal prisons. Sir William also conceded that there was no medical care provided for criminal lunatics held in normal jails. More than a decade later the Royal Lunacy Commissioners for Scotland reported that sheriffs, legal officials and doctors were all backing the idea of a single institution to hold criminal lunatics. But the fact was that successive governments had little sympathy for the plight of the insane. For decades the Dundee asylum was the only institution offering to accommodate criminal lunatics.

More and more asylums were springing up, particularly after the government made the building of at least one in every county mandatory in 1845, but the problem remained of how to pay for their running. At one in Glasgow, men and women slept two to a bed while in one room three women had to share a bed. The Gartnavel asylum in Glasgow complained it was £37,000 in debt and banks were demanding repayment. Simply by handing over five guineas (£5.25) anyone could buy a vote for life on the management of the asylum. In some institutions patients were forced to sleep on the floor on filthy mattresses stuffed with straw chopped into tiny pieces so inmates could not plait it into ropes to escape or strangle fellow patients or members of staff. The Dundee asylum charged the wealthy parents of one family fifteen shillings (75p) a week for keeping their 'idiot girl'. When her father died, leaving the then enormous fortune of £50,000, the asylum told her family it was doubling its price, but one of the girl's brothers, who was handling their father's estate, refused to pay the extra and moved the youngster to a cheaper asylum at Perth.

Change, however, was on the way. Slowly society was recognising that while those suffering mental illness needed particular help, there were exceptions – men and women whose particular conditions meant that they posed a threat to the safety of those around them. In 1845, Parliament was petitioned by campaigners who pointed out that the law made no allowance for the financial maintenance of criminal lunatics in Scotland. Most criminal lunatics, but not all, were transferred to Perth jail, but the question of a specially built institution where they could be safely confined was put on hold. It would be twenty years before Skae, Sir William Rae and others finally had their way with the opening of a criminal lunatic department for the whole of Scotland. It was sited at Perth jail, originally built between 1810 and 1812 to house French soldiers taken prisoner during the Napoleonic Wars but recently converted to take civilian convicts. The criminal lunatic unit would be separate. The new department was made up of three separate buildings surrounded by eleven acres of ground, most of which was to be used to employ inmates on gardening and agricultural work, the remainder serving as an exercise area.

In a report to the government published in 1866 the managers of the prison service in Scotland were keen to trumpet the existence of the new unit:

> The new department for the reception of the criminal lunatics of Scotland has been occupied since the 12th January 1865. We have every reason to be satisfied with this establishment, and its adaptation to its special purposes. It was rendered necessary by the enlargement of the classes for which the old lunatic department was available. This enlargement was made by statute for the purpose of comprehending all those lunatics who, by their conduct, have shown themselves so dangerous to the public that they must not only be detained in custody, but should be under the charge of a Government department. We have again to express our thanks to Her Majesty's Commissioners in Lunacy for their valuable advice in the re-arrangement of this department of the establishment.
>
> We have stated that recent legislation has had the effect of enlarging the class of lunatics capable of being admitted into this department. The number of its occupants is consequently gradually

> increasing. We forsee [sic] that the occupancy, according to present arrangements for admission, is likely at some time not far distant to press upon the accommodation. We are therefore likely, when such pressure approaches, to bring the matter under your consideration, with a view either to the restriction of the class of inmates who may be received within the department, or to the enlargement of the building.

At last the government had accepted that these individuals were too dangerous to be treated in normal hospitals and too unwell and unpredictable to be incarcerated in prisons because most had committed appalling crimes. Now they were being kept in a specially built high-security establishment, but the emphasis was on making sure they could not escape. Providing treatment to deal with their mental illnesses still took a back seat for several decades. And this division of emphasis gave rise to the fear that the chances of ever being freed from the new Perth unit were remote and so many of those committed to it determined to get free and stay free. The effect this had was to increase the pressures on and dangers to those guarding them.

2

BUYING FREEDOM

The generosity of the public in handing over cash to support asylums might have been motivated by fear as much as benevolence. While there was considerable sympathy for the insane, having an institution in which they were locked up protected the community by keeping them off the streets. Until the opening of the criminal lunatic unit at Perth, courts had been at a loss as to what to do with insane people who harmed others. In 1810, Margaret Robertson, a surgeon's daughter, was accused of poisoning her mother by dosing her with arsenic, a crime for which a guilty verdict would almost certainly result in her being hanged. During her trial at Perth it was said that when her mother briefly left the breakfast table of their Crail home, Miss Robertson mixed white powder into her tea. But the evidence of Margaret Horsburgh, a former family servant, saved the accused woman's life. The *Aberdeen Journal* reported her evidence:

> Miss Robertson, nine years ago, caught a fever from her mother, by her careful, assiduous and anxious attendance. One day, in 1805, she was, without any previous depression of spirits, suddenly seized with a delirium in church. She continued in that state for some time, and afterwards recovered. She often told the witness, after her recovery, that when first seized, she imagined herself capable of flying out of the roof of the church and, when taken hence, she thought the house on fire and her mother some monstrous creature.

The jury found poor Margaret insane at the time she poisoned her mother and as a result she was ruled not guilty. But, said the newspaper, the judge 'granted warrant for admitting her to prison, till caution was found that she would not injure herself or others, under the penalty of 1,000 merks Scots; which having been instantly found, she was dismissed from the bar'. The merk was a silver coin, equivalent to an English shilling, so for handing over £50 Margaret walked free.

Not every criminal lunatic was so lucky. In 1826, Archibald MacLellan from Degnish, near Oban, Argyll, who supported his ten children by fishing, suddenly went crazy and attacked and killed his daughter Christina, smashing her over the head with a stool while his helpless wife, Jeannie, watched through a window, too terrified to intervene. 'There was no struggle when we went in,' Jeannie said at the trial of her husband. 'He gave up his stool without a murmur.' Archibald escaped the gallows because the jury decided he was 'insane and deprived of reason' and he was sentenced to life imprisonment. Like Margaret, Archibald was offered a way to freedom. The judge told him that if 'Sufficient Caution and Surety' could be found, he could avoid spending the rest of his days in a grim jail cell. It meant coming up with a sizeable sum of money and somebody of note willing to take legal responsibility for him. Sadly, with nine children to feed Jeannie had no money to spare to buy her husband's liberty and working-class families like the MacLellans were far removed from the rich upper classes. The result was that, for the next thirteen years, Archibald lay untreated and unaided in Inveraray jail, where he was found dead in his cell in June 1839.

Sometimes cases where a man or woman was guilty of extraordinary and worrying criminal behaviour could only be dealt with by sending the perpetrator to a private asylum just to keep them off the streets, where they were a menace to themselves and everyone else. Typical was a terrifying series of incidents that caused panic in Edinburgh when a madman who up until that point had been a respectable city businessman running a firm of dyers went berserk. Imagining himself to be Lord Balmerino, a notable Jacobite beheaded at the Tower of London, he decided he needed to raise a huge army and wanted mounts for his cavalry units. The best war horses, he believed, were the result of crossing the Barbary breed with grey mares and so he set about purloining grey mares. Spotting one dragging a cart in the Canonmills area of Edinburgh, he tried pulling it free from the shafts, at which the owner set about him with a club, forcing the crazed businessman to flee.

In Princes Street, he leapt on the back of a grey mare belonging to a clergyman and galloped off, eventually stopping and knocking on the door of a wealthy family in Queen Street. When it was opened by a footman, the lunatic rode in through the house, scattering servants and terrifying the owner and his children. He only agreed to ride off after being given a shilling to help pay for the equipping of his army. He later reached Piershill Barracks, home to a number of cavalry regiments, where he dismounted and was arrested.

Reporting this amazing trail of havoc in 1825, the *Caledonian Mercury* revealed there was even worse to come:

> He believes the whole of Caltonhill to belong to him; and is determined to root out all the tenants on the Regent Bridge whom he describes as mere plebeians, because they will not pay him rents. He has promised grants of land to all who will support his just rights; and, in addition, to stock their lands so granted with Irish goats of an excellent breed, which yield each seven pints of milk daily.

The businessman was sent off to a house that took in lunatics, but had an asylum for criminal lunatics been available that is where he would certainly have gone. He was lucky, because he could easily have found himself walking on to a scaffold. Plotting to raise a private army was treasonable, punishable by beheading.

The glaring need for a dedicated criminal lunatic department was shown in April 1844 when Peter Campbell, a schoolteacher, was accused of killing his aunt. For some time before the terrible incident, in which he also tried killing his mother at their home in Craignish in Argyll, friends had noticed Campbell becoming increasingly erratic. He complained of voices in his head telling him his mother and aunt were witches who had to be stopped from chasing him. The voices ordered him to cut the women's throats and he was doing just that in January that year when the owner of a nearby public house heard screams and interrupted the attack on Campbell's mother. The teacher was holding a cut-throat razor dripping with blood. His mother survived, but his aunt bled to death in hospital from dreadful injuries to her face, neck and arms.

When he appeared in court, he was deemed not guilty of murder through being insane. Campbell was obviously dangerous; nowadays he would have been immediately hauled off to Carstairs, but because there was no facility for criminal lunatics he was ordered to be held in Inveraray jail, where he stayed for three years before being moved to Perth, by which time the prison there was managing to hold the likes of the teacher among ordinary inmates. The building of the formal unit for criminal madmen was two decades away.

The need for it was growing. In January 1844, concerns about the mental health of Adam Sliman from Burntisland in Fife led to a warrant being issued authorising his removal to an asylum. Town constables who tried to serve it on him at his home found themselves threatened with a knife. Later they tried again, but one of the officers, Thomas Corstophin, was stabbed and died. Sliman, aged thirty-three, was charged with murder. At his trial in Perth, his father said Sliman had been acting strangely ever since he was hit on the head by a winch on board a ship in Leith. He was convinced men were using a huge telescope to watch his movements and even see into his heart. The jury found him guilty but insane and he was committed to jail at Cupar in Fife.

His case was raised in Parliament the following year when his MP, Edward Ellice, complained Sliman was still in Cupar prison. Ellice said:

> The man is now dangerously insane, and yet remains in the criminal prison, where the necessity of keeping him from doing mischief precludes the possibility of giving him the air and exercise necessary in his disease. The surgeon has certified that he is literally dying by inches under the restraint, and yet there is no remedy. On one

occasion when he was let out in the yard among the other prisoners, he became furious and it took the united strength of several men to secure him and convey him back to his cell.

Were, he asked, any steps being taken to send him to an asylum or the penitentiary at Perth? The government spokesman told him, 'He is a most dangerous lunatic and a murderer, although not responsible for his crime. No private asylum was willing to take him and no public asylum could be forced to find him a place.' Sliman's case highlighted the need for an asylum for criminal lunatics. Eventually he was moved to the lunatic wing at Perth jail, where he died in 1857, eight years before the unit to which he would have gone was opened.

Pressure on the government to build a separate criminal lunatic unit was becoming intense. In 1852, the Earl of Shaftesbury told the House of Lords:

> It is unjust to ordinary patients to associate them with persons branded with crime. The lunatic is generally very sensitive, and both he and his friends feel aggrieved and degraded by the association. The moral effect is bad. The conduct of criminal patients is frequently very violent; their habits and language are frequently offensive and their influence on other patients injurious and pernicious.

Criminal lunatics, he went on, didn't enjoy mixing with normal lunatics either: 'It exposes them to taunts from other patients and the stricter confinement imposed on themselves irritates them. They are irritated also when other patients are liberated and they are left in confinement.' Not everyone agreed. The superintendent of Bethlem admitted that not keeping criminal and ordinary lunatics apart disturbed routine and discipline, but at the same time he rejected the idea of a single state criminal lunatic asylum.

However, the opening of the new, separate unit at Perth for criminal lunatics went ahead, meaning courts no longer had the problem of what to do with dangerous lunatics. Yet just as at Carstairs a century later, asylums would face criticism when the release of a patient went wrong. In June 1867, the family of Alexander Bisset, a dyer from Dundee, were so worried about his bizarre behaviour that they had him committed to the city asylum. He was there until 10 October, when doctors decided he was well enough to rejoin his family in Annfield Road. His unmarried sisters, Euphemia, a power loom weaver, and fifty-year-old spinster Margaret, who worked for a local grocer, were unhappy at the decision because their brother continued his strange antics, sometimes walking off in his bare feet or muttering prayers for hours on end. Clearly he was unwell and he'd been back at home for just over a fortnight when it was decided to arrange to have him taken back to the asylum. It was a Saturday and nothing could be done until the Monday. That night Alexander launched a terrible attack with an axe on Margaret, fracturing her skull. She died three days later without ever regaining consciousness. Her brother was charged with murder but during his trial questions were asked as to why he had been freed from the asylum only to kill seventeen days later. He was acquitted of murder through insanity but sent to the new unit for criminal lunatics at Perth.

This department was being well used: too much, according to the annual report for 1877 on prisons in Scotland, which revealed it held fifty-seven inmates, forty-one men and sixteen women. According to the report there had been 'no material change during the year in the methods of discipline obtaining in the prison'. It also added, 'Want of accommodation in the lunatic department is still complained of.' Overcrowding was always a potential source of trouble. It was perhaps with this in mind that the government decreed that contraband tobacco, seized during raids by Customs and Excise officers, should be dished out to inmates of criminal lunatic departments. However, the longing by inmates to be free was an ever-present danger to warders. There were occasional breakouts, but invariably escapers were soon recaptured. Sometimes, though, it was hard not to feel a smidgeon of sympathy for an inmate determined to get away.

Three men fled from the criminal lunatic department at Perth in August 1925. Two were back inside in a very short time, but the third, William McKee, made an audacious and inventive attempt at putting distance between himself and his pursuers. He was caught the day after he got away when a retired police officer, who had been reading newspaper appeals for the public to be on the lookout for the lunatic, spotted him at Esplanade Station in Dundee. Challenged by the pensioner, McKee immediately admitted who he was and put up no resistance.

After climbing the prison wall he thumbed a lift in a passing lorry. He persuaded the driver to swap his well-worn tweed trousers for McKee's prison-issue corduroys. He knew Dundee well, having once lived in the city, but his plan was to get to his sister's home in Motherwell. He was confident of being able to hitch a lift south but needed to get out of Dundee city centre quickly before he was recognised. Police had set up roadblocks around the city perimeter and McKee realised his best hope of getting around these lay in a railway crossing of the River Tay. Once over the Tay he was confident of finding a driver willing to give him a ride, but he needed money for a train ticket. The city was busy with Saturday afternoon crowds. McKee began singing outside a local bar, relying on the generosity of drinkers. He was not disappointed. Soon he had enough to buy a ticket to Wormit, south of Dundee. However, as he crossed to his platform the former policeman saw him and he soon found himself back in the criminal lunatic unit in Perth. The fact that he managed to cover the twenty-two miles to the railway station showed how desperate and clever a lunatic could be.

Each year Perth prison governors continued to complain about overcrowding in the criminal lunatic unit. Slowly the message was getting home that a new, bigger institution was needed and word was that conversion of a former military camp near Carnwath in Lanarkshire was the cheapest alternative. In a written question in February 1935, the MP for Glasgow Govan, Neil Maclean, asked if it was true that the criminal lunatic unit at Perth was being transferred to Carnwath 'in the near future', if the government had made a grant available for the rebuilding work and 'if this proposed transfer is responsible for the appearance and insanitary conditions prevalent in the old quarters' at Perth. The response from the Secretary of State for Scotland was:

> The question of providing a criminal lunatic asylum and a State institution for defectives elsewhere than at Perth prison is receiving my active consideration. Legislation will be required before expenditure can be incurred on a scheme of this nature. The condition of some of the old quarters at Perth is unsatisfactory, but the buildings are not suitable for reconstruction.

The urgency of having new premises was demonstrated by the fact that just a month later the government moved the Second Reading of the Criminal Lunatics (Scotland) Bill to provide for the erection of a new unit on 217 acres of land at Lampits Farm, Carstairs. In moving the Bill, the government representative said:

> The Bill will enable a much-needed improvement to be effected in the conditions under which a considerable number of mentally afflicted persons in Scotland, whose detention is essential in the public interest, will be housed and employed, and will provide better facilities for treatment in trying to help them, wherever possible, towards mental recovery and a return to ordinary life.

If staff and inmates were looking forward to new, bigger surroundings, they were in for a disappointment. Plans for the rebuilding at Carnwath – it would eventually simply become known as Carstairs – got under way, but oddly enough an Austrian interrupted them. His name was Adolf Hitler and the certainty of war followed by years of bloody conflict meant the government had other uses for the site. It was not until 1956 that the first inmates entered Carstairs.

Meanwhile, Perth continued to have its troubles. In a mass breakout in February 1941, seven male inmates escaped, resulting in a major investigation into clear flaws in the security arrangements. Just two warders had been on duty, and when one was called away, one inmate overpowered the other, locked him in a cell and used his keys to unlock the cells of six others. The second warder was then bundled in beside his colleague. The escapers used keys to unlock the clothing store and help themselves to civilian outfits. They then seized a warder patrolling the outside of the unit and literally walked away. One of the escapers hitched a lift to Falkirk, where he was spotted by a policeman as he was thumbing another ride, hoping to reach friends and family in Glasgow; three others were planning to cross the River Tay to Dundee by stealing a fishing boat, but when a fisherman spotted and challenged them they ran off, only to be caught after passengers in a passing bus saw them and told police. The others were recaptured locally soon after this.

It was becoming increasingly difficult to prevent more escapes. Many of the brighter and more alert warders had been conscripted into the armed forces. In September 1942, James Mackenzie, aged forty, whose home was in the north of Scotland, fled from a warder while he was being allowed a few hours of escorted freedom in the centre of Perth. He hitched lifts to Dalry in Ayrshire but after sixty hours, tired and hungry, let himself be recaptured. Five years later another escape would have potentially serious consequences. Two convicts fled but were caught on the outskirts of Perth. As they were being taken back to prison in a police van, they suddenly attacked the two officers guarding them and fled. They stole a car and sped away chased by police. When the motor crashed the prisoners again ran away but were overpowered soon after. Both needed hospital treatment for injuries incurred in struggling with officers. Memories of this incident would be stirred more than thirty years later with the spectacular and deadly escape of two patients in 1976, the story of which is told in chapters 19 to 25.

The escapes went on. In November 1949, convict Hugh Thomson, aged twenty-four, from Glasgow, gave himself up just four hours after getting away from his escort. In November 1949 while in November the following year later Thomas Walker was at large for three days before being found in a house in Edinburgh. Just a month later another escape ended in tragedy when Thomas Howie from Dundee, who had been held in the criminal lunatic department for five years, ran off from an escorting warder. His pursuer ordered a butcher to drive after him in his van, but when Howie realised he was being chased he tried to swim across the River Tay, only to be swept to his death. But just as his life had ended, so that of the unit from which he had fled was fast drawing to a close.

3

DISAPPOINTMENT IN MARRIAGE

It had taken hundreds of years and the generosity and determination of a relative handful of individuals to bring about a revolution in the way Scottish society viewed lunacy. Finally, asylums were springing up in many of the leading towns and cities, allowing the mentally ill to be segregated from those suffering physical and more obvious sickness. And enlightened physicians such as David Skae had at last won the argument for the setting up of a dedicated criminal lunatic department where the most dangerous maniacs could be incarcerated. It would be almost a century before Carstairs was opened but, in the meantime, facilities for the treatment of those with psychiatric illnesses were basic, to say the least.

There was sympathy in plenty. However, the days when patients suffering relatively minor mental problems, such as breakdowns or depression, could be sent home to recover were many decades in the future. In effect anyone acting abnormally, no matter how trivial their seeming eccentricity, would be sent off to the nearest asylum where treatment consisted largely of inmates being given a menial occupation while staff hoped rest and quiet would bring about a cure. There was care and sympathy in abundance, but little or no understanding of the causes of mental illness.

Nowadays doctors can categorise its various forms and degrees of severity. Different hospitals specialise in treating particular types of disorder. Not all criminally insane find themselves in Carstairs. Some become patients at other hospitals where security is less strict. But a century and a half ago anyone suffering from mental illness, no matter how slight, was likely to find themselves in prison, the workhouse or an asylum. And very often, as a set of unique records show, the reason for a man, woman or even child being taken from their home to an asylum could be remarkably trivial.

On 19 May 1864, the Northern Counties Lunatic Asylum opened its doors at Inverness to admit its first patient. It would act as a catchment for those in the Highlands and north of Scotland who had demonstrated signs of mental abnormality or whose behaviour was simply out of the ordinary. The asylum, which later became known as Craig Dunain Hospital, kept details of everyone it admitted in a 'Register of Lunatics' and these records, now retained at the Highland Archive and Registration Centre in Inverness, make for fascinating reading.

The very first patient, number one in the 'Register of Lunatics', is mariner Donald Davidson, aged forty-two, who was described as a pauper from Inverness. Two doctors had convinced a sheriff that Donald's strange behaviour, which had caused his wife increasing worry for three years, meant he needed to be locked away from the public. He had suffered a partial paralysis and was said to be suffering from dementia, a common diagnosis in those days, covering a wide variety of mental illnesses that in reality might be simply a mild breakdown or the consequences of a series of strokes. In his case, the latter probably accounted for his paralysis. Donald, it was said, had become insane through money worries. His condition worsened in the asylum where he died five months later.

The first woman admitted to the asylum, four days after Donald, was Catherine Camsran, the fifty-seven-year-old wife of a joiner. She was suffering from 'Melancholia', a term which covered a number of illnesses but most generally depression, a common problem in those difficult times dominated by poverty, hunger and anxieties about the ability of families to keep a roof over their heads. Some believed that unfortunates suffering from the most severe forms of melancholia had had their minds and thoughts taken over by the Devil. Catherine's journey to the asylum from her home in the village of Kilmonivaig, fifty miles to the south, would have been arduous and most probably by horse and cart.

DISAPPOINTMENT IN MARRIAGE

A day later came the arrival of William Macaulay, described as a waiter aged twenty-seven, from Conan Village. The register reveals he was diagnosed as suffering from 'Mania' caused by 'Religious Excitement'. A more detailed examination of his treatment suggests he had suffered a breakdown. Doctors did their best, but sixteen months later, even though his condition had not improved, he was packed off home. Breakdowns blamed on religious fervour were commonplace and affected all ages. On 31 May, a local woman, Catherine McIntosh, aged just twenty, was admitted. She had suffered a breakdown – once again categorised in the register as 'Mania' – nearly three years earlier and would remain at the asylum for the next twelve years, spending her time knitting and reading her Bible.

Typhoid fever, often the outcome of poor sanitation and hygiene, leading to a victim eating or drinking contaminated food or water, was a common killer. And despite every effort by those running the asylum to keep it clean and germ-free, the risk of disease was constantly there. It was a problem for all asylums in which patients lacked the will or intelligence to stick to basic rules of cleanliness, and that at Inverness was no exception. The disease took the lives of three patients transferred at the end of that first May from the asylum at Montrose: Mary Matheson, a domestic servant aged thirty-seven, who died twelve years after being admitted; Peter Davidson, a clerk who died in October 1867, and John Davidson, thirty-one, a labourer who spent twenty-one years at Inverness before his death in June 1875. All were said to have been suffering from 'Dementia'.

While it was the poor who were most commonly victims of mental illness, very often those who might be thought of as relatively comfortably off found themselves inside the walls of the asylum, their freedom to move about severely restricted. Anyone wanting to escape would be quickly chased by staff and, if necessary, the police. The strict security must have made schoolmaster William Brodie, aged sixty, feel as if he were a pupil back in school. He died in the asylum in 1868. Robert McFarquhar, a fifty-year-old accountant, remained at the asylum for nineteen years before his death in 1873. Both were said to be suffering from dementia when they were admitted in those early days.

CARSTAIRS

Carstairs holds men, and formerly women, who – often for a seemingly mild problem – have snapped and committed hideous acts. In the same way, the reasons why men and women found themselves in the asylum at Inverness were many and varied and sometimes almost humorous. The Register shows that Grace Fraser, a spinster aged thirty-eight, had been employed as a domestic servant when she entered the asylum in June 1864 suffering from melancholia. The cause? It was recorded as 'Disappointment in Marriage' and in the years that followed that same theme would lead many other sad women to follow her. Grace spent three months in the asylum before being discharged apparently recovered from the loss of her bridegroom.

Hector Munro, a shepherd aged twenty-one, found himself admitted as a result of probably the most unusual reason of any of the many hundreds and thousands who spent time or even most of their lives in the asylum. Hector, from Skye, had been taking part in one of the many Highland Games that were a feature – and still are – of community life when he suffered a breakdown during an argument over one of the competitions. The register records his form of mental disorder as 'Acute Mania' and the supposed cause of insanity as 'A quarrel at Putting the Stone'. He missed the remainder of the Games season after being locked in one of the asylum wards but was discharged almost exactly a year later in June, presumably in time for the next round of competitions. Friends of the young man would have been saddened by his sudden loss of control, but just as tragic, if not more so, was the case of Margaret Urquhart, a domestic servant from Kiltearn in Ross and Cromarty. In early 1850 when she was eighteen, she had been jilted by her fiancé. Margaret never got over the shock of not becoming a wife and in the years that followed showed increasing signs of sadness and depression. Finally her condition became so unpredictable that she was admitted to the asylum in late June 1864. The Register noted she was 'Very much exhausted by journey'. Her diagnosis was dementia caused by 'Disappointment in Marriage'. Sadly, the trauma of being uprooted from her home and journeying to the asylum took a terrible toll on Margaret. Her entry concludes, 'Patient died

DISAPPOINTMENT IN MARRIAGE

3 days after her admission, from exhaustion consequent on her removal.'

Jessie Polson, a spinster of forty-seven from Fearn near Tain in Easter Ross, had, like Margaret, suffered twelve years of misery and depression after being left at the altar. Officially she was diagnosed as a victim of dementia, but her nightmare would continue for another nine years before she was discharged. Like her, Andrew Ross, aged forty-two from Lairg in Sutherland, was a dementia victim. He had been a sufferer for fifteen years and a hint as to the cause came in the register's record of his occupation. It said simply, 'in a spirit dealer's shop'. He died in the asylum in January 1895 having spent the last thirty years of his life there. Andrew Ross, forty-one, a labourer from Edderton, Easter Ross, had also fallen to dementia, but in his case the cause was listed as 'forcibly removed from a smallholding of land'. He never recovered and died eleven years later.

Sunstroke was a common problem among farm labourers in particular who were expected to spend long hours in the fields, especially during harvest time, without respite or proper protection from the burning rays of the sun. Victims often went mad. One such was Kenneth McDonald, aged twenty-five, a labourer from Glasgow, who was admitted suffering from 'Mania' caused by 'sleeping exposed to the sun'. He recovered and was discharged in March the following year.

Each patient arrived as a result of his or her own very personal tragedy. Sixty-two-year-old Ann Mackenzie suffered melancholia caused by the 'sudden death of her nephew'. She died eighteen months later. Angus Baillie, aged only thirty-three and a labourer from Clyne, Sutherland, spent nineteen years in the asylum being treated for dementia caused by 'Religion' before his death in 1883. Donald McPherson, a mason and seventy-one-year-old widower, died two and a half years after being admitted suffering from dementia resulting from 'loss of money'. Margaret Fraser, aged thirty-seven, a servant from Kiltarlity near Beauly, Inverness, was stricken by dementia after giving birth to an illegitimate child and died of exhaustion in July 1877 after spending thirteen years in the asylum.

Few cases though are more tragic than that of Margaret Kennedy from Boleskine on the shore of Loch Ness. She was admitted in July 1864 suffering from dementia. The cause? Three years earlier, within a few hours of each other, her husband had died and then she gave birth to a baby. The trauma had been too much for her mind to absorb and she spent the remainder of her life locked away in the asylum, a sad figure wandering the corridors of the asylum until her death in 1874.

A quarter of a century later Boleskine would come to have a reputation for a different form of madness when it was bought by Satanist Aleister Crowley. There he practised black magic rites and sorcery before selling it in 1913. During his ownership a drunken employee tried to murder his own wife and children one night, the ten-year-old daughter of Crowley's lodge keeper died suddenly at school and a year later the employee's fifteen-month-old son died suddenly of convulsions as his mother dandled the baby on her knee. Even after Crowley was long gone and dead, the insanity went on. In 1960, Major Edward Errick Grant, aged fifty-one, who had bought Crowley's Boleskine home, shot himself in one of the bedrooms.

Ann McKean was sixty, a spinster and teacher who was admitted to the asylum in September 1864 suffering from dementia. The cause was listed as 'Excitement from anticipated marriage'. It was a wedding that should have taken place thirty years earlier. She died in 1870. James Cowie, a soldier, had suffered epileptic attacks as a consequence of 'Coup de Soleil' – sunburn. His eccentric behaviour had resulted in his being jailed, but in Inverness prison his antics so worried staff that he was transferred to the asylum in 1864 suffering from mania. He died there in 1876. David Morrison, twenty-six, a coastguard volunteer from Ross-shire, spent thirty-six years in the asylum until his death in 1900. He had been admitted suffering from dementia caused by 'Excitement of Drill'.

Schoolteacher Angus McLeod, aged thirty-two from Alness, Ross and Cromarty, was admitted with chronic mania, the cause said to be 'Over study' during the previous seven years. He died in the asylum. Married Margaret Wilson was only twenty-three and a pregnant domestic servant from Fodderty near Strathpeffer. She was listed as suffering from mania caused by 'Jealousy' but recovered and was discharged fifteen months later. John Holm, aged twenty-six, of Avoch on the Black Isle, was admitted in March 1865 with mania, the cause given as 'Loss of means and disagreement with wife'. His record ambiguously stated he 'Has been frequently excited'. He died five years later. May McDonald, thirty-four, a domestic servant from Inverness, was afflicted with mania having suffered from 'Removal of teeth' in April 1865. She recovered and went home two months later. Jean Chisholm, a forty-five-year-old wife of a farm worker at Urray, Ross and Cromarty, was taken into the asylum after cutting her throat. She was categorised as being suicidal and suffering from melancholia, the cause being simply 'Change of residence'. She recovered. Kenneth Kennedy, aged twenty-three, from Croy, Inverness, became a patient in the asylum in January 1865 after being diagnosed with mania. The cause was 'Want of work'. He never left, dying five years later. Angus McDonald, a ploughman aged twenty-five from Sleat, Skye, was admitted with mania caused by 'Disappointed love' in September 1866. He was released the following year. Thomas McGill, aged nineteen, a gardener from Dornoch, Sutherland, arrived at the asylum diagnosed as melancholic. The cause, according to the register, was simply 'Masturbation'. He would not be the last.

John Bennet Munro was not the first clergyman to find himself in an asylum. Munro's wife was so concerned by his behaviour at their Speyside manse after her fifty-five-year-old husband was told he was having an assistant who would become his successor imposed on him that she had him admitted. Doctors put his illness down to melancholia. He was discharged three weeks later. Another clergyman, the Reverend Andrew Douglas, aged twenty-eight, from Inverness, was admitted suffering from mania in May 1873. The cause was 'Wounded vanity'. Efforts to treat him failed and when he was discharged three months later it was said he was 'Not improved.'

Security at the asylum was strict. Occasionally patients ran off. One such was Robert Mackenzie, a labourer aged twenty-seven, who was committed to the asylum by a sheriff in April 1874 suffering from mania. His record states that he escaped four years later, but was discharged on his recapture. William McLamman, a seaman of twenty-one from Avoch, was another admitted on the orders of a sheriff, suffering from mania, the cause listed as 'Supposed to be a fright in connection with a police chase' four months earlier. He died a year later. Mary Mackay, aged thirty-nine and a farm worker, spent more than two years in the asylum after suffering attacks of melancholia caused by 'Immoral life and consequent disgrace'. Janet Scobie, a married washerwoman of thirty-nine from Inverness, was kept in the asylum for two years after suffering melancholia, the result of a 'Broken heart'. Effy McLeod, sixty, a domestic servant from Portree, Skye, was admitted suffering from mania. The cause was a typical symptom of the day – 'Poverty and insufficient nourishment'. She died a year later of exhaustion.

The roll call of patients of any asylum was evidence that here the rich mingled with the poor, the famous with the unknown, the old with the young. All had a common illness – that of the mind. No one was safe from gremlins that tunnelled into the brain. James Munro was a colour sergeant with the 93rd Sutherland Highlanders when, at the age of thirty, he won the Victoria Cross for saving the life of a wounded officer at Lucknow during the Indian Mutiny. After leaving the army he turned to drink to dull the pain of injuries and ended up in the asylum, dying a year later. Few on the other hand, had heard of James Stewart, a shoemaker from Logie Easter, Ross and Cromarty. He was admitted to Craig Dunain in 1894 where he died five years later at the age of eighty. James was convinced a young woman waited in the wider world for him to come to marry her and, determined to reach her, tried to escape ten months after his arrival but was foiled. However, two weeks later he did manage to get away, being discovered by a searching policeman the following day. But not all escapes of those thought to be mentally ill would end so innocently.

The records can give only the barest details of why each patient found him or herself in the asylum. But behind every entry lies a deeply personal drama, a tragedy caused by love gone wrong, wounded vanity, poverty and a thousand other reasons. For many, the moment they set foot inside the institution marked the end of freedom. But their often unwitting sacrifices were not in vain. It is true that in the vast majority of cases, those in the Inverness asylum held little, if anything, in common with the patients who would ultimately fill Carstairs. But the ways these Highland men and women responded to treatment and the results of studies on them by doctors would prove invaluable in researches into how to deal with the seriously disturbed at the State Hospital. Doctors in Carstairs are provided with the most sophisticated means of treating mental illness, methods that may not have been heard of when James Stewart waited vainly for his bride or Margaret Urquhart died without experiencing the marriage bed. But the work carried out in Lanarkshire today owes much to the trial and error of those Inverness doctors and their unhappy patients.

4

ESCAPE TO KILL

'The law is an ass', according to Mr Bumble in Charles Dickens' *Oliver Twist*, published in 1837. More than a century later a distinguished High Court judge would agree, although his wording would differ. His Lordship was not to know, however, that in a few decades' time, the case over which he presided was to play a highly significant part in the story of the State Hospital.

Before him stood the diminutive figure of Iain Simpson who faced two charges of capital murder and was technically on trial for his life. It was August 1962 and men were still being hanged in the United Kingdom, although the prospect of a date with a hangman did not deter murderers. Nor had the lesson of what befell others scared off Simpson from taking the lives of fellow humans.

Four years previously, in July 1958, American-born sex maniac Peter Thomas Anthony Manuel, whose parents were Scottish, had gone to the gallows at Glasgow's Barlinnie prison after being found guilty of committing seven murders between January 1956 and January 1958. The seven who officially died at his hands were Marion Watt, forty-five, her daughter Vivienne, seventeen, and sister Margaret Brown, forty-one, all of whom were killed in the Watt home at Burnside, Glasgow; Isabelle Cooke, seventeen from Mount Vernon, Glasgow, who was raped then strangled; and three members of the Smart family, parents Peter, forty-five, Doris, three years his junior and their son Michael, ten, who were battered to death in their Uddingston home. Manuel was also accused of the murder and rape of teenager Anne Kneilands at East Kilbride, although the charge was ultimately dismissed through lack of evidence. He was also widely believed to have shot dead taxi driver Sydney Dunn, aged thirty-six, in Northumberland. Criminologists wondered whether others had perished at his hands.

In the days during which he waited in the death cell at Barlinnie for the arrival of hangman Harry Allan, Manuel did his best to throw doubt on the views of psychiatrists that he was sane by secreting soap under his tongue and literally frothing at the mouth and then spending several days when he uttered only the word 'chips'. His posturing failed to win him a reprieve on the grounds that he was mad, but many continue to hold the view that instead of being condemned to the noose, Manuel's behaviour and the fact that he was a devious and conniving serial killer were enough to justify his being ordered to spend the remainder of his life in Carstairs. He was a known psychopath but some who have studied his case believe that while there were grounds for detaining him in the State Hospital, such was the extent of his evil and the public outcry over the cloud of death and terror he threw over such a heavily populated area of Scotland for two years, that to have spared him would have aroused massive fury directed at the government of the day.

A year and a half earlier, Anthony Miller had been put to death by hangman Allan at Barlinnie, despite pleas for a reprieve on the grounds that the killer was only nineteen. And almost exactly a year after Iain Simpson was due to stand trial, Henry John Burnett, aged just twenty-one, was hanged at Aberdeen by Allan. Ever since Burnett's death, suspicions have remained that there were strong grounds for justifying a reprieve. It turned out he would be the last person to be executed in Scotland, but it was another year before the last hangings in England, those of Peter Anthony Allen and Gwynne Owen Evans in August 1964. However, while police hunted the killer of the two men whose names appeared on the indictment against Iain Simpson, believing that when they finally trapped their quarry he or she would undoubtedly dangle on the scaffold, once they had arrested Simpson it soon became apparent in interviews with senior detectives and then mental health experts that here was a creature who was little other than a dangerous madman and while many in the population called for him, like all murderers, to face the ultimate penalty, the law stated that those whose mental state meant they were not responsible for their crimes should be treated rather than punished.

But what made Lord Kilbrandon – the distinguished judge in the Simpson case – so uncomfortable was the emergence of a feature of the law relating to lunatics. He had some withering comments to make and no one was arguing with him. What was that feature? We shall see, as the incredible story of Iain Simpson – perhaps the most astonishing patient ever to enter the gates of Carstairs – unfolds.

Simpson was one of ten children born to his parents at Coatbridge, Lanarkshire. He was an unexceptional pupil at the local Kildonan Senior Secondary School. Reports describe him as being of below average intelligence and before he had reached the age of ten he had been caught stealing. Even at this early age, his mother Jean wondered if there was something wrong with her son. There seemed no motive for his stealing – sometimes he even gave back what he had taken. When he left school he could only get a job as an errand boy but his thieving continued and his conduct occasionally bordered on the bizarre. It was with something of a relief that Jean was there to help him when the postman brought him his call-up papers.

Conscripted into the Royal Army Service Corps, Simpson found himself mingling with young men from all sorts of different backgrounds: the strong, the weak, the decent and the dishonest. He watched the con men and twisters wearing the same uniform as him shamelessly steal and rob from the weak and vulnerable and abuse young women, and within him grew a disgust and loathing for what he regarded as their vile behaviour. When he took his views to army chaplains he came away feeling fobbed off, that they weren't interested in the opinions of a mere squaddie. But like so many with a religious fervour he was a hypocrite, berating sinners, thieving from his friends and lying and tricking all around him. What was remarkable was not just that a man of low intelligence became a practised and convincing confidence trickster who easily fooled others, but that while serving as a private in Germany he discovered a talent for learning the language, an asset that he would put to use once he was discharged. He practised his German on local women and for a while one of them became a regular girlfriend.

Back on civvy street, Simpson once again put his ability as a fraudster to the test. Posing as a respected and successful dealer in antiques he went back to Germany where, donning traditional Scottish dress including a kilt, he booked into an expensive hotel and told other guests he was a doctor and the son of a prestigious Scottish heart specialist. He even organised lectures on medical matters. They were well attended and no one doubted the credentials of 'Herr Iain' who managed to pass himself off as a relative of Wallis Simpson, the Duchess of Windsor, at one stage.

A Dutch antiques dealer who fell for his lies was persuaded to do Simpson a favour by haranguing customs officials into allowing a shipment of antiques to be sent to an address given by Simpson in Scotland. Needless to say the goods were stolen. The arrangement was that in return Simpson would supply the man with Scottish antiques and repay money the Dutchman loaned him for his fare home to Scotland. Neither antiques nor money ever arrived in Holland because, instead, Simpson embarked on a new career as a preacher, establishing his own church at Easterhouse in Glasgow, donning a dog collar to knock on doors in the huge housing scheme and even learning to cook so he could hand out food to hungry, hard-up members of his congregation.

At home he displayed many talents, painting and decorating and building a dolls' house for one of his siblings. Then one day he announced he had discovered a new interest – rambling. There was a hidden motive. It gave him the chance to roam Britain expounding his increasingly strong views on the immorality of his fellow man. But his antics were becoming ever stranger. On one occasion his mother discovered him in a graveyard near the family home digging up coffins. He began despising traditional religions and went back to stealing. Eventually he was persuaded to enter Crichton Royal Hospital at Dumfries as a voluntary patient to have treatment for what was, to his family at least, an obvious mental illness. A doctor there concluded Simpson was of unsound mind and potentially dangerous. However, the patient was anxious to be on the road again and, as was his right at the time, he left hospital.

However, his behaviour was attracting concern and he was committed to the Hartwood psychiatric hospital in Lanarkshire in 1960 on the grounds that he was a danger to the public. But in April the following year he escaped. Astonishingly, a law which had been passed a century earlier and never repealed meant that if he could avoid being caught for twenty-eight days then he could not be forcibly taken back. It was that law which would be the subject of stern comments from Lord Kilbrandon and raise demands for the introduction of emergency legislation to make sure there could be no repetition. But by then the damage had been done. Simpson meanwhile spent the next few weeks hitchhiking his way around north west England, staying outside the clutches of searching police. By the time he was caught stealing from a church in Dumfries, it was too late to have him recalled to Hartwood. In technical terms, by staying at large for more than twenty-eight days he had discharged himself and there was nothing anybody could do about it.

While he waited to appear before a sheriff at Dumfries on the stealing offence, Simpson tried to hang himself. Officers checking his cell rescued him and when he came to trial he was jailed for nine months. Doctors who examined him decided he was not suffering from a mental illness severe enough to have him certified, and so he spent the next few months sitting in a prison cell where he read avidly, occasionally walking the landings looking for fellow cons to lecture on the wickedness of the world in which they lived. A fellow inmate said at the time:

> He was a nice wee guy, but everyone avoided him like the plague because once he got started on religion there was no stopping him. It was pretty obvious he had a screw loose, that there was something wrong with him, but he was never violent, just a bit of a religious nut who got steamed up when anybody argued with him.

Simpson was freed in January 1962 and resumed his wandering mission to convert anybody who would listen. Mostly he hitched lifts, preaching to motorists who saw him thumbing rides and stopped to help. He moved to Manchester, lodging with Alice Bustin, telling her he was an antiques dealer. During one of his treks in February, he found himself in Staffordshire where he bumped into nurse Estelle Kierans, aged eighteen from Lancashire. Pretty Estelle quickly found herself being won over by the bright young man who told her he had graduated from Glasgow University and was now lecturing in theology, philosophy and psychology at the University of Manchester. She had no reason not to believe him and over the next few weeks he wooed her with tales of how he loved her and wanted to spend the rest of his life with her in a dream home in the Cairngorms.

In a letter dated 22 February and written just days after they had met for the first time, Simpson told Estelle:

It is a strange, exhilarating pleasure to write in affectionate terms to you, strange for the simple reason that it is a new and wonderful experience I am having, exhilarating for the glorious uplift in spirit (non alcoholic!) that has dawned with our most happy meeting. However, perhaps, I am being a bit presumptuous, you may have decided against our friendship, have you? I will, at any rate, proceed on the assumption that I have found the one who fulfils my ideas of womanhood, with high hopes that our feelings will someday have mutual aims. These words simply indicate a certain conviction of rightness, or truth or of beauty that has come to me. It is as if the mind had suddenly 'clicked' and with the 'click' I must end this very inadequate letter.

He signed off with 'Your Slave, Iain'.

They met regularly and in a loving letter while he waited for her to join him for a love tryst in Scotland Simpson wrote, 'I will have a lot to look forward to this week, it is almost like a year until Saturday, but it will pass. Then I will be with the woman I love.' Privately, he was in no doubt that his feelings for Estelle were mirrored in hers for him. He wanted to marry her and take her north to meet his parents. It might be the picture of a man who had left his torment behind and discovered true contentment and happiness. And for that reason what followed was all the more bewildering.

In early March he arrived at her home, driving a black Ford Anglia car. The registration number was YUM 552. 'Where did you get that?' asked Estelle. 'It's my brother's. He's loaned it,' she was told. It was a terrible lie. In fact, until a couple of days earlier, the car from which Simpson climbed had belonged to thirty-year-old electrical engineer George Green, who had driven north from his home in Leeds to spend a week skiing in the Cairngorms, leaving behind his fiancée Sheila Wild. It would be a last fling for George; the couple were to be married that summer. Like many other motorists he had been warned by Sheila and his family to be wary of hitchhikers. At the time George set off for the long drive into Scotland, James Hanratty, a twenty-five-year-old petty criminal was in prison awaiting execution in April after being convicted of abducting a couple as they sat in a car in Bedfordshire. Hanratty was said to have climbed in and ordered scientist Michael Gregsten and his mistress Valerie Storie to drive to a lonely lay-by at a spot named Deadman's Hill off the A6 road, where he shot Gregsten dead, raped Valerie and then shot her, leaving her for dead. She survived and was the prime prosecution witness at Hanratty's trial. 'Don't let strangers into the car George,' had begged his family. 'Remember the A6.' His black Ford Anglia had a couple of minor indentations in the rear. 'I'm having a holiday in Scotland. I'll get these sorted when I'm back,' he had told his local garage.

The A9 was, and still is, the main road leading to the spectacular Highlands. At the same time as George was at the wheel of his five-year-old black Ford Anglia turning on to it, Iain Simpson was hitching up it, also heading north, possibly to look for a Cairngorms lodge where he might entertain Estelle at some future time. From Leeds to the Cairngorms meant a trip of almost 400 miles. Perhaps George became bored, but for whatever reason he ignored the advice to be careful and stopped when he spotted the well-built but small hiker thumbing a lift. In the motor the men introduced themselves and chatted. Tragically, Simpson at some stage turned the conversation to religion and morality. His strict views were not those of George and the two argued, the dispute becoming more and more heated until George stopped the car near the village of Carrbridge and told Simpson to get out. Instead, his passenger pulled out a gun and shot him dead, pulling the lifeless body into the passenger seat then heaving himself behind the wheel, turning the car around and driving south back down the same road they had travelled minutes earlier. He was looking for a quiet spot where he could dump George's body and found what he sought when he came across a lay-by outside the village of Newtonmore in the shadow of the Cairngorms. Simpson may have been mad, but he was clever enough to do his best to make sure that in the event of the body being found, there would be nothing on it to identify the victim. He stripped George of everything except his stockings and shoes and, fearing another motorist might decide to make a stop at the same spot, hurriedly pushed the dead man under leaves and debris. But he had been careless and in his haste made a fatal mistake.

He drove off, heading south, and would ultimately meet up with Estelle. She had no reason to suspect anything was wrong. 'Jock' Simpson was his normal, confident self, telling her how much he loved her and persuading her she needed a holiday. Later that month he arrived for a date with her and when she asked why he did not have the car told her it was in a garage being given a respray. In fact he needed to disguise the motor.

Because he had said he would be missing for up to a fortnight, neither Sheila nor George's family had any reason to worry over his absence. But eight days after he had left Leeds, his body was discovered by a former police officer who had by chance stopped at the lay-by. Within minutes, detectives had sealed off the area and begun searching for clues. Who was the dead man? An examination of his shoes revealed the smooth spot on the right sole so common to drivers who spend much time pressing the accelerator pedal. That meant he had been a motorist. But what had become of his car? Simpson's carelessness would provide the answer. In dragging out the body he had failed to notice he had disturbed a map and, despite being dirty and wet, officers were able to read that it had been stamped with the address of a garage near George's Leeds home.

CARSTAIRS

When workers there were given a description of the murder victim, they immediately identified him as George Green who drove a black Anglia with the registration number YUM 772. The dead man's distraught family confirmed he had told them he was going to Scotland. Now the hunt began to find the car.

Coming so soon after the A6 killing, newspapers were publicising the near copycat murder on the A9 and carried police appeals for news of the car. Posters were circulated to garages throughout north west England and Scotland giving a description of the Ford Anglia and the indentations that needed repairing. Simpson knew he needed to disguise it and did a partial colour change himself, crudely using a brush to alter the appearance to grey and red, although when it rained the original black began showing through in parts. But he didn't bother repairing the dents. His deadly mission to put the world to rights was not yet completed. He carried on driving the murdered man's motor and at one stage Estelle had joked, 'Maybe you're the A9 killer' to which he had calmly replied, 'I could be, dear.' The couple had laughed because to her he had showed only politeness and kindness, and she would tell friends, 'Jock is a real gentleman, he's a lovely guy and I'm going to marry him. He's going to take an honours course at Glasgow University.' In fact, Simpson was studying the art of murder.

In early April he had been motoring along the north west coast of Scotland when, near the Kyle of Lochalsh, he offered a lift to hitch-hiker Hans Ruedi Gimmi, twenty-four, a student studying textile design, who had been touring Britain on a walking holiday as part of a break from his studies in his home city of Zurich, Switzerland. Hans had been hiking around Skye. He had based himself in lodgings in Edinburgh, but his tour was coming to an end and he was due to return home via a temporary base in London, but on the way planned to visit Paris. He accepted a ride from the bogus university lecturer who offered to drive him to London. When Gimmi told him he had to collect his belongings from lodgings in Edinburgh, Simpson even said he would take him to the capital, a considerable detour. That night they booked into a youth hostel at Ratagan, on the shore of Loch Duich in the shadow of the spectacular Eilean Donan Castle.

From there, Hans sent a postcard to a girlfriend in Edinburgh, telling of his meeting with the kind lecturer. Next morning, they drove south and then went on to Edinburgh where Hans packed his bags and they set off for London, crossing into Dumfriesshire, Simpson saying he needed to call in to his Manchester digs.

They had gossiped amiably enough, Gimmi speaking excellent English, but at some point the subject had moved to religion and, as in the case of George Green, Simpson lost his temper. Not far from Lockerbie, he pulled off the main road and drove into Twiglees Forest where he produced a gun and blasted the student dead. Blood spattered the car and he hastily wiped the windows and seats then rolled the body into undergrowth and rejoined other traffic on the road south. Reaching the Manchester lodgings, landlady Alice was surprised to see him park around the rear of the house, strip everything from the car and vigorously wash and clean the interior.

Callously he resumed his courtship of Estelle, as though nothing had happened. While police appeals for help in tracing the killer of George continued to appear, nobody was aware that Gimmi had been murdered. For all anyone knew, he had been driven off from his Edinburgh lodgings by a kind friend who would take him south to catch his flight home. Simpson may well have carried on killing had it not been for a teenage second-hand car dealer in Manchester whose attention was attracted by the badly painted Anglia. In his father's garage, police had pinned up one of their appeal notices giving details of the car they were convinced had been used in George's murder. Its registration number was YUM 772 and the car that Simpson had brought in had YUM 552. The young man called the police, who then stopped Simpson, but for some reason were satisfied by his explanation that his was not the motor they were seeking.

Officers let him go, but back at their station did more detailed checks and realised he needed to be interrogated. They raced to his lodgings and found him packed and about to leave to keep a rendezvous with Estelle. The couple had planned a trip to Scotland for the weekend, to hike and walk and enjoy the company of one another. Instead Simpson was locked into a police cell and then driven north to be questioned about the murder of George Green. He admitted being the killer but then shocked detectives by telling them, 'There's another one.' He accompanied them to Twiglees Forest where he showed them the decomposing body of Hans Ruedi Gimmi. Simpson said the original registration plates for the Anglia had been thrown into Fernilee Reservoir in Derbyshire, from where they were recovered by police frogmen. His gun was dumped into the River Mersey.

While Estelle and others who had known and liked Iain Simpson, and family and friends of the two men he had brutally slaughtered, tried to get on with their lives, he was held in Porterfield prison, Inverness, where his visitors included his parents, his younger brother Donald, a deep-sea trawlerman and psychiatrists. After their 420-mile round trip to see him, mum Janet told friends:

> I didn't know what to expect; nobody wants to think of their son as being a wicked murderer. At first we found it hard to speak, there were police officers in the room with us but we ended up talking around what he was said to have done; instead we chatted about his brothers and sisters and the weather.

When he appeared in court in August 1962, Simpson faced two charges. The first alleged that:

> Between 7th and 16th of March on the Inverness to Perth Road between Dalwhinnie and Carrbridge, both in Inverness-shire, or elsewhere in the county, he assaulted George William Green, electrical engineer of Leeds, discharged a loaded firearm at him shooting him in the head and robbed him of a motor car, camera, a wallet, £40, a watch, driving licence, cheque book, suitcase, two holdalls containing clothing and murdered him.

The second accused that:

> Between April 8th and May 6th in Twiglees Forest, Eskdalemuir, Dumfriesshire owned by the Forestry Commission, or elsewhere in

the county, he assaulted Hans Ruedi Gimmi, trainee student of Zurich, Switzerland, discharged a loaded firearm at him shooting him in the head and robbed him of a pair of shoes, a camera, flash equipment, a watch, wallet, railway ticket, sum of money and other articles and murdered him.

By the time of his trial later in the month, psychiatrists were convinced he was insane, too mad to plead to the charges. One said:

> At one stage he started a church of his own and was concerned in the theft from other churches of communion vessels. He seemed to feel he really had achieved something by the killings and to feel he was doing it to impress people that the world had a wrong standard of values; the victims had not been killed but merely what Simpson called 'changed'. He said he was carrying out a divine mission but has no sense of the gravity of his situation. He seems almost to feel a sense of triumph. He said he would have achieved more in the same direction if allowed. I regard him as a very dangerous person. There is no question of his just feigning the symptoms of insanity.

And a colleague told the judge:

> I have found in him a religious type of motivation. He posed as a minister for nine months and as a doctor on another occasion. His life became an increasing fantasy, a very considerable amalgamation of religious and criminal factors mixed up together. But gradually the homicidal impulse replaced the suicidal. He seemed to have a compulsion to discuss moral values and if people did not measure up to the standard he required he was compelled to destroy them to purify society. He only interrogated men; women were never in danger. He wanted to carry on as long as possible what he regards as good work.

But it was the comments of the judge that caused a sensation. His Lordship was told how Simpson had been certified and committed to mental hospital and was sent to Hartwood, from where he escaped. But according to the Lunacy (Scotland) Act of 1862, which was then continued in the Mental Health (Scotland) Act 1960, by staying free for twenty-eight days there was nothing the law could do to send him back and so he was free to go where he wanted and do what he wished. His madness saved him from the gallows; however, the judge had no alternative but to send Simpson to Carstairs. Lord Kilbrandon said:

> I am not blaming anybody but if it is the system that was at fault and this has given rise to serious public anxiety, then I am not in the least surprised. I hope this case will never be forgotten by those who are responsible for this country's mental health administration.

His words struck home. James Dempsey, MP for Coatbridge and Airdrie, immediately announced that as soon as Parliament reconvened after the summer recess, he would table a Question seeking the law to be changed to make sure the Simpson situation could never happen again: 'It is ridiculous that because somebody avoids detection for at least twenty-eight days they cannot be sent back to the mental institution from which they have escaped. Something must be done.'

But the stable door was being shut after the horse had bolted, and two men had died needlessly as a result. Yet that would not be the end of the killing or the suspicion that not all of Simpson's victims had been found. As is often the case, serial murderers become easy targets in any long unsolved case involving extreme violence. In his case, after his committal to Carstairs, his name was added to a long list of men suspected of involvement in the disappearance of twelve-year-old Moira Anderson in February 1957 from Coatbridge, Lanarkshire. But most have since dismissed the theory that he could have been responsible.

5

SUFFER LITTLE CHILDREN

Five innocent trusting children who moments earlier had been excited at the promise they would see and cuddle a litter of newborn puppies. Now, one by one they fell, screaming, their little arms flailing until five tiny bodies lay on the pavement, their bones smashed and blood pouring from their broken heads. Forty feet above them, the madwoman who had thrown them from the window of her home looked down and waited for the police to take her to a meeting with the hangman. The anger and blame that followed this nightmare was directed at the crazed, miserable wretch named Jean Waddell who had dropped the children to their terrible fate. But was she alone the culprit? There are many who, to this day, feel others escaped just judgement.

It was the evening of Monday, 27 March 1961 when the eyes of the world were suddenly cast on Toryglen Street, a nondescript road in Oatlands, Glasgow. An off-duty police constable walking past a tenement block noticed a crowd gathered outside and many of the spectators were weeping. Curious, he marched over and was met with a sight that would haunt him for the rest of his days. On the pavement lay five children, some motionless but in others there was slight movement. 'What's happened?' he asked and was told, 'A woman threw them out of her window.' Emergency services had already been summoned and when ambulances arrived doctors began the tender task of looking for life. One child was already dead, but the others would recover from appalling injuries.

The toll could have been much worse. Hearing the screams of the first to be thrown, a near neighbour rushed over and was in time to break the fall of the last child to be hurled into space. Detectives who immediately began investigating interviewed another resident of the block where Jean Waddell lived and he told how after racing to the flat from which the children were falling, he burst through the door and as he did so, a little boy rushed out past him sobbing for his mother. At least the child was spared the ordeal of the others. The fall from the flat on the third storey of the block killed Marjorie Drummond Hughes, aged four. Doctors would later tell her heart-broken family that, if she had suffered, her pain had been brief because she died almost immediately. The four who survived were Felix Francis Lennon, aged six; Margaret Mary Lennon, five; Thomas Downie Devaney, four; and seven-year-old Daniel O'Neill, whose condition gave most rise for concern, but he would recover. All the children lived close by Waddell's home.

In the immediate aftermath of the horror, the knee-jerk reaction of many in Scotland was to demand that thirty-seven-year-old Waddell should hang. At the time capital punishment remained an option for courts. Just three months before the Oatlands tragedy, Anthony Miller had been executed and by the time Waddell appeared in the High Court Victor John Terry was in the condemned cell at Wandsworth prison, London, waiting to keep his appointment with the hangman. Admittedly the outrage over the execution in Holloway, London, of beautiful Ruth Ellis in 1955 for shooting dead a boyfriend had effectively ended the hanging of women and no female had gone to the gallows in Scotland since Susan Newell in 1923. She had killed a young boy and was clearly mentally ill, although an attempt by her defence to save her on the grounds of insanity was rejected by most of the jury. What would save Waddell, however, was the fact that by the 1960s politicians and most of the public had lost the stomach for marching a female to the scaffold and there was much more sympathy for someone like her who was clearly mad. When the full story emerged, questions would be asked about whether others responsible for keeping the public safe from lunatics should be made to account for their actions.

SUFFER LITTLE CHILDREN

News of the Oatlands outrage had appeared in newspapers everywhere and the eyes of the world were on Scotland. In early May, Waddell appeared in court but was found insane and unfit to plead to charges that she murdered tiny Marjorie by lifting her through a window and dropping her to the pavement whereby she was so severely injured that she died and also that she attempted to murder the other youngsters in the same way.

These were horrible crimes yet the woman who committed them had at one time been happy, bright and capable. She had worked as a hotel receptionist and shorthand typist. But it all changed after the break-up of a short-lived marriage at the end of the Second World War to serviceman Floyd Oakman. Suffering a total breakdown, she had been taken to a sanatorium to be treated for tuberculosis, but while there she assaulted a nurse and was transferred to a mental hospital. She suffered delusions imagining she was about to conceive an illegitimate baby and lived in a near permanent fantasy world in which she was convinced police were forever watching her, monitoring her every movement. She was admitted to Hawkhead mental hospital in Glasgow – now better known as Leverndale Hospital – where, imagining herself to be the Empress of Japan, she was subjected to electric shock treatment that had a devastating effect. It terrified her and her nine months there left her with a morbid fear of being taken back, a fear so great that she would rather die than undergo the treatment again. However, to the astonishment of those who knew her, she was released.

But her mental agonies remained. To her, death would be the only release, and one day went shopping for a gun, but at the very last moment had second thoughts and instead tried killing herself by taking an overdose of tablets. There was even worse to come. After the suicide attempt she was taken to the psychiatric unit of a hospital in Duke Street, Glasgow, but merely by telling staff she felt better was discharged after a short stay. A few days later, believing that if she committed a murderous act the State would condemn her and end her wretched life, she lured a number of local children to her flat by telling them she wanted to show them a litter of puppies. It was an attraction no child wanted to miss and they were thrilled to follow this real-life Pied Piper of Hamelin. What followed in the next few minutes was the stuff not of legend but of horror.

To the man in the street, it was glaringly obvious that she was unwell, a fact of which her family were all too well aware. But formal confirmation of just how ill she was came from consultant psychiatrist Dr Hunter Gillies. What he had to tell stunned the packed public benches:

> At no time did she express sorrow for her actions which she described to me in detail regardless of the damaging nature of her admissions. She is a chronic case of paranoid schizophrenia from which she has been suffering sometimes overtly and sometimes inconspicuously since 1947.

He said a report from Hawkhead hospital stated she suffered bizarre delusions of a sexual nature, typical of patients who were paranoid schizophrenics. The judge, Lord Strachan, had no alternative but to send her to Carstairs.

So who did allow Jean Waddell to walk from a psychiatric hospital to kill? Among those demanding to know was Gorbals MP Alice Cullen, no stranger when it came to trying to get to the bottom of bizarre matters. Seven years earlier hundreds of children, some as young as four and armed with sticks and stakes, invaded the Southern Necropolis cemetery in Glasgow in search of a vampire with iron teeth. They had been influenced by graphic cartoons in American horror comics sold in Britain portraying violence and terror and Mrs Cullen led demands to have these banned. The result was the introduction of the Children and Young Persons (Harmful Publications) Act of 1955, which made it illegal to sell to children publications showing incidents classed as repulsive or horrible. But it was one thing to take on comics salespeople – another to eke out secrets from the medical profession, with the result that whoever had authorised the discharge from psychiatric hospital of Jean Waddell was able to remain anonymous behind the customary curtain of confidentiality. As for the killer, she too was able to fade into anonymity and obscurity, living to the ripe old age of eighty-six before dying in Dumfriesshire in 2009.

Carstairs had admitted its first female patients in 1959, when five women were transferred there from the lunatic unit at Perth jail. Men outnumbered women by eleven to one at the State Hospital and a report published in the highly respected *British Journal of Psychiatry* examined why they were there and how they had fared. The article appeared on pages 445–7 in the issue of November 1975 (No. 127) and was entitled 'A Fifteen-Year Review of Female Admissions to Carstairs State Hospital', by Patrick W. Brooks and Geoffrey Mitchell. It revealed that up to the end of December 1973, of a total of 934 patients detained in Carstairs over that period, sixty-six were females, most of them aged between twenty and thirty, the youngest being only sixteen. Among a number of conclusions, the authors said:

> There is an impression that the number of persistently violent patients coming from other hospitals may be increasing, yet at the same time our results suggest that our ability to change their behaviour, either while in-patients at the State Hospital or subsequently after transfer, may be limited under present conditions. At present the hospital appears to be offering these patients a temporary, albeit more secure, place of asylum, at the same time thus providing a period of relief and respite for the staff of the ordinary psychiatric and subnormality hospitals, whose therapeutic efforts on behalf of the majority of their patients can be so seriously disrupted by such persistently violent patients.

Surprisingly, this doubt in the usefulness of Carstairs went unnoticed. The reason for the admission of a woman tended to produce a high degree of emotion, as in the case of Jean Waddell. Very often the crimes that led them through the gates of the State Hospital involved children. Among those covered by the survey was Catherine Duffy, aged twenty-five, who had been ordered to be detained in Carstairs without limit of time in January 1972, after she pleaded guilty to killing her daughter Clare, ten weeks old. She had admitted that after hitting the baby on the head with her hand after the tot was crying, the infant struck her head against the arm of a chair and died from a subdural haemorrhage. Sympathisers suggested it had been an accident but the baby's father told how his wife claimed a lamp had fallen on the child. Then when he rushed from their home in Shettleston, Glasgow, to get help, she chased after him begging him not to tell anybody what had happened. By the time he returned to the tragic scene after calling for police and an ambulance, he found Catherine sitting fondling the family's pet dog as though nothing out of the ordinary had taken place. In reality, this distressing story had begun two years earlier when the tragic loving mother underwent a personality change. Now mental illness had severely diminished her sense of responsibility. Doctors certified her sane, and fit to plead, but at the same time described her as a psychopath.

Four months later, Catherine was joined at the State Hospital by grey-haired grandmother Wilhelmina Thorburn who had sparked off a huge city-wide manhunt when ten-month-old Louise Kilmartin, who had been sleeping in her pram outside her home in the Calton area of Glasgow, disappeared without trace. The search ended at Bargeddie with the discovery of the baby's body lying on the Glasgow to Airdrie railway line beneath a bridge.

Who could have snatched a sleeping infant then thrown her to her death? Police were at first baffled but then officers making routine inquiries of women wanting a child of their own followed up a series of advertisements placed in shops in the east end of Glasgow. The advertiser was offering to take care of babies while their mothers were at work and, although she was not a suspect, detectives became interested in her because of her sheer persistence and seeming determination. But within minutes of knocking on the door of her home in Easterhouse, Glasgow, the forty-one-year-old burst into tears and confessed she had taken Louise.

Yet again questions would be asked whether the murder should have been avoided. Because it emerged that the mother-of-three had a long history of mental troubles going back more than two decades. She had told staff in one mental hospital she loved her babies so much she wanted to eat them and, as if to demonstrate how, had attacked nurses, trying to bite them and suck their blood. When she appeared before the High Court in Glasgow, accused of having stolen and murdered Louise, a psychiatrist said that Wilhelmina had told him that she took the child because she was lonely but could give no explanation for what happened after that. He said she showed no emotion or remorse and at one point had said she did not know why she was in prison and expected to be released soon as she had done nothing wrong. The doctor said, 'This woman is mentally ill. It is likely that it is that form of insanity, schizophrenia.' Found insane and unfit to plead, Wilhelmina, the granny who loved too much, was sent to Carstairs.

It was a sad tale, but distressing too was the case of Eveline Livingstone. Eveline's story offers a stark lesson in why society should learn to listen to those whose tormented minds cry out for help. Just a month after Wilhelmina was committed, another grandmother was keeping a careful watch on nineteen-month-old Judith Clark who lay happily in her pram in Allison Street at Govanhill, Glasgow. It was the sort of street where families had good reason for being wary. Most remembered a terrible incident in a flat there almost three years earlier when bank robber Howard Wilson, a former policeman, had shot and killed constables Angus Mackenzie and Edward Barnett when they tried to arrest him. Fellow cop Inspector Andrew Hyslop was shot in the head, surviving but carrying bullet fragments in his brain for the remainder of his days.

Little Judith was enjoying the sunshine and her grandmother frequently popped out to check on the baby. Passers-by laughed and played with the child. But one had a sinister purpose as she neared the pram, watching until Judith's grandmother had gone indoors. Eveline Livingstone was aged thirty-nine and a schizophrenic who, for many years, had been treated for the condition. Suddenly, the sleepiness of the sunny summer day was shattered by the shrieks of the youngster who was discovered covered in blood. A woman was spotted running off. She was quickly arrested, but despite their efforts doctors were unable to save lovely little Judith who had suffered shock and blood loss. Her injuries were horrendous. She had been stabbed more than fifty times and died the next day. By then police had arrested and charged Mrs Livingstone.

It was a callous murder. But then it began emerging that there was much more to it than simply a case of a crazed woman lashing out at a helpless baby. Eveline Livingstone had screamed out for help and had been denied. During her late adolescence she suffered from depression and in her early twenties was admitted to a mental hospital in Glasgow to be treated for schizophrenia. For the next seventeen years she was in and out of hospital, once being dragged back just as she was about to hurl herself out of a ward window; on a couple of occasions she had tried to gas herself. She married and had a daughter, but the relationship with her husband and child, although loving, could not drag her from the depths of despair into which she so often plunged.

She telephoned a psychiatrist, telling him, 'I have these strange feelings coming over me. I need help,' and begging to be taken in to a mental hospital where she would feel safe. She claimed his response had been that she ought to wait until her next outpatient appointment or arrange to visit her family doctor. The morning after that call, having seen her husband off to his work, evil thoughts began forming telling her to commit violence. Trying to fight the urge by killing herself, she put her head in a gas oven but then, desperate to feel normal, went to a hairdresser. Back home in Govanhill, for a while it felt as though the Devil had been denied but then she once more felt strange, picked up a pair of scissors and went for a walk. She was still blood-stained when she told police what happened next: 'I knew I was going to do something wicked. It didn't matter to me who this was done to. I saw the child and had a great urge to strike her.'

Psychiatrists told Lord Wheatley, the judge at the High Court in Glasgow, that despite the hospital treatment, Mrs Livingstone's condition was prone to periods when it became worse. They said her 'dangerous, violent and criminal propensities' meant it would not be safe to admit her to an ordinary mental hospital and confirmed she was insane and unfit to plead to the charge. In an unusual ruling Lord Wheatley sent her to Carstairs and ordered the accusation that she murdered Judith to be temporarily deserted. It meant that if doctors decided at some time in the future she had recovered and was sane, she could still be tried for murder. While they mourned for Judith, the baby's family and friends generously sympathised for her killer, echoing the opinion of many by pointing out that had she been taken into hospital as she had asked, a little life would have been spared. Sadly society had failed Eveline Livingstone.

The crash of the blows inflicted by Ann Dunn on her own daughter and another youngster was so loud that it awoke upstairs neighbours who would later tell police how they heard whimpering. Next day a relative of Dunn who called at the house in Stonehouse, Lanarkshire, found Dunn's five-year-old daughter Erin lying motionless in a blood-soaked bed. Beside her was a blood-stained claw hammer and in a pool of blood on the floor of another room lay the unconscious body of the dead child's ten-year-old friend, pieces of broken bone sticking out of her skull. She was rushed to hospital where despite appalling injuries she recovered, although the attack left her scarred for life.

Fearing she had taken an overdose, Dunn, thirty-six, was led off to hospital where she told nurses, 'I killed them. I don't want to be here any more. I am going to prison.' How could a devoted, loving mother snap and kill the human being most dear to her? After her relationship with Erin's father broke up Dunn sank into despair and was prescribed drugs for neurotic depression, but had stopped taking the medication because she thought she no longer needed it. At her trial where she was accused of murdering little Erin and assaulting the other youngster, the Crown accepted her plea to the reduced allegation of culpable homicide on the grounds of diminished responsibility. Her defence advocate said:

> She was a very caring and concerned mother and everyone who knew her could speak to that. The suddenness and shock of the incident made it all the more horrible. If and when she comes to realise the tragedy and awfulness of the event it will be a real life sentence for her.

Ann was sent to Carstairs. By killing children, Catherine Duffy, Wilhelmina Thorburn, Eveline Livingstone and Ann Dunn gained only misery and wretchedness.

Jennifer Byrd was sent to Carstairs because, motivated by greed, she took the life of her elderly mother to obtain riches. Had Byrd shown patience, she would have inherited a fortune. As a youngster she wanted for nothing. Educated at fee paying schools and winning awards for her brilliance in the Russian and French languages at Glasgow University, she fell in love with and married American student Patrick Byrd. The couple had two sons, but the breakup of the marriage was a blow that sent her into a pit of depression from which she sought refuge in drink and then went to live with her mother, Ann Baillie-Scott, the wealthy daughter of famous Arctic explorer William Laird McKinlay. Ann had announced that when she died her £400,000 fortune would be equally divided between Jennifer and her sister Patricia, but then Patricia died in a car accident meaning the entire amount would be left to Jennifer.

In October 2003 Mrs Baillie-Scott, aged eighty-four, was found dead. A soft toy had been stuffed in her mouth and she had been strangled. Days later her surviving daughter was charged with murder. However, after doctors confirmed Jennifer, fifty-one, was suffering from depression, her plea of guilty to culpable homicide was accepted and she was sentenced to four years' detention which would begin in the State Hospital. If her condition improved she would be transferred to prison to serve out the remainder of her sentence.

Jennifer Byrd had been lucky enough to have a privileged upbringing. It was in total contrast to that of Margaret Maxwell Davidson Henderson. An orphan at the age of just thirteen, Margaret was sent to Dykebar mental hospital where she would remain for the next seventeen years surrounded not, as were the friends she had known at school, by happy giggling adolescent girls who fantasised about boys and marriage and babies, but by the mentally sick. After being discharged she was moved in and out of at least half a dozen psychiatric hospitals in England and Scotland. Police in Scotland discovered her friendless and sleeping rough and she was admitted to yet another mental hospital, Heathfield on the outskirts of Ayr, because she was found to be suffering from fits. There she suffered depressive mood swings and tried committing suicide by slashing her wrists.

During her recovery she met fellow patient, retired schoolmistress spinster Margaret Cassells, aged sixty-seven. It was as though fate had brought them together. The women became friends, chatting as though neither had a care in the world and the cordiality of their relationship impressed hospital staff. Their friendship might also solve a problem. The teacher would need someone to care for her when she was discharged and sent home, while Margaret Henderson would need a job and somewhere to live. Why not as housekeeper to the schoolmistress? Miss Cassells was all for the idea. And so the two women went to live together in Ayr, but the decision to let Margaret look after her elderly employer would end in tragedy.

One day, not long after the arrangement began, she had cooked a meal and as she was clearing the dining room table, her employer asked her to switch on the television set. That simple request was enough to spark a murderous attack with a bottle. Henderson told a psychiatrist, 'The next I knew I started to hit her on the head with the bottle. I had a funny feeling all day and felt the need to do something. This feeling has often come over me in the past few years and when it does I usually run away.' She ran, too, after the bottle attack and was spotted by a coalman who, not unnaturally, thought she wanted to order a delivery from him. Then he noticed her arms covered in blood and heard her screaming, 'I've killed my employer.'

When she appeared at the High Court in Ayr in October 1968, she denied culpable homicide of the teacher on grounds she was insane at the time of the killing. Another psychiatrist who examined her said she had no clear memory of what happened before she discovered the bottle in her hand. He said, 'She remembered hearing her employer screaming and beginning to moan and thinks she ran out of the house to get help. She can give no reason for the attack.' A jury found Miss Henderson, forty-three, guilty but insane and she was detained in Carstairs. But like so many others whose actions had led to death, it was significant that a woman who so obviously was mentally unwell had been allowed to leave hospital.

That was the same question asked by those who pondered on the case of Joanne Wilkie in 1998. A confirmed schizophrenic she had been admitted to Dykebar Hospital ten times in the previous six years. Following her eleventh admission she announced she was discharging herself. Doctors pleaded with her not to leave, pointing out she was still unwell and the course of treatment they had diagnosed was not complete. But their advice went unheeded. Twelve days later Wilkie, twenty-seven, asked if she could take a friend's nine-month-old baby son for a walk. The friend agreed and, almost by instinct, Wilkie headed back towards Dykebar. But she had not changed her mind and was seeking help from staff there. Instead while pushing the toddler in his pram through the grounds she noticed he had fallen asleep. For a reason she would never be able to explain she put her hands around the child's neck and began to press. The kiddie woke up and began crying at which Wilkie picked him up, carried him over to a burn running through the grounds and threw him in. The boy crashed off rocks and rolled into the freezing cold water. Leaving him struggling for his life, she ran to the hospital and told a male nurse, 'I think I have killed a baby. I am not sure, he may still be alive.' The man ran in search of the child and hearing a scream saw the little boy lying under a bridge, only his head above water level. His quick thinking saved a young life.

Doctors who treated the infant discovered he had suffered a fractured skull and X-rays revealed blood clots caused by his head having been smashed against the rocks. Yet almost miraculously he survived. Police asked Wilkie why she had thrown the baby. 'I didn't want it to be living,' was her reply. The judge at the High Court in Glasgow, Lord Nimmo Smith, told her, 'It is lucky he didn't die.' Wilkie admitted attempted murder and the judge sent her to Carstairs without limit of time.

Carstairs no longer treats women patients, primarily because it is felt unnecessary to hold females under the same conditions of stringent security that apply to males. And so women have gradually been moved out and into a range of other psychiatric hospitals where security remains strict, but is relaxed enough to allow them greater freedom. While Carstairs retained female inmates, the emphasis was on endeavouring to provide them with as close to what would be regarded as a normal home environment as possible. Women were encouraged to cook and sew, received training in managing a household budget, were occasionally allowed shopping expeditions accompanied by staff and even had regular hairdos from outside hairdressers.

Regrettably an all too common theme was the need for counselling to help women inmates come to terms with the consequences of having been abused, often sexually, in their childhood or youth. Did the therapy work? Were many – or any – of its one-time female inmates able to return fully to family life? Sadly we will never know. The shadow of secrecy prevails.

6

ON THE WORD OF THE DEVIL

For years, garage mechanic Phillip Givens felt the Devil trying to take control of his mind. Like so many wars, it was the innocent who suffered and this was no exception. The extraordinary battle ultimately claimed the life of happy schoolboy Freddy Dowden who died simply because he trusted his killer.

There have been many cases of men who kidnap and abduct youngsters. Mostly the motive is money. A child disappears, a telephone call is made to the victim's parents demanding ransom, payment is handed over and the young person returned home. Very occasionally it all goes wrong. The target perishes, as was the case of seventeen-year-old Lesley Whittle who died a terrible and lonely death after Donald Neilson, known as the 'Black Panther', left her naked and bound down a drainage shaft in 1975.

A dozen years earlier such a similarly appalling fate was that of Freddy, aged fifteen. There was never any doubt that Givens was the killer. However he said he took the boy's life not because he wanted to, but because the Devil living in his head ordered him to do so. Freddy was not the first youngster abducted on the instructions the evil voices relayed to Givens. A few weeks earlier Philip Martin, sixteen, had been attacked. Luckily for him he managed to escape, and in doing so he set off one of the most remarkable manhunts in Scottish criminal history, one in which supreme dedication and skill by police officers would bring to a conclusion the terrifying reign of the Devil in Phillip Givens. But none of the hundreds of policemen and women who sought Phil Martin's attacker could have realised he had already struck and his helpless victim lay dead. Or that had they not succeeded it was almost certain that another youngster would have perished as Givens obeyed the Devil's commands.

Philip Christopher Martin from Dalmuir, Glasgow, had found work as an apprentice slater after leaving school. The job was based in Greenock and even though it meant daily travelling he was happy to be earning money and able to join his mates on nights out. On the afternoon of Thursday, 19 July 1962 he was walking along a road in Clydebank when a black car pulled alongside and the driver wound down his window and leaned over. 'Hi, you fancy earning ten shillings [50p]?' he asked. He was a stranger, a receding hairline exposing a scar on his face but Phil thought he might have been sent by work colleagues who knew the young man would pretty certainly be short of cash as he was not due to be paid until the following day. 'What's the job?' Phil asked. 'Oh, I have to shift a fireplace and need somebody to help me lift it. It'll only take a few minutes and it's ten bob in your hand when the job's done, then I'll take you home.' It sounded simple enough. 'Okay,' he said, opening the passenger door and climbing in.

As the stranger drove off, Phil asked where they were heading. 'Just up the road to Glasgow. We'll be there in no time.' The journey passed quickly, the two chatting amiably before the car pulled up outside what seemed to be a disused shop in the Finnieston area of the city. Producing a key, the driver took him inside. It was dark and the youth noticed the windows appeared to have been painted over black, presumably to stop anyone seeing inside. His host lit a candle and Phil saw the grate of a fireplace. 'Okay, where are we moving it to?' he asked. And when he turned he saw the other man was holding a gun. Phil would later tell a friend:

> He ordered me to stand against a wall. I started laughing because I thought this was a laugh, but then I looked at his face and saw it was no joke. He ordered me to strip then pushed me into a chair, tied me to it and put a length of sticky tape across my mouth. I was terrified.

Givens, his attacker, snuffed out the candle, chillingly told his victim,

'Be brave' and left, locking the door. Phil was already bumping his way in the chair over towards the window and by using his teeth pulling down his gag. However at that point Givens, hearing the noise of the chair crashing on the floor, came back in, replaced the gag and left for a second time. Once again Phil crashed towards what he hoped would be safety and this time children playing outside heard the racket and ran to their parents for help. Local people smashed their way into the shop and rescued him. A crowd gathered and among the curious onlookers was Givens who had intended returning once more to the scene of his attack to check whether his victim was still helpless only to find his way barred by dozens of neighbours.

Stunned and shocked, the teenager made his way home and blurted out his story to his dad. 'Come on, we're going to the police,' his father told him. At their local police station it was quickly obvious to father and son that Phil's story, especially when it came to his describing having a gun pushed into his back, was being regarded with a good deal of cynicism. However when officers went into the empty shop and found evidence that backed up the boy's story, together with the fireplace and an empty can of black spray paint, he was taken seriously. But who was the attacker?

Inquiries with agents acting for the shop owners revealed the premises had been rented by a 'Mr Green' who had paid cash for a short-term let. The home address he had given was checked out and found to be false. At least the description the agents gave of Mr Green was remarkably similar to that given by Phil of the stranger who had tied him up. Detectives found fingerprints in the shop. They were able to eliminate Phil's, but those on the strands of tape and chair matched none in criminal records. They had come up against every detective's nightmare, a first-time offender. There were other clues. Phil helped a police artist draw up an identikit impression of the fat man with the scar on his face. When it was shown during a television appeal for anyone who might know who it was to come forward, witnesses who had already been interviewed were taken to a concert specially laid on by police to avoid accusations that they had been influenced by seeing the TV show.

ON THE WORD OF THE DEVIL

Then there was the car. Phil knew it was black but didn't know the registration number and, hard as he tried to be helpful, could not be sure whether it was a Ford, possibly a Ford Anglia, or an Austin. At the time, just about every car on the British roads was black. He was shown photographs and was able to refine the model of the motor down to one manufactured between the start of the Second World War and 1946, but in those seven years 80,000 black Anglias and Austins had been produced, and 10,000 of these were owned in Scotland. Every one of the owners would have to be traced and interviewed. It was a staggering undertaking and the sparse evidence police had to go on, coupled with the fact that at the end of the day, apart from getting a fright, Phil Martin had not been injured, hardly justified the time and expense that would be involved. While the incident was being treated seriously, some detectives reasoned it may have been a one-off or even an attempt at a sick joke that went wrong, with the scar-faced man deciding against a repeat. Others took a more pessimistic view and were convinced the attacker would try again. Their theory would be proved tragically accurate. But in the meantime as the days moved into weeks the inquiry was gradually overtaken by other matters categorised as being more pressing and likelier to be solved.

Then in the late afternoon of Tuesday, 7 August, Frederick Douglas McElvogue-Dowden disappeared from his home in Drumchapel, Glasgow. His engineer dad Frederick had more reason than most to be concerned. His son had taken the death of his mother Mary badly and the father and son were especially close. Apart from the fact that a few neighbours said they had seen the boy getting into a black car – again, possibly a Ford Anglia – there were no other clues for police to work on. Had the driver picked up the youngster as part of a pre-arranged rendezvous and had Freddy run away? Police carried out routine searches of Freddy Dowden's usual haunts, they questioned school friends and pals, checked hospitals, looked for any signs of the boy having taken suddenly ill or fallen into the River Clyde and they wondered if maybe he had decided to embark on an expedition to the city and had fallen into bad company. No stone was left unturned but there was not a sign of the teenager.

By early October, although the search for Freddy was in the process of being scaled down, the fact that there still was no trace of him heightened the determination of the police to discover what had become of him. Officers on the beat were ordered to retrace their steps and interview witnesses again. Then a sharp-eyed beat constable carrying out a routine check of a disused doctor's surgery in the West Bridgend part of Dumbarton realised that for some strange reason somebody had covered the windows in black paint. It was an odd thing and must have been done to hide something going on inside. His curiosity aroused, the constable decided to take a closer look and, climbing up on to a ledge, peered inside. What he saw made him retch. He rang his station then smashed in the door. Tied to a sink, an overturned chair at his side, his mouth and nose covered tightly by adhesive tape, was the near naked decomposing body of Freddy. Nearby was an empty black paint aerosol. A pathologist reported that he had died mercifully soon after being abducted and taken to the empty building. He had not been assaulted, beaten or sexually abused. He would not have suffered for long.

What had been a search for a missing boy now became a murder investigation. The then Scottish Murder Squad, based in Glasgow, and led by the legendary crime fighter Detective Chief Superintendent Tom Goodall, who had arrested serial killer Peter Manuel four years earlier, descended on Dumbarton. Manuel had been hanged and now Goodall was on the trail of another murderer who might find himself dangling at the end of a rope. The squad came up with some terrifying clues. There were fingerprints on the chair and tape. They did not match those of anyone with a criminal record. But they were identical to the prints of the man who had tied up Phil Martin. And when agents looking after the surgery were asked to check their records and report whether the building had been rented to anybody, an astonishing fact emerged. A man who identified himself as 'Mr Black' had paid cash to use the premises. His description matched that of 'Mr Green'. That was proof he had struck twice. Would there be a third abduction, another possible murder of a youngster? Senior detectives knew they had to find the man responsible.

ON THE WORD OF THE DEVIL

Letting agents all over central Scotland were visited, shown the artist's impression drawn with the help of Phil Martin, and asked whether it looked like anyone who had been trying to rent an empty building. That part of the inquiry came up trumps. Around the time Freddy had disappeared a 'Mr Blue' had paid cash for the short-term use of an empty shop in Plantation Street, Govan, Glasgow. Armed with the address, detectives quietly surrounded the shop and, using a duplicate key, went inside. They found a chair, lengths of rope, a black paint aerosol and a roll of adhesive tape. There was nothing to suggest anyone had been held there, but experts found fingerprints matching those of 'Mr Black' and 'Mr Green'. A discreet watch was placed on the shop in the hope of catching the elusive 'Mr Blue', although he never showed up.

Now the case took on a new and more desperate urgency. It was obvious Freddy's killer planned another abduction and so he had to be caught, and quickly. Desperate to build a picture of the perpetrator, senior officers called in a criminal psychologist and gave him complete access to the thin file they had so far built up and asking what sort of man he thought the attacker might be. It is well worth remembering his answer: 'He will be over thirty, not married and still living at home probably with a single parent who is most likely to be his mother.'

Experienced senior detectives reasoned the best chance of finding the killer lay in tracing the owner of the black car. It would mean taking bobbies off other important duties and running up hundreds of thousands of man hours but an unpredictable madman remained at large – one who, having got away with his attempt to abduct Phil Martin, and having succeeded in murdering Freddy Dowden, was evidently trying again. The perpetrator had to be found and commanders of a number of surrounding police forces agreed to transfer men to help out. The painstaking work of elimination began.

Meanwhile, police officers burning the midnight oil in their hunt for the owner of the black car were narrowing the number of possible owners. Two months after Phil Martin was snatched, they had managed to get the figure down to around 1,500 potential owners. Individual cops were being issued with a list of between twelve and twenty people living on their beats to check out. One by one their names were crossed off as owners came up with convincing and truthful alibis for the day of the attack on Phil. Then a constable knocked on a door in Darmarnock, Glasgow, to ask the owners of their black Ford Anglia where they had been on 19 July. 'In Canada,' they told him and in answer to further questions went on to tell the officer that while they had been holidaying in North America they had loaned their car to a friend, Phillip Givens, the mechanic who regularly serviced it. 'You'll probably know him,' said the couple. 'He looks after a lot of police cars.' They were asked to describe him and the reply sent the hairs on the back of the policeman's neck on end. 'Oh Phil's a bit on the fat side and he has a wee scar on his face.' The constable went off to Given's home only to be told he was at work. There, one look at the mechanic sent the policeman rushing to his bosses to tell them he had found the killer kidnapper.

Givens was arrested. His fingerprints matched those of 'Mr Green', 'Mr Black' and 'Mr Blue'. It emerged that the criminal psychologist knew his stuff – Givens was thirty-five, a bachelor and he lived with his married sister Margaret. At an identification parade, he was picked out by Phil and the various leasing agents. The beast who preyed on youngsters became a slobbering mess of a broken man, begging for help and claiming he never meant Freddy to die, only wanting a sexual thrill from the act of tying him up. He claimed he had gone back to the surgery to free the lad, but finding him dead panicked. When he was asked why he had not ended the misery and suffering of the youngster's family by telephoning police to say where the body was, Givens replied that voices in his head told him what to do and they had said nothing about informing the police.

In Barlinnie prison, where he awaited his trial, he begged his sister to take care of his beloved pet dog Bruce. Margaret told a friend:

> I am glad he was found out for I know he would have gone on killing and hurting little boys until he was caught. He just couldn't stop. I know he was mad. He said he heard the voice of the Devil ordering him to do the things he did. He was frightened of what would happen when he died and came before God.

ON THE WORD OF THE DEVIL

When he appeared at the High Court in Glasgow the following year, Givens faced two charges – that he assaulted and murdered Freddy and that he assaulted Philip Martin, pointed a revolver at him and tied him to a chair. He admitted both offences.

The extent of Givens' madness was revealed by consultant psychiatrist Dr Hunter Gillies. He reported that the lunatic had got sexual kicks by tying himself up and had decided to see whether he would be thrilled to the same degree by doing this to boys. Until he was arrested he had shown no open signs of madness, but then his behaviour had become increasingly bizarre. Gillies said, 'He is an abnormal personality, a psychopathic personality with an illness almost amounting to insanity although I do not think he is insane.' Another psychiatrist said Givens had a pathological sexual development which gave him satisfaction in tying himself up then freeing himself. 'Givens thinks of his abnormality in religious terms, of the conflict between the Devil and his good self inside him. He has had no girl friends at all. He has no interest in women. He is basically rather a timid person.' By a strange quirk, the madness inspired by the Devil saved Givens from hanging. Instead of condemning him to death, the judge, Lord Mackintosh, sent Givens to Carstairs without limit of time and told him:

> In view of the medical evidence which has been led, I hold that you are suffering from a mental illness. I further hold that you, being a person of dangerous, violent and criminal propensities require treatment under conditions of special security.

Givens would never again terrify or kill boys. He finally found out whether he would be rewarded by the Devil or face his Maker in 2006 when he died aged seventy-eight.

7

GOOD SAMARITAN SLAYER

It was famous as the city that grew up on a diet of 'jute, jam and journalism'. Dundee prospered with sixty jute mills giving work to 50,000 Dundonians. Its Keiller's marmalade could be found on breakfast tables worldwide while comics such as the *Dandy* and *Beano* and the one-time bestselling *Sunday Post* newspaper, featuring the antics of Oor Wullie and The Broons, were a must for young and old. The city is the birthplace of internationally renowned actor Brian Cox, music hall star Will Fyffe and suffragette Agnes Husband. It is where RRS *Discovery*, the boat in which Captain Robert Scott and Ernest Shackleton sailed to the Antarctic in 1901, is berthed, and Dundee will house the new Victoria and Albert Museum of Design.

Scotland's fourth largest city has much about which it is entitled to boast but it has also known terrible tragedy. The Tay Bridge disaster of 1879, in which the first rail bridge collapsed as a train passed over, immortalised in the poem by William Topaz McGonagall, cost an estimated seventy-five lives. Yet it was the deaths of three other innocents that threw a cloak of horror over Dundee it can never shake off. In 1968 Hazel Phin, aged twelve, was strangled; a year earlier Robert Mone had shot schoolteacher Nanette Hanson dead; and then in 1974 six-year-old Pauline McIvor was abused and throttled with a skipping rope. Robert Mone would play a leading part in the greatest of all the Carstairs dramas and his crimes are investigated in detail in chapters 19 to 25. Like the senseless slaughter of any child, the killings of Hazel and Pauline have left an equally unforgettable legacy.

GOOD SAMARITAN SLAYER

Schoolgirl Hazel had finished lessons at St John's Roman Catholic school in Dundee – the same school where Robert Mone had been a pupil – and was walking past a close in September 1968 when she vanished, her disappearance sparking both a huge search and mass panic. She was not the sort of child to run off and police quickly came to the conclusion that she had been abducted. The thought that brought terror to parents was the prospect that a child killer was on the loose because as the hours passed with no sign of Hazel, the chances of her being found alive diminished. The ordeal of her family, in particular that of her mum, was terrible as the Phins waited for news of the child with hope running out as each minute dragged by. The following day a search of homes, attics and outbuildings in the streets around her home proved fruitless until an anonymous tip-off that they should look at a particular building outside the search area produced the gruesome discovery of her body in a cellar several hundred yards from where she had lived and been loved.

The dark, dingy room that was her last resting place had been converted into a workshop by Karl Anderson Tonner, aged twenty-three. It lay below the flat where he lived with his mother Euphemia and his seventy-three-year-old grandmother. In it he would spend most of his time tinkering with motorcycles. Now, surrounded by scrapped parts, oily tools and grimy rags and beneath a filthy sheet lay the little girl. She was naked, dead and bound hand and foot. Wound tightly around her neck was a length of rope. A post-mortem examination revealed she had been strangled but if there was any consolation for those whose hearts had been broken by her murder it was that at least she had not been sexually abused. Tonner made no attempt to deny he was her killer. He told the police:

> The girl was passing through the close. I took her to the washhouse converted into a workshop. I was going to have intercourse. When I got her there I did not feel like it, so I killed her with the rope and covered her up.

It was a callous, cruel epitaph to his helpless victim. When Tonner was brought before a sheriff in the city, the prosecutor revealed, 'It appears she was originally taken to the cellar for some sort of sexual relations, but nothing of that sort took place.' He was sent to the High Court in Edinburgh to be sentenced in November, by when a charge that he murdered Hazel had been reduced to one of culpable homicide because of his mental state. One psychiatrist told the judge, Lord Grant, 'He suffers from a serious personality disorder characterised by an abnormal degree of indifference to the feelings of others.' Another doctor said Tonner had been sane when he killed but added, 'He is a person of continuing dangerous, criminal and violent propensities requiring treatment in conditions of security,' the standard formal expression necessary to give a judge authority to commit an accused person to the State Hospital. Tonner was sent to Carstairs where he revealed himself as a sexual deviant with an especially unhealthy interest in children but at the same time was hell-bent on getting free so he could take out his sexual frustrations on gullible and trusting women.

Other patients were discovering loopholes in European legislation that enabled them, by arguing their condition was untreatable, to demand courts in Scotland let them either go free or successfully apply to be switched to prisons where they would have the opportunity to request parole. Tonner left it up to lawyers to work on his discharge. He had other irons in the fire. In 1997 the *Daily Record* newspaper told how sly Tonner had been answering lonely hearts advertisements, avoiding mentioning the fact that he was held in an institution for insane lunatics by simply giving his name and his address not as Carstairs but Lampits Road, the street on which the State Hospital was sited. What was particularly vile was that he managed to persuade unsuspecting mothers to send him photographs of their children and at night, alone in the privacy of his room, he would pore over his sick collection. The hoard was eventually discovered during a search by staff, but not before he had compiled more than a hundred snaps of youngsters.

Tonner failed to get out by claiming there was nothing the hospital could do to treat his condition but he had another ploy in mind, one in which his lonely hearts letters would play a part. If he found a woman willing to marry him, he could then argue he had a settled environment to which he could move. He built up a coterie of women who wrote to him regularly, in some cases for many years, under the impression he was in hospital suffering from a nervous complaint. One of these pen friends visited him at Carstairs and gave him photographs of her teenage daughter. He was allowed to send another youngster dolls made in one of the hospital workshops and permitted to use mail order to buy jewellery that he sent to her mother.

The woman was horrified when a friend told her the truth about Tonner. 'Oh, my God,' she said and promptly dumped him. Incredibly, social workers wanted to pay the fare of another woman to travel from England to meet him at Carstairs. Then yet another woman, this time from London, agreed to become his wife until she too discovered his past. She said after scrapping a planned marriage, 'I was about to marry a sick killer who had killed a little girl who was the same age as my own grandchildren. It makes me sick to my stomach.' When she learned the truth about his past, one of his pen friends threatened to take Carstairs to court if they did not stop him contacting her. A politician said he would want to meet hospital management. 'I want to know what is going on,' said MP Jimmy Hood. He was not alone.

Tonner finally won his freedom in 2007, nearly four decades after his arrival, but he did not leave in the manner he had wanted. He was carried from the State Hospital in a coffin after collapsing in his room following a heart attack at the age of sixty-one. He had lived well at Carstairs. While others outside the hospital walls struggled to survive, taxpayer-funded Tonner tucked into hearty meals while his body ballooned. His few pals believed he topped two hundred and eighty pounds, the sort of weight more appropriate for a heavyweight all-in wrestler and that obesity had contributed to his death. A friend of Hazel's family said at the time, 'Good riddance. Nobody who knew Hazel has any forgiveness in their heart for this madman.'

A year before Hazel was killed, the McIver family, who lived half a mile away, had been celebrating the birth of a daughter. They named the infant Pauline Jane and mum Alison, a nurse, looked forward to watching her daughter grow. Like her neighbours she had read and heard all about the tragedy suffered by the Phins. 'Lightning never strikes in the same place twice,' Alison's friends would assure her. In the months that followed Hazel's death, parents were especially watchful, accompanying their youngsters to and from school even if that meant rearranging work shifts. However with the passage of time and the fact that Tonner was locked up eighty miles away, their vigilance relaxed and trust returned to the community.

It wasn't that anyone was forgetting little Hazel. Mums and dads would continue to keep an anxious eye out for their children as soon as school ended for the day and began looking at their watches and worrying until the kiddies hove into sight. In the case of the McIvers, Alison had other children to take care of, a son Scott and a daughter Karen. Because the youngsters had arrived within a relative short period of time they had an especially close affinity, almost the sort of relationship parents associated with twins.

With time, the terror that had gripped the city with Hazel's death diminished. Sadly, it would return. In mid June 1974 Pauline McIver, now aged six, had decided to play with a school friend when they were told by teachers classes were over for the day and they could go home. The two often played together briefly before going indoors for their tea. It meant that if Pauline was a little late in getting home her mum need not unduly worry, although it was always stressed to the youngster she should not stay away too long. Her friend was the daughter of Michael Wilkinson and, for legal reasons, her name and her age cannot be given. That Monday afternoon the two pals walked off from school together and went into the Wilkinson home to play. An hour after the close of school Pauline had not arrived home and Alison began to fret. Time passed and with no sign of the little girl her parents began to retrace her probable route from school. It took them to the door of the tenement flat where Michael Wilkinson had brought up his daughter since his marriage ended. His explanation seemed reasonable. He told Alison that, yes, Pauline had been to his home with his daughter. The two had played in the flat but about half past four he had told Pauline it was time to go for her tea and she had left.

The McIvers drove around, called at the homes of other of Pauline's friends and knocked on the doors of neighbours, asking whether anyone had seen their daughter but, with each negative reply, their worry increased. At home they discussed what to do. As far as they could ascertain, Wilkinson had been the last person to see Pauline and so, some time after ten o'clock that night, the girl's father returned to question Wilkinson who repeated his earlier version of events. It was time to call in the experts, the police, something they ought, they decided, to have done much earlier, although as events turned out the delay would have made no difference. Officers immediately began house-to-house inquiries following Pauline's likely route and, because it was the last known spot where anyone acknowledged having seen her, much of their effort was concentrated on the tenement block where Wilkinson and his daughter lived.

An hour after midnight a police officer made the terrible discovery of a child's body. It lay in a recess used to hold refuse bins and no attempt had been made to hide it. It was obvious she had been sexually assaulted. A post-mortem examination would reveal she had been beaten on the head and body and then strangled. Bus driver Wilkinson, twenty-seven, was arrested and taken to a police station where he at first made statements reiterating what he had told Alison McIver. Officers would later say he seemed uncomfortable and uneasy and finally said, when again asked how he thought the body of the child had come to be found so close to his house, 'I know I'm going to get the blame. Let me think. I will have to tell somebody anyway. I think I must have killed her, but I can't remember doing it. It was me that done it.'

He told detectives that after putting Pauline's body behind the bins he had gone back home to watch the comedian Harry Worth on television and had then gone out to a public house where he drank three pints of beer before returning home. When he was charged with murdering Pauline who, it was confirmed, had been sexually molested, Wilkinson replied:

> I don't remember how I did it. I put her in a case and carried it downstairs and left her at the back. I went back to the house and washed her clothes in bleach then threw them out the back.

In addition, he was accused of using lewd and libidinous practices towards two other girls both aged twelve.

While he was on remand awaiting his trial Wilkinson was examined by a series of psychiatrists who disagreed about his mental state. When he appeared in court it was not him but his daughter who caused a sensation, because she was called as a Crown witness to give evidence against her father. What she said was crucial. She and Pauline, her best friend, had, she said, been playing cards in her home when her daddy took Pauline into the bedroom: 'He closed the door and I heard screaming after that.' Eventually the bedroom door was opened and she saw her friend lying on the floor. 'Daddy told me to get a skipping rope which was on the bed. He put it round Pauline's neck and pulled it tight.' The court had been cleared when the child gave her evidence, but the horror of what she said next caused total silence. She said her daddy put her friend's body in a suitcase and said to her, 'If you tell anybody, I'll do the same to you.' She was asked, 'Is he a good Daddy?' and 'Do you love your Daddy?' and to both the infant replied, 'Yes.'

A girl aged thirteen who had called at the Wilkinson home around six o'clock said she left after hearing screams from a bedroom. She went back an hour later to discover his daughter spraying the flat with an air freshener and she noticed he had marks on his trousers. 'I thought they were blood,' she said.

Because of his mental state the charge had been reduced to one of culpable homicide and Wilkinson had pleaded not guilty on the grounds that he was insane at the time Pauline died and could not be responsible for his actions. Five psychiatrists gave evidence. Those called by the Crown said the accused man had a normal intelligence but a doctor for the defence said Wilkinson appeared to have a mental block, a missing period between going to the bin recess and coming to, kneeling beside the child's body. 'It is impossible to say with absolute surety what his mental state was at the time the girl died,' he said. The jury unanimously convicted Wilkinson of the culpable homicide of Pauline and guilty by a majority verdict of the indecency offences against the twelve-year-old girls. He was sent to Carstairs.

These were dreadful offences. Yet there was a remarkable contradiction to the character of Wilkinson and it showed that good was possible even in those capable of great evil. In 1972, he had read of the plight of a family in Cambridge, England, whose twelve-year-old daughter was desperately ill and, without a kidney transplant, it was feared she would die. Her family along with doctors and nurses were frantically appealing for a kidney donor and Wilkinson, who had a daughter of his own, offered to make the sacrifice. Elsewhere throughout Britain, others had come forward and a donor was ultimately selected from a volunteer living nearer to the sick schoolgirl. Nevertheless, considerable praise was heaped on Wilkinson.

When investigating potential donors, doctors would have made detailed checks on the backgrounds of likely volunteers. It would never be revealed whether, apart from the distance factor, there were other reasons why the Dundee man had been rejected. If his medical file was shown to doctors at Cambridge, it would have shown worrying features. Around this time he had needed treatment at psychiatric units in Scotland after it was found he suffered from epilepsy associated with a personality disorder. Such a condition would not necessarily have made him an unsuitable kidney donor, but it would have been taken into consideration when assessing his likely reaction following the donor operation. Still, it had been a wonderful gesture by Wilkinson for whom there was a lot of support and sympathy in Dundee. Here was a man who, like the family of Hazel Phin, had known the sorrow of losing a child. In 1971 he and his wife Alice had helplessly been forced to endure the lingering death of their son Martin, aged just two, because of a liver complaint. The tragedy affected Wilkinson who began a deep interest in witchcraft and the occult, an obsession that led to the breakup of the marriage.

By 1997 he had been held at the State Hospital for twenty-three years and itched for freedom. He had seen how others used flaws in the legal system to argue for their discharge and now he followed the same route pointing out that he was not suffering from any mental disorder which meant he could not be treated and thus there were no grounds for keeping him locked away. Part of his plea had been heard at Edinburgh's Court of Session, which involved him being escorted there by three male nurses from Carstairs. But it would be a painful experience. Despite the long passage of time, feelings in Dundee remained high against him for what he had done and one man especially had, what most believed, good reason to be bitter. For legal reasons his identity cannot be given but as Wilkinson was leaving the court during a luncheon break, the man appeared as if from nowhere and laid into the child killer, punching him on the face and body and knocking him to the floor where he was dragged away while police seized his attacker who was later admonished by a sheriff after he admitted assault.

The distress of that appearance doubled in 1999 when appeal court judges threw out his efforts to leave after deciding he was in fact suffering from a mental disorder and so needed treatment. It was ruled his illness was 'characterised by an anti-social personality disorder' which justified the need for him to stay at Carstairs. However, in 2005 he did get his wish to leave the Lanarkshire institution, but it was not to freedom. The *News of the World* reported that he and fellow child killer Alexander Miller who had been at the State Hospital since 1976 had been secretly moved to low-security Ailsa mental hospital at Ayr. The newspaper said the move was 'causing outrage among worried locals who claim the monsters could easily escape,' and it quoted a local mother:

> We've been told that there is no threat from the patients but having two such appalling child murderers on your doorstep is very frightening indeed. People who do these acts should never be allowed out. It's not fair – they are even being housed near a school.

Yet again local people wondered why the men were being homed on their doorstep and were refused information by the Carstairs authorities. Word leaked from Ailsa Hospital that their transfer was authorised after doctors at Carstairs decided years of treatment had gradually lessened the extent of their respective mental illnesses – that each was no longer a threat, particularly to children. In any case, although security at Ailsa was at a much lower level than Carstairs it nevertheless existed and neither of them would be allowed outside the hospital confines without special permission. Even then, they would be accompanied by specially trained nursing staff. In the case of Miller, there was little sympathy for his plight at still being incarcerated while some in Dundee remembered Wilkinson's gesture at offering to place his own well-being on the line to help a family he had never met. Nevertheless the rejection by those at Carstairs of pleas for information about the mental state of the men led to suspicions that the authorities had something to hide.

8

BODY IN THE SUITCASE

They may have the minds of infants, the faces of babies and the needs of adolescents, but youngsters are locked away in Carstairs alongside hardened adults. As a former State Hospital patient admitted:

> Sexual abuse of vulnerable youngsters is rife in any prison or institution and Carstairs is no different. It might try to paint a picture of a squeaky clean hospital where everybody abides by the rules of morality, but kids in there are still at the mercy of predators who know they are never going to get out and therefore have nothing to lose.

The problem for the authorities is what to do with youngsters who suffer from mental illness and are classed as too dangerous to be treated in a standard psychiatric hospital where security is comparatively relaxed. Ordinary juvenile criminals can be sent to institutions specialising in handling young offenders but the NHS apparently makes no distinction between a dangerous lunatic aged sixty and one still struggling through his or her teenage years. Regardless of age, all dangerous males are dumped in Carstairs. The enormity of their wrongdoing leaves courts with no option. Still though, it is difficult to accept that there are a handful of youngsters capable of committing evil of the magnitude that shocks and horrifies older generations.

BODY IN THE SUITCASE

Take, for instance, the case of Ronald John Andreetti. From time to time, his parents had worried about his behaviour. Sometimes for no apparent reason, his temper flared. They had taken him to doctors who examined the youngster, but said they could find nothing wrong about which they should feel concerned. That did not satisfy his mother Helen, who remained convinced something was amiss with her son and that he needed treatment. But who was she to argue with specialists? The well-built youngster from Edinburgh had been adding to his pocket money by helping out at a garage while he awaited his end-of-term school examination results. If the results were reasonably good then an apprenticeship as a mechanic might be on offer, but one day in June 1968, his world, and that of two families, came crashing down.

Seven-year-old Katherine Mary Brown had been happily playing in the street with a friend. The Brown and Andreetti families knew one another and it was not unusual for the children of each to visit the Edinburgh homes of one another. On that day Andreetti was in his house when Katherine arrived. A neighbour had watched her enter, the child waving her hands as if suggesting they were dirty and she would wash them. Katherine was never again seen alive. When she did not return home, her family worried, searched for her and then called in police. One of the first to sympathise with them was fifteen-year-old Andreetti. 'Don't worry, we'll find her. I'll help you look,' he promised. The local community turned out in force to help, supplementing scores of police officers, tracker dogs and even a spotter aircraft and a helicopter. In newspapers and on radio broadcasts were appeals for householders to search their homes, gardens, sheds and coalhouses in case the missing girl had taken ill and felt tired, crawled inside and gone to sleep. Yet all drew a blank. As the hours moved into days, it became obvious to experienced detectives there was little hope of finding the girl alive.

The neighbour had told police of seeing Katherine evidently go into the Andreetti home and that naturally made Ronald not just a witness but a potential suspect. Yes, he admitted to officers, she came in wanting to wash her hands but he had told her to go to her own home and wash them there. She was alive and well when he watched her go off. Helpfully he even showed police around his attic bedroom, opening drawers and seeming to be helpful and concerned. The check of his room was cursory, but even if it had been thorough, it would have made no difference. The child was dead.

Three days after the kiddie vanished, Helen Andreetti and a home help were cleaning his bedroom when they moved a suitcase that had been pushed beneath his bed and almost immediately realised it held something that should not be there. Police were called immediately and when they opened the case inside lay the little huddled body. It was clear she had been attacked before her death. When he was questioned, Andreetti confessed he was responsible and he was charged with murder. However four months later at the High Court in Edinburgh, after psychiatrists agreed he was suffering from mental illness, he admitted a reduced charge of culpable homicide and of assaulting Katherine by striking her head against a table, stabbing her with a screwdriver and attempting to rape her.

One consultant told Lord Grant, the Lord Justice Clerk, that the teenager, although not insane, suffered from an infirmity of mind that impaired his judgement to such an extent that he was not fully accountable for his actions. It was a permanent condition and one liable to recur without warning and this diminished his responsibility. 'He has dangerous, violent and criminal tendencies,' the consultant said, and when the judge asked, 'Is this opinion based on the need for the protection of the public?' the expert replied, 'It is.' Lord Grant ordered Andreetti to be detained in the State Hospital without limit of time. It meant that finally he would get the specialised help his mother had always believed he needed. But the fact that she had been proved right was no consolation.

Following the case, lawyers stressed that the teenager's family knew nothing of his crime and were shocked when the body was discovered. Katherine's family moved away, too distressed by the attention her death had brought on them. A friend of the Browns said at the time:

Imagine what it was like for them to discover that for three days they had passed the house not knowing their little girl lay in there, dead in a suitcase. After it was over they had to cope with watching their child's friends go off to school every morning while knowing she would never again join them.

The case begged questions over whether more attention should have been paid to Helen Andreetti and more help offered to her son.

Four years later, another tragedy would raise similar issues. The innocent victim this time was six-year-old Gillian Anderson from Haddington in East Lothian and her disappearance in June 1972 sparked off a huge search lasting three days. She had vanished on her way home from school during the town's annual carnival. Gillian had just a quarter of a mile to walk, but she never reached her family. Police toured the area making loudspeaker appeals for help in finding her, but there was no trace of the missing child. One theory was that she might have gone off to play on the banks of the nearby River Tyne and fallen in. A local fisherman who knew the river well, pointed searchers to the stretch where he thought a body might be and the little girl, who had been savagely beaten about the head, was discovered. When news that she had been found spread local schoolboy Charles McCue went to the town's police station and said he had killed Gillian and thrown her body into the Tyne. Not unnaturally the murder caused considerable anger, but not all of it was directed at McCue. Many local people asked whether the role of social workers needed to be investigated.

A year before Gillian's death, McCue had appeared in court in connection with an alleged incident involving a girl of four. After the discovery of Gillian's body and McCue's arrest, worried parents of other children demanded to know whether social workers had been monitoring the schoolboy following the earlier attack. Their concern turned to anger when police and social work officials said legal restraints prevented them giving out any information. Their silence only increased speculation. Parents in the area who expressed disquiet turned out to have been justified in their calls for information when McCue appeared in the High Court in August that year. He had originally been accused of murdering Gillian by striking her repeatedly on the head with a brick and then putting her into the river, but a psychiatrist said he suffered from mental deficiency and marked immaturity of personality, as a result of which he was declared unfit to plead and instead the court accepted the plea put forward by his lawyer of 'insanity in bar of trial'.

However the psychiatrist's next words sent a chill through the courtroom. 'He is capable of repeating this type of crime again,' he said. 'He would be best committed to the state institution at Carstairs. That would be in his interests and in the interests of the public.' And he told the judge, Lord Cameron, that, despite having a history of mental illness, McCue had not received psychiatric treatment, adding that his condition was not something that had developed but had been there since his birth. In answer to a question by Lord Cameron about whether McCue had expressed any remorse, the psychiatrist said the boy knew he had done wrong but did not think his offence was serious. Lord Cameron ordered the boy's detention in Carstairs without limitation of time. Nobody knew it then, but many years later McCue would once again make headlines.

He spent twenty-one years in the State Hospital, and then a further two in a psychiatric hospital in Edinburgh before being given his freedom. However when he was forty-one he was convicted of two charges of a breach of the peace by propositioning a girl aged fifteen and her twelve-year-old brother. He was sentenced to three months in jail, but because he had already spent more than that time locked up awaiting his trial, it meant he would normally have been able to go free. Yet he had originally been committed to Carstairs without a time limit, effectively a life sentence, and so the Secretary of State for Scotland was able to recall him back to the Lanarkshire institution. Many, including politicians and members of the children's family, wondered who had originally recommended his discharge from Carstairs. They did not get an answer.

Should children be committed to Carstairs? In the cases of Andreetti and McCue, the trial judge was in no doubt that sending them to the State Hospital was the right thing to do. They were conclusions that were easily reached because both accepted they had done wrong even though they were mentally ill. A case in 1999, however, posed questions as to just what should be done with a youngster suffering from insanity. It followed the death from serious burns of nine-year-old Charles McFall from Uddingston, Lanarkshire. Another boy, then aged twelve, was accused of murdering him but the charge was then reduced to one of culpable homicide. The trial judge, Lord Caplan, said the accused youngster's IQ was so low that he would not be able to understand trial proceedings and that he was technically insane. At a later hearing the judge decreed the incident an accident and cleared the boy of any guilt, saying, 'Children can act recklessly and it may be they are even more prone to do so than adults, but their capacity to appreciate the dangers may not always be sufficient to attach criminality to their conduct.' It was a sympathetic, fact-based decision, but one that left the dead child's parents upset. Others wondered why young people who in the past had been declared insane and sent to Carstairs had not benefitted from such a ruling – that they too were too young to understand what they were doing. Sometimes defence teams and the families of accused boys and occasionally girls were content for youngsters to be sent to mental hospitals, even Carstairs, where they could receive treatment but also be kept in strict security and unable to commit more harm.

A similar argument in the Uddingston case might have been applied to that of another schoolboy, fifteen-year-old John Milne. The victim here, well-liked Helen Laird, also fifteen, was cycling from her work in a fishmonger's shop in 1968 when, just a mile from her home at Monzie, Perthshire, she was fatally stabbed by Milne, a former schoolmate, at the entrance to Sma' Glen, a local beauty spot. He then stabbed himself, but hospital doctors saved his life. Sadly nobody could save Helen whose death brought immense sadness to all who knew her. It emerged that Milne, a loner, had admired his victim from afar. He was charged with her murder, but when he recovered enough to appear before the High Court in Dundee, a consultant psychiatrist said:

> His unnatural emotional blunting presently showing his history of unusual shyness and solitary habits and the commission of such an act based on jealousy in relation to a girl he did not even try to get to

know, in itself indicates a gross derangement of thought and judgement not consistent with sanity.

In short he was suffering from a mental illness so severe that he was found insane and unfit to plead to the charge. The judge, Lord Leechman, sent him to Carstairs. From then on, the secrecy in which Carstairs cloaked itself meant the public was not to know what became of Milne, an attitude that still gives rise to major concern.

A century earlier reformers had argued against the locking up of children in the same prisons as violent adults, pointing out the risks of youngsters being corrupted by older criminals. They called for the opening of institutions specifically catering for the young. Now the same arguments were being applied in the case of the insane in an attempt to prevent schoolchildren and teenagers being shunted off to Carstairs to join and potentially be influenced by mature men and women criminals. Some felt this lack of separation was the fault of politicians who refused to make funds available to create separate facilities for the young. As things stood, judges had their hands tied in cases of young people whose mental condition made them a possible risk to the rest of society. There was simply nowhere to send them. The situation in England was no better, as was demonstrated by the horrific case of Mary Bell, whose Glasgow-born mother Betty had settled in the Scotswood area of Newcastle-upon-Tyne where Mary was born. When she was aged ten, Mary strangled four-year-old Martin Brown. Shortly afterwards she similarly killed Brian Howe, aged three. She was eleven when she was convicted of the manslaughter of the infants on the grounds of her diminished responsibility. The problem was what to do with Mary. There was nowhere appropriate to send her. Over the next few years, from her initial stint in a secure unit she graduated through a young offenders' institution, prison, then open prison, from which she briefly absconded desperate for a taste of teenage normality, and finally the terrifying Styal women's jail in Cheshire where she was at the mercy of hardened callous murderers and prostitutes until her final release from an open jail twelve years following her conviction.

This author knew Mary and her mother. He visited their homes and they his. Betty Bell, burdened by self-recrimination and blame for what had happened, frequently begged for her daughter to be given psychiatric treatment. Once she admitted, 'If this had happened in Scotland, Mary would have been helped. In England they've never had anything like this before and they just don't know what to do with her.' Instead Mary was abused and threatened while incarcerated. Nowadays she would almost certainly have been sent to a psychiatric hospital, very probably because of the severity of her crimes an establishment similar to Carstairs. Mary herself struggled to shake off the shackles of institutionalisation. Not long after leaving prison, she gave birth to a daughter, but she had spent her entire teenage years looking through barred windows and even in motherhood found happiness elusive. All that society has bequeathed to Mary Bell has been a lifelong legal guarantee of anonymity. Do the children of Carstairs find ultimate normality and happiness? We will never know. Is it possible for them to rejoin society? We are not told. Does society want them back in its midst? Would an average family feel comfortable knowing that the individuals concerned in the three cases that follow are their next-door neighbours?

Peter McCallion was aged fifteen when, while on leave from a List D school where he had been sent after committing assault and robbery offences, he attacked an elderly couple with a walking stick in their home at Greenock, Renfrewshire. Kate Webster, seventy-nine, was hit at least ten times on the head and body. In trying to defend herself, her wrist and fingers were broken. Her husband, Alec, a year older, had his right arm broken and died two months later although the death was not directly attributed to the attack. Any teenager who commits such a brutal attack is of course outside of the norm. With McCallion, though, this was especially the case. His nickname was 'Brenda' – it was one given to him by the police after he had dressed as a woman to carry out a previous attack. McCallion admitted breaking into the home of Kate and Alec and assaulting them to their severe injury, permanent impairment and danger of life. Two psychiatrists said he was mentally impaired and might be a danger to the public, so Lord Kirkwood sent him to the State Hospital without limit of time.

Harry James Munro was another who committed a crime while he was on the run from the establishment where a court had placed him. The apprentice butcher, aged seventeen from Edinburgh, used a wicked oriental-type knife to stab dead part-time barman Duncan Murray, fifty-seven, after failing to return to borstal from a home leave. Psychiatrists told a judge at the High Court in Edinburgh that Munro had been in approved schools and a borstal since the age of ten and had 'an impulse towards violence and an extreme personality problem'. One said, 'He is unable to control these impulses and numerous attempts to treat him have not helped.' Munro admitted culpable homicide and it was said he was suffering from diminished responsibility at the time of the killing, although he was now sane and fit to plead. He was sent to Carstairs without limit of time.

It is difficult to imagine the terror of two women who were put through a horrendous ordeal at the hands of Allan Williams in 1994. What made it all the more unimaginable was that Williams, from Greenock, was just eighteen at the time. The nightmare of his victims began when the two friends, aged thirty-seven and forty-two, went on a shopping trip to Greenock. In a car park Williams suddenly appeared as if from nowhere, pointed a gun at the two and ordered them into their motor, clambering in with them. He ordered one of the friends to drive to a remote country track near Kilmacolm, increasing their distress on the way by claiming he had killed another woman a few hours earlier.

When the car stopped, he ordered one of the women to tie the other up, then pointed the gun at the head of the second woman and ordered her to carry out a disgusting sex act. Producing a knife he cut the women's clothes off, robbed them and then pistol-whipped one. In the High Court in Edinburgh it was said that as he walked away from the car, leaving the women inside, he thanked them for a 'nice day' and grinned. One of his victims managed to run semi-naked for help but their ordeal lasted almost three hours. The teenage loner was said by a psychiatrist to have violent fantasies and a severe personality disorder, adding, 'He is dangerous.' Williams admitted abduction, assault and attempted rape and was sent to Carstairs without limit of time.

Campaigners who seek better help and facilities for young offenders with mental health issues point out that while a sane eighteen year old will almost certainly end up in a special facility catering for sixteen to twenty-one year olds, an insane youngster of the same age can be sent to Carstairs to come under the influence of older, more experienced men. According to the Mental Health Foundation, young criminals forced to share facilities with adults are more susceptible to being bullied and it says that 'mental health services for young people in custody are inadequate'. In other words, the situation in regard to the young criminally insane has changed little in two centuries. Courts prefer referring young people to routine psychiatric hospitals, but, year after year, teenagers continue to dribble into Carstairs.

Researchers are also quick to point out that youngsters committed to custody, to young offender institutions or to psychiatric hospitals, including Carstairs, are more likely to reoffend. Criminality is much more likely to rub off on vulnerable young people locked up with mature criminals. The State Hospital refuses to say what treatment is given to the young. Indeed, whether or not young lunatics ought to be in Carstairs is a question that politicians have conveniently overlooked.

9

CAIN AND ABEL

Few cases in which young people suffering from mental illness have broken one of the Ten Commandments can have been more dreadful than that involving Peter William Mackenzie, aged only thirteen. In this ghastly nightmare, there are similarities to the story told in the Book of Genesis of Cain and Abel, the two sons of Adam and Eve. Cain was a crop farmer who killed his brother, a shepherd. Peter Mackenzie killed his brother Ian. Both lived on a farm. The modern day remake went tragically much deeper into the pit of horror. Not only did Peter kill Ian, he also murdered family servant Mary Stephen, aged seventy-two, and tried to take the life of his own mother, Williamina. If it was possible to add to the disgust many felt, then that was certainly the situation regarding the death of Mary, because the old lady was deaf and dumb.

Peter and Ian were two of five brothers from Williamina's first marriage. She had another son, Charles, to her second husband, Hector, who owned a garage in Inverness, three miles from the imposing but rambling family home at Stratton Farm. Like so many youngsters growing up on a country farm, Peter was familiar with guns. From time to time he would be out in the fields and woods shooting at rabbits and vermin. He was a good shot, according to his friends. Then one night in August 1966, both his gun and his mind exploded. Panic erupted when Williamina, crying, breathless, fear-stricken and her face and body covered in blood pouring from a neck wound, turned up on the doorstep of a neighbouring family screaming for help. Weak from loss of blood she was barely able to blurt out what had taken place a few minutes earlier, but neighbours reacted instantly by calling police.

Officers from the force headquarters in Inverness and others from surrounding stations rushed to Stratton Farm where they discovered a horrendous scene. Ian, aged sixteen, was dead. Mary, who had been with the family for more than thirty years, lay moaning and covered in blood. She was rushed off to hospital by ambulance along with Williamina, who would recover while Mary died within a few hours. Thankfully Charles, aged three, was found still asleep and unharmed. Police found Peter still at the scene and arrested him.

It would later emerge that at the moment when Peter fired at his mother, she was so close that pellets from the rifle he held all penetrated a single spot in her neck. Had she been standing further away, their spread would have shattered her face. Yet immediately she recovered, this loving mother became a regular visitor to see her son as he was held at Craig Dunain hospital where he was examined by psychiatrists while he waited for his trial. When he entered the dock at the High Court in Edinburgh in November 1966, Williamina was still there to support him and very publicly show her love and forgiveness. Peter was charged with murdering his brother and Miss Stephen – with discharging a rifle and with attempting to murder his mother. One of the psychiatrists said he had come to the opinion that Peter was of unsound mind when the crimes were committed and was still unfit to plead. 'His state of mind is dangerous and his behaviour must continue to be unpredictable,' he said.

There was little else that Lord Grant, the Lord Justice Clerk, could do other than order Peter to be detained in the State Hospital without limit of time. However the judge also had the unusual task of deciding whether the youngster could be named in the media. The case had attracted huge interest, not just in Scotland, but all over Britain because of the tender age of the killer. Normally newspapers were restricted from revealing the name of someone of that age, but here was an exceptional case and Lord Grant explained why he was allowing Peter to be identified:

Having regard to the medical reports, it seems no coherent account of this could be given in the Press unless the name and address of the accused were disclosed. I direct that the Press may report the proceedings in such a manner as they think fit.

This twentieth-century version of man's first recorded murder produced huge sympathy within the community, most of it for Williamina who had, in effect, lost two sons and a loyal friend. Yet nobody was surprised by the loyalty shown to Peter by her and her husband. One family friend said:

Anybody who knows this lady will have expected nothing else from her but for her to stand by her boy. It has been terrible to witness her distress and heartache and yet she has never wavered in her love for Peter. She is aware that he just does not know what he has done. But how many other mothers could so very clearly show such forgiveness, even to one so dear?

There had been another remarkable demonstration of forgiveness the previous year in yet another case involving a youngster and the State Hospital. James Williamson, aged only sixteen, had been sent to Carstairs after killing an elderly loner, William 'Willie the Wasp' Townsley White. The victim was aged seventy-four and a well-known character in the Crossgates area of Fife, but known much more widely all over Scotland as the Gypsy King. He lived in a caravan near a tumbledown farm building on the outskirts of Crossgates and, although giving the appearance of being a pauper, was rumoured to have salted away a neat pile of cash for his savings. It was talk of that cache which reached the ears of teenager Williamson, a youngster who was always on the lookout for the chance to make easy money.

James was a likeable boy who would cross the street to avoid a fight and, while he had a tendency to run wild from time to time, he shunned violence. Unable to read or write, he was thought of as something of a scrounger, rarely with money in his pockets. Yet beneath his normally quiet exterior lurked a menace, a streak of evil bursting for freedom. Then suddenly he seemed to have money to burn. He was happily embarking on a spending spree. It was totally out of character and tongues began to gossip. Where had his windfall come from? Williamson wasn't saying, but when word of his unexpected wealth reached police, officers suspected they knew the answer.

One night someone had attacked Willie the Wasp, battering him senseless, and he died from his injuries. Detectives who investigated discovered his caravan had been ransacked and things were missing, including the old man's £200 savings, a treasured watch, chain and a set of medallions. Police were sure the windfall and the killing were not simply a coincidence and they arrested Williamson and charged him with murder. While he was on remand, he admitted to his dad, also named James, that he was a murderer.

When he appeared for sentence at the High Court in Edinburgh, he pleaded guilty to a reduced charge of culpable homicide. A psychiatrist said the accused teenager had the mental age of a child of seven. The doctor said, 'He is incapable of seeing the likely consequences of his own acts and of controlling his immediate emotional responses.' A Crown lawyer said, 'He requires special guidance and protection in conditions of special security.' The judge ordered Williamson to be detained in the State Hospital without limit and off he went to Carstairs. His story did not end there, however. In fact the book on his young life was closed just six weeks later, when a male nurse, carrying out a routine late night check of his room, discovered him dead. The boy had knotted one end of his bed sheet into a ball and pushed it through his window, then he tightly wound the other end around his neck, knotted it and strangled himself. Frantic efforts to save him using a resuscitator and intravenous injections failed to bring him back to life.

At a fatal accident inquiry, one of the doctors treating him said James was a quiet, well-behaved boy who suffered from a mental deficiency and personality disorder. He was not insane, though, and had shown no signs of being suicidal. In fact he had been quiet and co-operative. At no time, though, had he showed remorse for killing Willie the Wasp. Some among James' friends felt that sending him to

CARSTAIRS

Carstairs wasn't just for the protection of others but for him too. In that respect he had been let down. His own dad didn't see it that way, however. James senior, aged forty-one, had no criticisms for staff at the State Hospital over his boy's death and only forgiveness for the system that failed his son. Fighting back tears of sorrow he said, 'Nobody is to blame and I bear no grudges.'

10

THE BOX MAN

The police had a name for the maniac who for years had terrorised young boys in a violent city. They called him 'the Box Man'. The method he used to entice unwary youngsters into dark places where he could satisfy his twisted lusts was frighteningly simple. When he went on his sick trawls for victims, he would take a box and encourage victims to help him hide it. Natural youthful naivety and curiosity meant the trick rarely failed.

Frightened parents were worried to let their sons out of their sight. Boys were lectured in schools about the dangers of going with a stranger. Men innocently delivering packages were liable to find themselves stopped by police officers and ordered to account for their movements. Agents with empty buildings to sell or lease were encouraged to report on prospective takers. Yet the Box Man continued his vile campaign.

Desperate to catch him and regardless of the cost, police chiefs set up a special squad of hunters. It would mean delaying investigations into other minor crimes and sometimes patrols would be thin on the ground. As time went on and reports continued from angry mums and dads that their sons had come home crying and terrified after falling victim to the Box Man, the squad was increased. At its height 150 men and women made up its ranks. They worked overtime, missed days off, cancelled holidays, went without sleep and ate only snatched meals. In some cases the disruption to their home lives caused domestic problems – there was talk of separations, even divorce. Yet they carried on regardless, knowing that unless he was captured the danger remained that the Box Man might add their own sons to his long list of conquests. They would notch up more than half a million hours of conscientious, diligent searching before his disgusting reign was ended.

When that day arrived, the identity of the Box Man shocked a number of officers. Quiet bespectacled Leslie Johnston, twenty-nine, was more likely to be mistaken for a schoolteacher than a sexual predator. He was a hard worker, the pride of his parents. When he wasn't serving drinks and meals as a ship's steward and back on leave at home in Finnieston, Glasgow, he had an interest in the Lindella Club, a lively popular discotheque in Union Street where, in 1962, a fourteen-year-old girl named Marie McDonald McLaughlin had been discovered singing with her group, the Gleneagles. And so the career of Lulu and her band The Luvvers was born. Bobbies on the beat frequently called into the Lindella for a chat with Johnston or to share a cup of tea with him. There was nothing wrong in that, nor in them discussing with him progress in the Box Man investigation. After all any snippet of information from a well-informed young man like Johnston could be hugely important to the inquiry squad.

A year after Lulu was on her way to stardom, the Box Man had begun making headlines. Slowly at first and then in increasing numbers, boys told of the cheerful stranger who had come up to them as they were playing in Glasgow's West End and produced a box from under his coat. He would casually lift the lid and once he had the attention of a potential target hint there was something valuable inside and he wanted to hide the box in an empty property. It was the sort of mystery boys could not resist. They would accompany the stranger into an empty building and there suffer horrific sexual indignities. When it became apparent these were not occasional random incidents but the work of a determined paedophile, senior officers ordered a more serious approach. They listened carefully to the boys' description of their attacker, accompanied the youngsters, some just eight years of age, the eldest sixteen, to the buildings where they had been lured, carefully searched for clues and fingerprints and questioned agents and owners of the empty properties.

THE BOX MAN

That line of inquiry convinced them they were up against a sinister individual who was covering his tracks well. He always paid for the short-term rentals in cash and checks showed the names and addresses he gave were bogus. Was the fact that there were sometimes lengthy gaps between batches of attacks a clue?

For six long, vile years, the Box Man remained at large, but eventually a man answering the description given by dozens of boys was spotted, arrested and identified as Johnston. He made no effort to deny he was the maniac detectives wanted and when he appeared before Glasgow Sherrif Court admitted thirty-seven offences of indecent assault, lewd practice and breach of the peace between May 1963 and June 1969. A prosecutor said:

> Johnston's method was to induce boys to go somewhere in the west end of Glasgow by asking them to look at a box he carried. He became infamous during this time and became known among police forces that went to great lengths and extremes to find him as the Box Man.

Psychiatrists had examined Johnston before he was sentenced in early 1969 and one reported, 'He has told me he is likely to repeat these attacks on children. He is a danger to the public and himself.' The result was that Johnston was sent to Carstairs without limit of time.

But for many of his young victims, the memory of their ordeals would never fade, even with the passage of time. There was no thought of sympathy or forgiveness for the Box Man who had blighted the characters of so many at what ought to have been the happiest time of their lives. A police officer who investigated the attacks said:

> Had he not been caught he would certainly have carried on. All the time we were confident we were getting closer to finding who he was. We were determined to catch him and put him away. The distress of parents whose children were besmirched by this sick individual was sometimes terrible to experience.

While the net was closing on Johnston, police in Glasgow were also nearing the end of their search for another fiend. But it would not be for a further month after the Box Man went off to Carstairs that a lunatic who preyed on little girls would be captured and then join him in the State Hospital. In this case, too, the dragnet meant a huge effort by police, scores of officers, including teams drafted in from outside the city, giving an effort that went far beyond the call of duty. In fact they became so active in their search for the beast who sought thrills by assaulting and raping kiddies that for a lengthy spell he was scared off and when he resumed it was in a different area of Glasgow, London Road in the east end. If he had chosen to call a halt to his twisted desires, he might never have been discovered but in the end a tip-off led to his arrest.

The monster who brought terror was a married man, building site labourer James Ferguson, aged twenty-three, who had received treatment as a youth for mental illness. When he was only four years of age he had lived rough with his father for a time and had then spent many miserable years living unhappily in institutions and foster homes. Others who experienced similar sadness in their childhood and youth did not go down the same dark path his sick mind led him, dreaming up terrible and sordid acts. He committed his first attack in the north of Glasgow in October 1967, after separating from his older wife and for a year and a half terrorised the north and west of the city, creeping out from his lodgings in the east end to force little girls to endure sick ordeals. At least two of his victims faced years of having to relive the nightmare of his assaults.

What he did for two years to girls, some of whom were just two years old, before he was caged caused revulsion, disgust and outrage. Sneaking about the streets where the children of working-class parents lived, he looked for unsuspecting targets. Some were playing in the street near their home, others running an errand to a corner shop for their mother. In every case he seized the child or persuaded her to accompany him to the court behind the tenement where they lived and then on to some quiet spot, a close or basement, far enough from their home so no one could hear their pathetic whimpering and bleating for help when he struck before running off. In most of the cases investigated by police, the little victims were taken to hospital and some even needed surgery for their injuries. The most terrifying feature, and that which brought dread to detectives, was that Ferguson used a knife on some of the children.

Desperate to catch the ogre, police left no stone unturned no matter what the consequences. Lone men, out for the most genuine and innocent reason, found themselves seized and questioned by police demanding to know who they were and what they were doing. Kerb crawlers became particular targets of officers. Prostitutes were asked to report on clients who talked about children. In a handful of cases men whose car registrations were noted as being frequently seen in areas where children had been attacked were visited at their homes and faced embarrassing questions from wives and mistresses. Nobody was complaining because, after all, tiny children were at risk. Everyone except the perpetrator surely breathed a sigh of relief when he was taken. Ferguson's campaign of terror was halted because of the curiosity of one of his neighbours who, conscious of the police appeals for help or information plastered all over the city, realised he was showing an unusual and probably unhealthy interest in little girls. The man, his worries confirmed by children who told of being approached by Ferguson, visited the suspect's estranged wife who remembered her husband coming home with a ripped shirt. The date of that coincided with one of the attacks on the six-year-olds. The couple told their fears to police who nabbed Ferguson at his workplace. 'I'm glad you have caught me. Now I will get treatment. I am sorry for what I have done,' he said when he was arrested. A search of his haversack uncovered a knife, which experts said might have caused injuries found on some of the tiny victims. What was definite was that his fingerprints matched those taken from some of the attack scenes.

The charges he ultimately faced reflected his foul activities. He admitted five offences of attacking and severely injuring girls aged between two and six with a knife, two offences of raping two six-year-old girls, one of whom he hurt with a knife, and two offences of using indecent practices towards two girls aged five and eleven. The first attack had been committed in October 1967 and the second in September 1969.

At Ferguson's initial court appearance before a Sheriff, the advocate depute told how all police leave was stopped because of what he described as the 'monstrous assaults'. He said:

> Ferguson caused fear and panic among parents. Because of the ages of his victims the police had considerable difficulty in obtaining a description of the person who carried out the assaults. It was only after the fourth attack that Ferguson was seen by adults as he ran from the scene and a detailed description was obtained. Because of the nature of the crimes and the repetition of them, massive police inquiries were instituted and at one stage police from all parts of the city were brought into the west and north areas where the assaults were committed at first, in an effort to capture the assailant. A search of criminal fingerprint records was carried out and although the crimes were committed in basements and back closes, all the places were examined minutely in an effort to find fingerprints which might be traced. Thousands of telephone calls were received from members of the public, particularly in the north and west of the city, whose lives had been disrupted by the man's activities. Each case reporting suspicious circumstances was followed up and during the investigations many innocent citizens were placed in embarrassing situations until they were eliminated.

Psychiatrists who examined Ferguson reported they could find nothing to suggest he was insane and announced he was sane and fit to plead. Friends of the families of some of his victims pointed out that he could be facing a life sentence in prison, a fate many believed he deserved knowing the brutality sure to be meted out by other prisoners. Men who abused children expected no mercy in prison. However, the doctors concluded Ferguson was a feeble-minded mental defective with dangerous and criminal propensities, whose offences showed a pattern of abnormal criminal behaviour and who needed to be kept in a place of high security, not just in his own interests but for the protection of the public. Ferguson, at one time

THE BOX MAN

the most wanted man in Scotland, who became the most hated in the land, was sent to Carstairs. The special squad of police formed to net him could finally go home satisfied their own children and those of parents everywhere were finally safe.

11

CHILDREN YET UNBORN

The trusting little girl thought she had nothing to fear from the young man who took her by the hand and set off walking, chatting to the child while she trotted to keep pace with him. She was five years old and had often listened to her mother and others in her loving family warning her never to go with strangers but this man was a neighbour, someone she saw nearly every day, who sometimes waved to her. After all he had promised the youngster her mother had said it was all right to go with him. In her innocence she had no idea that there is evil in the world, even among those we think we can trust. And the man who held her hand, Samuel Glass, was mentally unstable and had evil deeds on his mind.

It was a Sunday and as the pair walked along they met others heading to church services, passers-by who saw nothing wrong in what was probably an older brother giving his little sister a treat. As if to show anyone who took an interest that there was nothing untoward he lifted the kiddie on to his shoulders, producing gleeful giggles from her. There were no screams or shouts from the girl as she was carried into a disused railway tunnel at Bridgeton, even though it was dark and there was no one about. She still had no reason not to feel safe. She was not to know her young life had just a few nightmare minutes before it ran out. In the blackness of that filthy spot, Glass first indecently assaulted her and then, to stifle her cries, grabbed her by the throat, ripped off her clothes and produced a needle with which, unable to control his vile lusts, he scratched and stabbed her. Then he strangled her to finish her off and went home to his mother Margaret as though nothing had happened, leaving the little, bloodied body of sweet Jean Hamilton lying in a state of grace in the dust and mud.

It was not long before Jean's family realised she was missing and began searching. One of those who joined in the hunt was Margaret Glass. At the back of her mind she wondered if her son might know something and her heart sank when children said they had seen him carrying Jean towards the tunnel. She passed on her thoughts to the police. It did not take long after the discovery of the infant for detectives to track down the beast who had killed her. When news of the murder spread, plenty of others came forward to speak of seeing Glass, aged twenty, taking Jean away from her home in London Road, Glasgow. What was more, he already had a terrible reputation for violence. The most telling clue that pointed police in the direction of a pervert who had committed unspeakable acts on the tiny body was that Glass had spent time in a mental hospital from which he had been discharged just three months before Jean died. Soon after being arrested he admitted he had first tortured then slaughtered the mite. Later on when psychiatrists probed his sick mind Glass would tell one doctor, 'When we were in the tunnel I seemed to hear this voice in my head, like the voice of a friend telling me, "You have got to do it".'

In the east end of Glasgow, where Jean had lived, there was real anger towards Glass. Decent families, with five-year-old children of their own, felt he deserved nothing more than to be put down like a dog. When details of his background emerged, some of the fury aimed at him dissipated and spread towards the doctors who had agreed to his leaving Gartloch mental hospital in Glasgow. If he had not been released, Jean would still be alive and the grief of her mum, also called Jean, would not have the devastating effect it was ultimately to have.

Samuel Albert Glass had been trouble virtually from the day he was born in 1947. It was common for a youngster in the tough, poverty-riddled east end to be a tearaway, involved in petty crime, but he soon had a reputation for viciousness and pure nastiness. He developed a bizarre obsession in the history of the Nazi movement, making his own Gestapo-style uniform and occasionally wearing it and parading by himself in the tunnel where Jean would die. Margaret Glass did her best to calm the spite that filled her son who seemed to prefer his own company and rarely made friends but it was she who felt the worst of his venom. As a teenager he smashed her on the head with a hatchet while she was sleeping, forcing her to seek hospital treatment and routinely having to admit the blow had been struck by her own son. She told the police she did not want to press charges but, despite this, he was sent to borstal. When he was released Margaret welcomed him back into her home even though friends warned her against this, but she was always the first to speak up for him. 'He's my son. I love him and I've forgiven him,' she said.

The warning signs were there and it was not only she who ought to have acted on them. After he left borstal his infant stepsister was discovered with blood seeping from her groin and taken to hospital where an examination showed she needed internal stitching. Police interviewed her son who said the injuries were caused when the baby fell. His explanation was accepted. Margaret Glass knew there was something wrong with her son, that he needed psychiatric help, but none was forthcoming and now there was worse, far worse, to come. Early in 1967, Glass again assaulted his mother and on this occasion was told that if he agreed to stay in a mental hospital for twelve months on a voluntary basis, then instead of being sent to a young offenders' institution he would be placed on probation. He agreed and went to Gartloch, but just over a week later doctors allowed him to go home. It was effectively a death sentence for Jean Hamilton.

At court in September that year, a charge of murder was reduced to culpable homicide after doctors reported that while Glass was sane and fit to plead he was suffering from mental illness. One psychiatrist described him as having a personality disorder and a 'persistent tendency to act aggressively from minimal provocation', adding, 'He has very probably always had these features in his personality and is likely to retain them for a great many years, if not for ever.' The comment that reduced the courtroom to silence was made by Glass's own legal representative, the distinguished and highly respected QC Lionel Daiches, who is considered one of the greatest Scots orators. He said, 'I am not only concerned about Glass, he is only twenty, but one must remember the position of children as yet unborn.' Glass, who admitted taking, assaulting and killing Jean, was ordered by Lord Walker to be detained in the State Hospital without limit of time. The story of the girl's death would be resurrected more than four decades later.

Long before then, psychiatrists had already been severely criticised for their decision to release a patient, this time from Carstairs, who would very soon commit another serious offence. And by a bizarre coincidence he too was named Glass, although he was not related to Jean's killer. Robert Bruce Glass had been sent to Carstairs in 1972 after being convicted of a sexual attack on a young girl. On 10 April 1975, he was discharged and went to stay with family members in East Lothian. Eight days later, two fifteen-year-old girls had been out for the evening to a discotheque and were walking home when they became conscious that a man was following them. Frightened, the teenagers started to run off but the stranger gave chase and tried to grab both of them. One girl managed to fight her way free and fled screaming for help. Glass viciously seized her friend by her hair and pressed her to the ground, using threats and force to try to make her strip. The youngster fought back bravely and tore a St Christopher medallion from Glass's neck, then scratched his face and bit one of his hands. Her cries and yells scared him into making off. Police were called and made a series of appeals for anyone seeing a man with scratches on his face to contact them and it was as a result of these pleas that when he went into a local bar Glass was recognised and arrested.

While he waited for his trial – at which he would admit attacking the girls with intent to ravish one of them – Glass, aged twenty-five, was examined by doctors who concluded he was sane, fit to plead and not suffering from mental deficiency. They also reported that he had a personality disorder which showed itself in irresponsible behaviour, aggressive moods and indulgence in deviant sexual behaviour. With this on record, why had he been allowed to leave the State Hospital without any conditions attached to his release?

Astonishing excuses were given on behalf of Carstairs – one being that he was a psychopath and 'psychiatry has little to offer the psychopath'. This was why he had been discharged. In addition the Carstairs medical sub-committee, which recommended his freedom, believed he had made good progress, a claim which seemed even stranger in the light of the fact that just eight days afterwards Glass attacked two girls in a near mirror of the assault that resulted in his originally being held at Carstairs. It was also said that Glass had appealed against his continued detention and the feeling was he would win as the hospital was unable to treat his illness so there was no point in trying to keep him in the hospital. When he initially appeared at a lower court, Glass's solicitor said:

> It appears inconsistent that a man who was incarcerated as a danger to the public should be released and then when seen by two psychiatrists after this offence found fit to plead. We have here a man who was, until 10 April, in a state mental hospital with a warrant saying he was insane.

Then just over a week later it was decided he was sane and he was allowed to walk out. The argument over Glass continued at the High Court in Edinburgh where he appeared for sentence. His counsel said prison was not the correct punishment because he would eventually be freed: 'Judging by his past conduct he would repeat the type of attack which has characterised his lifestyle. It is absurd to suggest he has recovered from a personality disorder. The penal system is inappropriate to deal with him.' He wanted Glass put into the closed ward of a psychiatric hospital. 'He will receive treatment while the public are protected.' Doctors, on the other hand, said the attacker should not go back to Carstairs but to prison where he could get psychiatric help.

Lord Wheatley, the judge, admitted the present system did not provide the treatment or safeguards that were needed but he said, 'I feel my duty towards the community and young girls . . . to keep you away from them for an extended period is the paramount consideration.' Then he jailed Glass for five years. The case raised the age-old question of why, yet again, Carstairs doctors appeared to have got it wrong. Understandably, the mother of the youngster who had fought so courageously demanded an inquiry into the hospital decision. 'My daughter was so distressed and upset that she said she would never have a boyfriend. She doesn't even want to go out at night,' she said. Even Glass's own mother Agnes was angry over his release. 'He needs treatment, not punishment,' she said. 'As far as I know he was given no treatment in Carstairs.'

Glass should have received help because had he been treated correctly then the attack on the two girls might never have happened. He received no treatment in prison either, which was another mistake with dire consequences. Following his release, Glass left Scotland and moved to the north west of England. If social workers and probation staff responsible for him hoped he would turn over a new leaf, they were in for a massive disappointment. Four years after the East Lothian scare, Glass, now twenty-nine, was back in court, this time at Manchester. Once again it was a teenage girl who had been forced to suffer a terrifying ordeal. She had been in bed when Glass broke into her home. She woke up when he put his hand over her mouth, ordering her not to struggle or shout out. However, as she tried to fight him off, her sister heard the noise and came into her bedroom. Glass was dragged off and fled. But he was arrested and jailed for fourteen years after admitting burglary with intent to rape.

Yet another who went on to commit a terrible crime after being allowed to leave Carstairs was James McLaughlin Laing. He had first been sent to a mental hospital at the age of only ten and later, after being convicted of a breach of the peace, was detained in Carstairs, a move that angered him and left him with a sense of injustice. He spent twenty-one years there, frustrated at not being able to draw attention to his being kept for such a long time in a high security institution for what was a very minor offence. He would later admit that when he was eventually transferred to Craig Dunain Hospital at Inverness he was convinced his rage would spill over and find release only when he attacked someone. And attack someone he did, beating another man with a spanner when they met in woods around Craig Dunain.

When he appeared in the High Court in Inverness to plead guilty to serious assault, Laing was desperate to avoid being returned to Carstairs and begged to go to jail instead. A psychiatrist said:

> He told me that for years he has this festering cancer in his mind that he might harm someone because he felt he has been wrongfully kept in Carstairs. He is on a knife-edge and with very little provocation could become quite dangerous to himself and others.

Told he was being returned to the State Hospital, Laing was said to have pulled himself up to attention in the dock and, looking at the judge, Lord Grieve, announced, 'Thank you my Lord, but you have just signed my death warrant.'

Although he would eventually be moved, Laing at one stage shared a ward with Sam Glass. So did hundreds of other crazed criminals. Some died, others were transferred, but Glass remained. Rumours that a move to a lower-security institution was being planned for him shocked the family of his victim and brought back terrible memories, not only of the day little Jean died, but of the heartbreak her killing inflicted on those who knew and loved her. In cases such as that of Sam Glass, offenders ordered to be detained in Carstairs without limit of time can only leave the State Hospital if a nominated government minister authorises their release or transfer. It is unlikely Glass will ever be allowed to return to the community, the most likely scenario being that when doctors decide he is too old and infirm to be incapable of inflicting harm, they will recommend to the government he be moved to a less secure hospital where he will remain until he dies. These cases highlight the difference between being sent to Carstairs and given a prison sentence. At Carstairs, life can really mean life – a patient cannot leave unless doctors agree he is no longer a threat and propose a move. A prison term, on the other hand, must allow an offender the opportunity of parole once he or she has been detained for a set period laid down by the judge, whether or not the offender has been rehabilitated.

Some question if it is right to continue to hold a man in Carstairs, with the vast expense that entails if, after a period of years, he has not responded to treatment. But where else can a dangerous lunatic be detained? Others believe there can be no salvation for those entering the State Hospital, arguing that no expert, no matter how experienced or astute, can guarantee a patient is cured and will never reoffend – the brain is a sealed unit. Too many mistakes in the past have shaken public confidence in Carstairs.

The debate over whether or not to release lunatics centres on the issue of whether the public have a right to know that a Carstairs patient, whether recent or not, has been accommodated within their midst. Sarah's Law campaigners demanded a legal right for parents to be informed when a released convicted paedophile had become a neighbour. Should that same right apply in cases of criminal lunatics? Should the atmosphere of secrecy prevailing within Carstairs extend to the wider community? At present the public have no rights in this issue. But is it not the case that suspicion, lack of confidence in Carstairs and lack of sympathy and support for those suffering mental illness will continue so long as secrecy remains?

12

SLIPPING AWAY

'What The Hell's Gone On At Carstairs?' asked the banner headline across the *Daily Record* newspaper on 25 April 1972. It was the question on the lips of most adults in Scotland but then, as now, the State Hospital would choose to keep its secrets. What prompted the fury of the bestselling tabloid was not just the escape the previous day of a couple of twenty-two-year-old patients, Malcolm John Angus MacDougall from Oban and Alexander Lewis Reid from Perth who took advantage of an appalling and disgraceful lapse in security to slip away. The real anger was because Reid was the brutal slayer of a young mother while MacDougall had been labelled a potential murderer. They had been sent to Carstairs because the public were entitled to be protected from them. Although staff would later be slapped on their wrists for allowing two dangerous men to get free, it was obvious that not for the first time Carstairs management were closing the stable door after the horse had bolted. They had not learned from previous mistakes and nor would they, with terrible consequences, learn from this incident.

Why was so much criticism levelled at the State Hospital? It had been opened to hold men and women suffering from mental illness who were dangerous and was meant to be totally escape-proof. Even before it took its first patients, many local people had wondered about the wisdom of opening such an institution just one mile from the main railway line to London. Slow goods trains were continually using the track and it would be easy to clamber onto one and be out of the area, the country even, before they were missed. There had

SLIPPING AWAY

been a plethora of escapes from the start – thirty-eight up to 1964 and a further nine between then and 1967. The institution was quick to point out that none of the escapees had been at large for more than a few hours, but that missed the point. Nobody was supposed to be able to run off. There ought to have been a full inquiry after each escape and measures taken to ensure the same breach was not repeated. Clearly that had not been the case, leading to considerable and justifiable local disquiet.

Confidence in the Carstairs management was shaken by these escapes, but it was about to be rocked yet again. In the early hours of 20 May 1957, John McGhee from Greenock and John McDade of Glasgow smashed a little window in a dormitory and managed to wriggle though then drop to the ground. Both aged twenty-one and fit, they easily climbed over a twelve-foot-high boundary fence despite its being topped with barbed wire and fled. It was nine hours later before they were seen three miles away. Police who had been drafted in to search the area chased after the pair, discovering them hiding in bushes. Neither resisted and they were driven back to the hospital. If anyone expected a closer eye to be kept on the young men after that, they were in for a disappointment. Astonishingly, just six months later, McGhee, committed to the State Hospital from Greenock in 1954 after being convicted of assault and robbery, escaped again.

Clad in hospital-issue blue battledress and grey trousers he was in a working party being escorted by two male nurses back to his ward from the workshops with a dozen other inmates when he ran off, clambered over the fence a second time and vanished. Despite the alarm being sounded immediately, no trace could be seen of him in the immediate area and it was believed he might be heading to link up with friends in the Edinburgh area. He was eventually recaptured, but red-faced hospital officials faced awkward questions. His escape was not unnoticed by Lanark MP Patrick Maitland, who wrote to the government demanding stricter security. 'Something must be done to close these all too common escape gaps,' he said and, for starters, proposed electrifying the fence around the institution.

CARSTAIRS

The response from the Scottish Office gave little cause for encouragement or reassurance. It was standard glib government excuse material: steps had been taken to improve safety; others were being considered; measures to improve security were constantly being reviewed; extra staff had been recruited; the present warning system was adequate and the matter was being kept under review. It missed the point. Carstairs was intended to have the very best of security, but the standard would always depend on the competence of staff. What was needed was an experienced, skilled security professional capable of training up the rest of the staff to a high level of awareness. Until such an appointment was made, nobody could feel safe. Most remarkable and surprising of all, however, was that the idea of an electrified fence was turned down on the grounds that, even if desirable, there was no guarantee it would be fully effective.

The escape of Reid and MacDougall caused outright fear in the vicinity of the hospital. The former was only sixteen when he was sent to Carstairs after carrying out a killing that caused horror and revulsion throughout central Scotland. Angela McCabe was aged twenty-two and a month earlier she had given birth to a daughter, Margaret. She was looking after the infant in the back garden of her home in Bishopbriggs in May 1967, enjoying the sunny weather and waiting for her husband Gerard to return home from work. She had everything to live for and her happiness radiated from her ready smile and the kindness she showed even to total strangers. It was natural then that she was anxious to help when a young man knocked at her door wondering if there were any odd jobs he could do for her or if she knew of any neighbours who were looking for someone to do work. Asking the visitor to wait while she fetched him a glass of lemonade, she went off to think up some little job she might ask him to do. The reward for her generosity was for him to return to the house a few hours later and when Angela answered the door viciously plunge a knife into her heart and as she lay dying callously go inside, look for her purse, empty it of fifteen pounds and make off.

Her body was discovered by Gerard who rang police and was then locked up on suspicion of murdering his wife of eleven months.

He was only freed when Reid was arrested and confessed. When he appeared in court he admitted the culpable homicide of Angela. A psychiatrist who had interviewed him said he was suffering from mental deficiency and had the mental age of a ten-year-old, adding, 'I feel he would be too dangerous a person to be detained in an ordinary hospital.'

Slightly built MacDougall had a long history as a scary troublemaker. When he was a teenager he had been sent to approved school near Montrose. He escaped from the establishment in 1966 and while on the run with another miscreant broke into a house and threatened the wife of a doctor with a knife. After his recapture, a report from the approved school headmaster had a chilling ring. It warned, 'MacDougall is a potential murderer.' He was ordered to be detained in a young offenders' institution and moved to Dumfries. But after just a few months there, he and a crony escaped and during almost two weeks at large while police nationwide hunted for them, they first took six people hostage in a house in Dumfries, keeping them at knifepoint for five hours before making off. They stopped an unwary motorist who was forced to drive them to Lancashire. From there they eventually moved on to Epping Forest in Essex where they forced their way into the home of an elderly woman before returning north to Edinburgh to terrify another family in their home.

When he was sent to borstal, the staff were so worried by his behaviour that they requested he be examined by psychiatrists and as a result MacDougall was transferred to Carstairs where he met and became friendly with Reid. As the relationship developed the talk between the two ultimately turned to escape. It would transpire that getting out was as far as their forward planning went. Even so, what they achieved caused ructions.

They waited until after midnight when most of their fellow patients were asleep and unlikely to give them away and staff numbers had been reduced before acting. A male nurse patrolling the corridors was grabbed and dragged into a toilet. Taking his keys they literally let themselves out, clambered over the fence and vanished into the darkness. They had no idea of what lay outside the hospital but before their escape had spotted a well-known landmark, the 2,600-foot-high Tinto Hill, in the distance. Their reasoning was that from the peak they would be able to see the surrounding countryside and then work out their next move. The hill was six miles off and they headed towards it and began climbing. What was astounding was that it was not until six in the morning, four hours after they had gone, that it was realised one of the nurses was not around. A search discovered him still locked in the toilet. He was unharmed.

The alarm was sounded and police swarmed into the area. Tracker dogs appeared from cars and vans. Householders in the vicinity were rudely awoken by police officers knocking on their doors, asking them to search sheds and outbuildings for any trace of the two young men. Lorries and coaches were stopped and checked. Farmers discovered policemen swarming across their fields and it was a sheep farmer who spotted Reid and MacDougall on the summit of Tinto Hill and pointed search teams in their direction. Realising they had been seen and watching as police officers, some with dogs, began the slow climb upwards the fugitives attempted to get away by running down the opposite side of the hill, unaware a dog handler was heading towards them. Releasing his Alsatian dog, the officer shouted to his quarries to give up, at which MacDougall threw a knife into bushes then both lay down close to a waterworks and waited to be handcuffed. They had been at large for nine hours and were driven back to Carstairs while the rumpus caused by their brief spell of freedom exploded.

Announcing an internal investigation the Scottish Office claimed:

> Obviously the hospital takes account of every escape and no doubt they will look at the circumstances to see if any lessons can be learned from them. At the moment we have no idea how they got over the wall or the wire.

Senior hospital management were under pressure to be seen to act, not least because Judith Hart, the MP in whose constituency Carstairs was situated, made it clear she had been watching events at the hospital for some time, including allegations that patients had been ill-treated. She said she had passed on some of her evidence to the

Scottish Council for Civil Liberties, recommending an investigation by the Mental Welfare Commission – a body which defines itself as protecting and promoting the human rights of people with mental health problems, learning disabilities, dementia and related conditions. Clearly something had gone wrong, but who was to blame?

Within hours, three male nurses at the State Hospital were suspended. Following a brief inquiry one of the men was downgraded, a second formally reprimanded and the third cleared. The then Secretary of State for Scotland, Gordon Campbell, announced, 'I am determined to ensure that any lessons which could be learned from the escape would be put to good use to improve security at the hospital.' They were words that would return to haunt many.

Among those convinced that all was not well inside Carstairs was MacDougall's mother, Flora. She said he had escaped because he was not receiving any treatment for his psychiatric illness; 'He broke out because they wouldn't help him; he was just looking to get help. He was living a life of hell in there.' Friends of the family suspected her words hit home and wondered if he really had not been getting treatment because shortly after the escape doctors decided he was well enough to leave. Unfortunately he was unable to change his flirtation with crime. Three years after the breakout MacDougall was jailed for four years for stealing four mailbags from the Glasgow to Oban mail train.

Reid remained at Carstairs for a further thirteen years before doctors decided he had recovered sufficiently for him to be moved to a less secure establishment, Sunnyside Hospital near Montrose. He was allowed an occasional day out, but showed he could not be trusted by trying to abduct a child aged eight from a caravan site toilet block and, declared sane, was jailed and then returned to Carstairs. His determination to be free of the institution would continue and he began a series of legal challenges arguing that because, after years in the State Hospital, psychiatrists were changing their definition of his condition to one of an untreatable personality disorder there was no reason to hold him there. During a succession of court hearings, rulings in his favour were overturned by appeal judges.

At one early hearing in 1998, Lord Hutton pointed out that judges were being asked to rule dangerous patients could be released regardless of fears for the safety of the public. He felt it was up to politicians to debate changing the law:

> I consider that the balancing of the protection of the public as against the claim of a psychopath convicted many years ago that he should not continue to be detained in hospital when medical treatment will not improve his condition is an issue for Parliament to decide and not for judges.

By 2007, forty years after he was first committed to Carstairs, Reid had asked to have the terms under which he was held changed so he could be transferred to prison from where he could apply for parole. After initial rejections he was finally granted his wish at a hearing by appeal court judges in Edinburgh in November 2012. Carstairs psychiatrist Dr Natasha Billcliff said Reid was disruptive, took up more time and needed more attention than any other of the men in her care and dismissed efforts at therapy. She said the hospital could do nothing to improve his condition. The judges changed the terms under which he went to Carstairs to a life prison sentence with a ten-year tariff. Because of the time he had already been locked up it meant he could immediately seek parole.

The decision was hurtful and distressing to the many friends of Angela McCabe who pointed out that they too had been suffering a life sentence – only in their case there was no relief or freedom from it. Reid was ultimately shipped to a prison cell and almost immediately he challenged the prison service, complaining that he was not being allowed to attend rehabilitation classes which would let him show the parole board he was ready for freedom.

13

THE PHANTOM

He gloried in the nickname of 'The Phantom', a fictional comic character who used a mixture of brute strength, subtlety and brains to fight and destroy criminals. It was a complete misnomer as far as Alexander Stewart was concerned. For a start, he hardly looked the part. The comic Phantom was tall, handsome and with muscles that brought wishful glances from pretty women. Stewart on the other hand was unattractive, had a receding hairline and was developing middle-aged spread. Worst of all was his profession, as far removed from a crime fighter as it was possible to be. He was a prolific thief, a nasty sneak of a burglar who crept into the homes of unsuspecting, decent hard-working folk with few possessions and crept away sometimes with little things, ornaments, a watch, a ring for which they had saved and which meant so much. There were mementoes of dead sons and sisters, all stashed away in his grimy pockets and sold for a few pounds in dingy bars or to second-hand shops. This Phantom was a thoroughly rotten, heartless individual who preyed on the helpless. In one dreadful nine-month wave of crime he was blamed for a mind boggling ninety-three housebreakings.

At least, the meagre few who made up his friends would point out, he wasn't as bad as his brother Frank. What were a few burglaries compared with killing a man, which was what Frank had done? In 1969, Frank had disturbed night watchman William Gerry Thain. He always protested that he never meant Thain any harm, but the fact remained that the watchman died. What caused so much ill feeling towards the Stewarts in Aberdeen, where they lived and Thain had died, was that the victim was seventy-three years old and had never stood a chance against the much younger thirty-one-year-old Frank. Memories in the Granite City were still fresh of what had happened just six years earlier when Henry John Burnett had been hanged for killing a man. And for a time Burnett had lived less than a mile from the Alexander family.

Courts came down harshly on killers and when he initially faced a murder charge Frank was looking at the possibility of spending the next couple of decades in a prison cell. However, he was saved from prison by his mental state. After doctors confirmed he was suffering from psychiatric illness, he was convicted of the reduced charge of culpable homicide and sent to Carstairs. Lord Kissen, the judge, stipulated that he would remain there without limit of time only to be released with the approval of the government. While that now meant a 300-mile round trip to Lanarkshire whenever his mother Joan or anyone else in the family wanted to visit him, at least he was better off in the State Hospital than in a grim jail even though that prison would probably have been Peterhead, a bus journey to the north of Aberdeen.

It was to Peterhead prison that Alexander Stewart was eventually taken in 1969 after police brought an end to his housebreaking spree by arresting him and hauling him in front of a sheriff. At first he was held in Aberdeen's own prison, Craiginches, where there were concerns about his mental state, but then he was moved up to Peterhead. The jail there was the pit of the prison system, a stark, antiquated dump where the amenities were little better than those in a medieval dungeon. It was where the prison service sent the worst of the worst to fester in damp, cramped, overcrowded cells. Forced to spend hour after hour banged up amid the stink of their urine and faeces lying in open pots until slopping out time, Peterhead was a spawning ground for depression. And Alexander Stewart had more reason than most to slide down into deep melancholy.

If anything good could be said of him, it was that he worshipped the ground on which his wife Shirley walked, and idolised their three sons. He had told friends when she accepted his marriage proposal in 1963 that he was the 'happiest man on God's earth', but it didn't take Shirley long to have doubts as to whether she had done the right thing. After leaving school, her husband had been taken on as an apprentice butcher in Aberdeen. At eighteen, he joined the Royal Artillery. Most young men benefitted from the discipline of life in the armed forces, but, after six years as a soldier, Stewart left and simply became a criminal specialising in housebreaking.

The fact that he quickly became a target for police made him a minor hero in the Aberdeen underworld in which younger crooks tagged him 'The Phantom' because of his apparent ability to ghost in and out of the homes of victims. He was proud of his nickname, but what he failed to appreciate was that the bigger his reputation among small-time criminals, the greater a police target he became. His marriage to Shirley produced the boys, but she was determined her sons would not follow the path of their father into Scotland's prisons; she was constantly pleading with her husband to stay on the straight and narrow. Her own happiness, though, gradually turned to disappointment as her words fell on deaf ears and she looked elsewhere for solace. Shirley was an attractive woman. There were plenty of men about who admired her, although she had given them no encouragement. However, there was one exception and it was in his arms that she found comfort. His would become fatal embraces.

When Alexander Stewart was arrested, the prospect of another prison sentence for her husband was the last straw as far as she was concerned. She worked for butcher Gordon McWilliam who owned a couple of shops in Aberdeen and he had become the other man in her life. Gradually he became the only man. He was married with two teenage children but Shirley became his mistress and he her lover. While Alexander Stewart was detained at Craiginches to await his sentence, he wondered why Shirley had not visited him. The answer came through the prison grapevine; she had left him and set up home with McWilliam. His response was to throw himself from a landing in a pathetic effort at suicide, although most saw it as an attempt to win his wife's sympathy. If that was the motive, it failed. He was sent off to Peterhead where, in the miserable surroundings of the bleakest, most unsympathetic jail in the country, he brooded, building up an intense anger over what he saw as the injustice of his treatment by someone he still loved deeply.

In mid October 1970, he was released and made his way back south to Aberdeen to piece together what had become of his wife and children. His mind was a turmoil of brooding jealousy. By four days later he knew the name of the man who was sharing her bed and set about taking a terrible revenge. His first call, he had decided, would be to the butcher's wife Daphne. At the age of forty, she too had seen her life shattered by her husband's affair. Perhaps Stewart felt that in her he would find condolence. Maybe he hoped she could help him to win back his wife by persuading her husband to return to her side. No one would ever know why she agreed that Stewart could come to her home. They would be able to talk frankly because, with the children at school, she was alone. Her children would never again see their mum alive. Not long after her visitor arrived, she was dead, viciously battered and stabbed, a coat carelessly slung over her body. The terrible and unexplained deed done, madman Stewart set off on the next stage of his mission of mayhem to look for McWilliam and Shirley, hoping to find them together in the shop where Shirley worked. After a two-mile journey across Aberdeen, he discovered her lover wasn't there, but Shirley was.

Moments later the thirty-two-year-old ran screaming from the shop pursued by her crazed husband who lunged at her again and again with a knife until she collapsed in the street. Stunned passers-by would later tell how, as she lay bleeding to death, he had leaned over her and whispered, 'I love you.' Then in a frightening act that was both of frustration and another suicide attempt, he smashed the plate-glass window of a nearby shop with his bare hands and sat down to await the arrival of police. Meanwhile as Shirley's body was gently taken away the McWilliam children were wondering why there was no response from their mother to their knocks after arriving home from school, no smile and answering hug and no tea on the table. The youngsters, aged sixteen and thirteen, knocked on the door of a neighbour, wondering if perhaps their mum had popped in there for a chat. The neighbour, concerned at the eerie silence from Daphne's home, climbed in through a window to make the dreadful discovery.

In January the following year thirty-eight-year-old Stewart appeared at the High Court in Aberdeen but he was too mad to plead to the charge of double murder. Psychiatrists said he was suicidal and too insane to give instructions for his defence. The judge, Lord Cameron, committed him to Carstairs to join his brother. A sheriff had once told Alexander Stewart, 'Don't think because you were given the name of The Phantom, you are a romantic figure. You have shown yourself to be a petty criminal.' The truth was that a man's petty jealousy had grown into a terrible thirst for vengeance that took the lives of two loving mothers, one of them a complete innocent, and left five children with the terrible memory of a day when their world collapsed.

Was it his impressive nickname that led Alexander Stewart to believe he had the right to act as he pleased – a course that other ordinary mortals were not allowed to take? Lots of criminals regard a nickname as a status symbol, even glorying in names that to others might be offensive or degrading. Owen Bonner's looks, his black moustache and Van Dyke beard brought comments from cronies that he looked like the Devil but he took that a stage further. 'I am worse than the Devil', he told two terrified women in a chicken plant after taking them hostage at knifepoint in 1994, sparking a five-hour siege during which he demanded a £10,000 ransom. Yet could the women have been spared their appalling ordeal? Once again doctors at Carstairs found themselves in the firing line after it was revealed Bonner had been a patient in the State Hospital, where he had been sent after his mind became distorted through heavy drug taking. What is more, they had allowed him to go free twelve months before the chicken plant scandal.

He had been given a job in the plant at Coatbridge, Lanarkshire, but pulled out a knife and ordered co-workers Geraldine Henderson and Louise Ward to recite the Lord's Prayer and warned them he was worse than the Devil. In addition to the huge cash demand, he insisted television cameras were to be allowed through a police cordon to film him and he wanted a Michael Jackson album and one of the singer's outfits. Louise was able to escape, but only after he cut her. Geraldine too was injured, Bonner slashing her across the forehead and threatening to cut her throat. In order to be given her freedom and the knife she was forced to kiss her captor, who then let himself be arrested. For these vile acts, Bonner was sent back to Carstairs after psychiatrists said he was insane, and once more politicians insisted there should be an investigation into his release. Geraldine said, 'I thought I was going to die. He must never be freed again.' It was a view that had widespread support. But the hospital would face yet more embarrassment as a result of his antics.

A year later, senior staff allowed the holding of a ceremony in which Bonner married a mother-of-three who quickly decided she had lost interest in him. He appeared to have abandoned his wedding vows three years later when he was caught having sex with a female patient. In 2006, through lawyers, he placed a newspaper advertisement asking his wife to get in touch because he wanted to divorce her.

In 1999 Bonner claimed damages from the Criminal Injuries Compensation Board after nicking himself with an electric razor. The absurd action was thrown out, but on the day he appeared before the Board in Glasgow to be told of the decision, he escaped from escorting nurses. Fortunately for his minders he was captured, thanks to a member of the public who spotted him hiding behind a parked car. By January 2014, Bonner, now aged forty-seven, had been transferred to Rowanbank Clinic in Glasgow, where security is less strict but once again he left his guards with red faces, escaping in the centre of Glasgow during an escorted shopping trip. He later gave himself up.

The Devil has played a busy and significant role in the Carstairs story. In 2013 schizophrenic student Paul Glenn, aged twenty-one, tried to drown a man in a Glasgow pond after a voice in his head told him his victim was the Devil. He had been allowed out of Gartnavel Royal Hospital, but a judge decided he should be kept under much stricter security and he was sent to the State Hospital.

That same year Gordon McRobbie bludgeoned a woman working for a mental health charity in Kirkcaldy, Fife telling her he was the

Devil. Earlier he had watched the horror film *Shaun of the Dead*. He was convicted of attempted murder and sent to Carstairs.

Armed robber Gary Simpson believed himself to be the son of the Devil. He had been in Carstairs seven times and it was during one of those spells that it was alleged he dreamed up a plot with a fellow patient to murder one of the ward managers. He had insisted he wanted to be moved from Carstairs to a prison where he would have the opportunity to apply for parole, and at a hearing to assess his application to leave, a psychiatrist who submitted he ought to remain at the institution said:

> He needs medication to control his schizophrenia, depression and violent mood swings. He said he is the son of the Devil and that the Devil speaks to him. He can be a charismatic personality who is able to recruit followers, but he continues to have delusions.

Simpson failed in that attempt, but later on was shifted to Glenochil jail near Tullibody in Clackmannanshire. However when he asked for a transfer from there to Greenock prison so he could be nearer family members he was refused, one of the grounds being his claim to be related to Satan.

The Devil is traditionally associated with evil, and there could be no other word to describe the horror in 1998 that was laid at Satan's door. Telling them he was the Devil, student Kenneth McCaskill, aged twenty-seven, a schizophrenic, stabbed to death his father Simon, a Royal Navy commander, and then repeatedly plunged the weapon into his mum Katherine at their Edinburgh home. Prosecutor Raymond Doherty described the nightmare that had followed a happy family meal with friends:

> Kenneth told his mother he was Lucifer – a statement she was used to hearing since he had read a book about Devil worship. She told him not to be silly. He told his parents he wanted to take over the house and ordered them to leave, again telling them he was the Devil. When he was refused the keys to the family car he threw an ashtray across the room and ran into the kitchen to pick up a large knife.

His mother tried to stop the murder of his father, hitting her son with a frying pan. Doherty continued:

> When the father fell to the floor McCaskill diverted his attention to the mother and stabbed her. He stabbed her on the arms before plunging the knife into her chest and she fell to the floor with it still in her body.

Doctors said Mrs McCaskill was lucky to survive, but was this brave lady really so fortunate? She lost a loving husband, was left with dreadful memories and saw her son sent to Carstairs for the remainder of his life.

14

THE JANITOR'S SECRET

Who can say with certainty that a psychiatric patient who has committed acts of violence can be safely rehabilitated into the community with no danger of reoffending? Each year a handful leave Carstairs, most moving to hospitals where security is more lax and occasionally a man is given his total freedom but can these former patients be trusted? There have been too many cases that have left mortal doubts over the wisdom of those authorising releases, too many instances of the families of victims wondering just where the sympathy of the state lies.

James Lawless was only seventeen in 1956 when his bizarre behaviour was giving so much concern to friends and family that he was committed to a mental hospital at Larbert in Stirlingshire. It became clear doctors there could not control his illness and it was decided to move him to Carstairs. During permitted short breaks from the State Hospital he fathered a son Joseph and in 1962, when the boy was ten months old, Lawless was released on licence. It was a decision that ended in tragedy and the snuffing out of a little life that had hardly begun. The child was beaten to death by his father. Naturally questions were asked about who it was who had allowed the killer to go free. They would never get an answer. When he appeared in court, psychiatrists said Lawless was likely to commit further crimes and would be a danger to the public if he were allowed the freedom that a prison sentence would eventually guarantee him. After hearing their reports the judge, Lord Grant, made an order restricting his discharge indefinitely by sending him back to Carstairs without limit of time.

Despite what the judge had ruled, eight years later he was again given permission to leave the Lanarkshire institution. This time his destination was Bangour Village Hospital near Dechmont in West Lothian and despite being a killer he was placed in a ward where patients were free to come and go. In Carstairs he had met and fallen in love with a fellow female patient. She had been freed and was living on the east coast of Scotland. Lawless was allowed to leave the asylum each morning and travel to the Edinburgh area where he was found factory work, returning to Bangour Village at night. In 1971 he married his new love and was told he could spend weekends with her. The following year doctors approved a two-week holiday for Lawless provided he stayed with his new bride in Edinburgh. He was allowed out on licence.

However, alarm bells began ringing when he did not return to the asylum and police who called at the Edinburgh address discovered he was not there. Few had forgotten that on a previous occasion when he had been given leave from a mental hospital his baby boy had been killed. The Scottish Home and Health Department was quick to defend itself against any allegations of slackness should another tragedy be discovered, issuing a statement claiming: 'On the medical advice available to us we do not consider this man to be dangerous.' Two days after he disappeared, a nationwide manhunt was called off when Lawless, aged thirty-three, walked into Bangour Village Hospital. Nobody had been hurt but the question as to whether it had been right to let him enjoy a fortnight of total freedom was never answered.

It was as though lessons were never learned. While police everywhere were searching for James Lawless, the gates of Carstairs were being opened to let James Gibson leave. He headed back to his hometown, Dundee, a city that had borne more than its share of tragedy. Dundonians remembered the name of Gibson, a man with a lengthy criminal record, and wondered whether they might read about his release in their morning newspapers. They would not have long to wait.

THE JANITOR'S SECRET

Gibson's troubled past deeply worried the local police. He had a history of mental illness and because of the seriousness with which his condition was regarded he had been sent to Carstairs in 1958 when he was aged twenty-six. He was not there for long and when doctors concluded that despite his having the mental age of a boy of ten, there was nothing further they could do for him, he was freed on licence, returning to Dundee where family friends raised their eyebrows at his appointment as assistant janitor to a girls' school in the city. Was it appropriate for a man known to have suffered such serious mental illness to be mingling with girls? The answer was not long in coming.

Following his release from the State Hospital he had met and set up home with a local woman, forty-seven-year-old Mrs Mary McConnachie Saunders, who was estranged from her husband, a jute works labourer. At times the relationship was stormy – Gibson was prone to moods and could be argumentative. In late January 1960 a drinking session led to yet another argument that ended when he picked up a scarf, wrapped it around the throat of his mistress and strangled her. She died from asphyxiation. After his arrest, the killer admitted the culpable homicide of Mrs Saunders and, following psychiatric reports describing him as feeble-minded and mentally abnormal, a judge returned him to Carstairs.

This time his stay in the institution was longer. He was there for twelve years, yet once again doctors took the decision to allow his release in 1972. At first, he went to live in London but, unable to settle in the English capital and homesick, he went back to Dundee. His freedom was short lived. In February 1974, his father John, eighty-one, was found dead at his home in the city. Earlier that night Gibson had been drinking with relatives when a friend came to the bar where they were enjoying themselves and said the old man had locked himself out and needed help. Gibson left and climbed through a window to open a door and let his father into the house. Then he returned to join the other drinkers. Later the elderly man was found dead.

At first, both a doctor and the police believed he had died from natural causes. He had been in poor health for some time and his death had come as no surprise. For some days, friends sympathised with Gibson over the loss of his dad. Then he began muttering that he had killed his father. At first nobody took him seriously. However when he rang police from a coin box and claimed he was a murderer, the matter took on a very different significance. Officers recorded his call then went to find and arrest him. In a remarkable confession the former Carstairs patient said, 'I murdered my father by placing a pillow over his mouth and killed him. Now, wait a minute, he was eighty-three and I was just helping him.'

By the time he appeared in court the murder charge had been reduced to one of culpable homicide because of his mental background and the fact that the victim was in poor health and could have died at any time. Psychiatrists who examined Gibson said he was sane and fit to plead and more treatment would 'not be beneficial'. The advocate depute Donald Macaulay said, 'A matter of paramount importance is the question of danger to the public. In fairness to Gibson he should be kept away for some time for his own protection and to allow him to receive treatment.'

It was a situation that upset the judge, Lord Stott, who clearly felt the members of the medical profession were dumping their dirty washing on him. He said:

> It seems absurd that this should be treated other than a medical case. But doctors have washed their hands of you. It seems crazy that a man who has been described as mentally abnormal and feeble-minded should be sent to prison as a criminal. But there is no alternative. I must deal with you as a criminal. The crime is a minimum culpable homicide for if your father was not at death's door, he was very near it. It would not have required much force to kill him. Balancing all these things as best I can, there is nothing I can do but send you to prison for three years.

Gibson had been freed from prison by the time yet another recent release from Carstairs killed someone. James Moore was a self-confessed alcoholic whose conduct had resulted in his being committed to Carstairs. After they treated him, psychiatrists recommended to the Secretary of State for Scotland that he was well enough to be released and as a result he was given an absolute discharge from the State Hospital in 1974. Within two years of his freedom, he had killed. The victim was Thomas Brown, aged fifty-one.

Brown and his forty-seven-year-old sister, both alcoholics, had been living in a flat in Springburn in the east end of Glasgow when one night in a local bar they met up with Moore who had just been discharged and was living in a nearby block. The three chatted, shared drinks and went back to his flat. He invited the Browns to move in with him but it was not long before they were regretting their decision to take advantage of his hospitality. The trio would spend nights in bars before heading home armed with more bottles of drink, to booze, fight and drunkenly sing the early hours away to the disgust and anger of neighbours whose complaints were met with obscenities and insults. Often they would sleep away the daylight and frequently when he appeared Thomas would be sporting black eyes with cuts and bruises about his head and face, and reluctantly admit Moore had been the culprit. Friends begged him to go to tell his story to the police.

Then one morning in May 1976, a fight in the flat between the two men got out of hand and as was usually the case it was a tiny spark that ignited it. The trio had been drinking heavily in the living room, having spent their social security benefits on wine, spirits and cans of beer. Two days earlier Moore had washed a coat belonging to Brown's sister but that fatal morning he flew into a rage after noticing one of her pet dogs had brushed against it, leaving hairs sticking to the fabric. The woman was the target for his rage and when Thomas went to her rescue he was attacked by Moore with a brick and smashed on the head. He collapsed behind a door with blood pouring from his injuries, and lay motionless while the other two carried on drinking, the woman finally falling into a drunken stupor in a chair. She and Moore were so drunk that neither realised her brother was lying dead.

It was not until twelve hours later that he was discovered, still lying where he had collapsed, with the killer and his sister just feet away. Neighbours had heard the screams and shouts of the fight and the sound of a man apparently falling and much later, when nobody answered their knocks at the door or emerged from the flat, decided to call police. As the body of the dead man was being carried out, an officer who had been delegated to collect empty wine bottles from the living room announced to superiors his count had reached sixty. Moore, aged forty-three and described in court as a brutal and sadistic bully, denied murdering Thomas and repeatedly assaulting him in the year before his death. He was found guilty and jailed for life.

15

THE CRACKED MIRROR

'Please, please not Barlinnie' begged Thomas Wallace as he was dragged from the dock in 1976. 'Please don't send me to Barlinnie.' The thin-faced, dark-haired accused man had good reason for not wanting to be sent to the Bar-L, Glasgow's infamous Big House, the largest and reputedly toughest prison in Scotland.

He had just been given a life sentence for the cruel killing of a friendly little boy. Other prisoners, many with families and sons of their own, would show no mercy on any brute who harmed children. In fact they'd be waiting with homemade weapons and clenched fists to exact their own punishment on Wallace. He knew he was in not only for a beating but could expect urine in his tea and over his bedding, faeces in his food and a kicking in the exercise yard. And, at the age of fifty-nine, he no longer had the strength to fend off the attacks of younger, stronger convicts.

Of course he could ask to be placed in solitary confinement under the official Rule 48, which read:

> Where it appears desirable, for the maintenance of good order or discipline or in his own interests, that a prisoner should not associate with other prisoners, either generally or for particular purposes, the governor may arrange for the prisoner's removal from association accordingly.

Despite this, the now quivering wretch who was being hustled out of sight of the court knew like every other inmate and member of the prison staff that was no guarantee of safety. Somebody had to bring his meals and it was the work of just a moment to contaminate them. He knew he wouldn't be at Barlinnie for long before being sent to Peterhead where he would at least have the relative protection of other long termers who, like him, were there because they had murdered or molested youngsters. The spell he faced in Barlinnie would nevertheless be a living hell.

It was Monday, 26 April 1976 and he had just become the most hated individual in Scotland – the mad, twisted perpetrator of a crime so appalling it churned the stomach just thinking about it. True, Wallace's life until that day had been as miserable as the crime for which he had just been jailed, but if he hoped for sympathy he was on a loser. Christopher Doyle, the boy he slaughtered, was a lovely trusting kid who died simply because his killer blamed him for being responsible for a tiny crack in a bicycle mirror.

Wallace had always been a blemish on society, someone who offered and gave nothing. As a teenager he was shunned by others, a bully who took out his unpredictable bursts of violence on younger children, an adolescent with no interest in girls. When he was twenty, he picked an argument with a boy aged nine in Ayrshire. The child tried to get away but Wallace was having none of it, punching and kicking him then trying to drown him. Thankfully the child survived and was able to tell police about his ordeal. Wallace was arrested and charged with attempted murder. It had long been suspected there was something wrong with him. 'He wasn't the full shilling,' said a police officer who investigated his background. By the time he appeared in court, where he was ordered to be detained at His Majesty's Pleasure, he had been examined by doctors who concluded he was mad and as a result was moved to the criminal lunatic unit at Perth prison. It was 1936, the year when plans were being discussed to open a State Hospital for the dangerously insane at Carstairs. By the time the hospital began taking patients in 1957, Wallace, still locked up and regarded as a potential menace, was among them.

Two years later, he was transferred on licence to Dykebar Hospital in Renfrewshire where security was much more relaxed. At the time some wondered whether it was really possible for such a deeply crazed character to make what amounted to an astonishing improvement. It would not be the last time the judgement of the Carstairs management would come into question. Those who knew him raised their eyebrows even further when in 1971, twelve years after he arrived at Dykebar, he was given an absolute discharge – freedom to rejoin the society he had abused three and a half decades earlier. Because his original sentence had been the equivalent of detention for life, permission for his liberty had to come from the then Secretary of State for Scotland, who basically rubber-stamped the recommendation of hospital doctors and psychiatrists. Were they right? Time would tell.

The problem for Wallace was that he had nowhere to go. Nobody wanted him or wanted to remember him. He was homeless, friendless, jobless and hopeless. At Dykebar, managers took pity. They gave him an attic room above one of the hospital blocks and even a paid job as a domestic, cleaning, scrubbing and performing simple maintenance tasks. His became a familiar face around the hospital. He spent his free hours and days wandering aimlessly and riding the bicycle he had bought out of his wages – his pride and joy and his first real possession. He had even fitted it with a mirror for which he had forked out a few pence. He spent hours polishing the machine and making sure the mirror was crystal clear. Now and again he tried making friends but because of his mental health problems and because he was institutionalised he found it difficult to gel with other adults. It was then that his old penchant for youngsters re-emerged.

Wallace eventually found friendship with Christopher, bright and never without a smile. The schoolboy's parents, who lived in a cottage in the hospital grounds, both worked at Dykebar. Dad Joseph was a male nurse while mum Monica was a trainee as well as caring for their three children. Like other parents they had warned them about the perils of talking to strangers and they had made it clear to Wallace they wanted him to stay away from Christopher. It was a friendly warning but it was not heeded. The friendship continued, Wallace allowing the child to ride his bicycle. Then, one day in January 1976, he noticed the cracked mirror. It was tiny, but enough to reawaken a long dormant temper. In his sick mind he planned what he felt was deserved punishment – death. At a deserted outhouse he hid a hammer and length of tape then lured his young victim with promises he could ride the cycle. When unsuspecting Christopher arrived, Wallace launched a horrendous attack, smashing him on the head with the hammer, the force so powerful the tool broke, until he fell unconscious at which point Wallace wrapped tape around the youngster's neck pulling it tight and strangling him. When he was sure the boy was dead he threw his body into a stream, the Tod Burn that ran through the grounds of Dykebar.

Christopher's absence was soon noticed and a search started, but it wasn't until the next morning that his mutilated body was discovered. Nearby, police found the broken hammer head and shaft and two lengths of blood-stained tape. Wallace was arrested and admitted:

> I don't know what came over me, but I hit him twice with a hammer over the head and the head came off the hammer. He started shouting for help and I put a tape round his neck and strangled him. I regret it, but it's too late now.

At his trial Wallace pleaded guilty to murder. A psychiatrist said, 'He has no control over his aggression. He is likely to over-react whether or not he is provoked. He should never be allowed out of an institution again for the rest of his life.' Wallace's defence team warned he would be in danger in an ordinary prison and a defence psychiatrist said, 'I believe he will fulfil a threat to kill himself if he is sent to prison.'

Before he was sentenced Wallace twice asked to be allowed to speak but was denied permission by the judge, Lord Thomson, who said he was imposing the mandatory sentence for murder – life imprisonment – at which Wallace suddenly burst out, 'Aye, in Barlinnie' and began struggling, shouting and pleading. He tried clambering out of the dock into the well of the courtroom but was hauled back by three policemen, two of whom had drawn their truncheons. As he was hustled down the steps leading from the dock to the cells below the courtroom his screams could still be heard.

The fact that the killer had been caught and would never again experience freedom was no consolation to Joseph and Monica Doyle. 'You can tell a child not to speak to someone, that that person is bad, dangerous. But children forget warnings very quickly,' Monica said. 'Wallace should never have been allowed freedom. The tendencies were there and people better trained and more knowledgeable than us should have seen them.' Her sentiments echoed those of parents everywhere, and MP Edward Taylor demanded action. He said:

> This case is just one in a series where people who have been released from mental institutions commit either soon afterwards or much later very serious crimes. I feel there has been a much too liberal policy adopted by psychiatric advisers to the mental institutions.

While the controversy over his release continued Wallace was, as expected, moved to Peterhead. Its grim walls had once held the toughest convicts in Scotland. Now it housed sex offenders, rapists, paedophiles and a handful of men felt to be in need of protection. He had made no secret of wanting to be returned to Carstairs, but it was pointed out that doctors said he was sane. He spent six miserable months at Peterhead and then one day strung himself up in his cell, a fate that many believed he deserved. He would harm no more children.

The brutal killing in January 1961 of little Jane Patricia Cruickshank set off a huge manhunt. Jane was just six when she was found lying in a lane only one hundred yards from her home in Aberdeen with blood pouring from a slash on her neck. The child had been running an errand to a corner shop when she vanished. A horrified churchgoer discovered her and ran for an ambulance but it was too late for hospital staff to save her. Not surprisingly the news that a maniac was at large brought terror to parents in the Granite City. Police had the unenviable task of searching for the killer while at the same time warning he might strike again. Extra bobbies patrolled the streets, mums and dads were too scared to let their charges out of their sight and teachers refused to allow pupils to leave schools until a family member had arrived to escort them safely home.

After a while, the search was scaled down although a team of detectives continued the investigation. Then just over two years later the murderer struck again in identical fashion. This time the victim was little George Forbes, aged seven, who had disappeared from his Aberdeen home. Police and volunteers spent four months searching for him. Theories abounded as to his fate, including the possibility he had been kidnapped and taken abroad by a childless couple. Always in the background, though, lay the memory of what had happened to Jane, and in July 1963, four months after he was last seen, George was found partially buried under the floor of an allotment shed. He had been slashed on the neck.

James John Oliphant had been on the police list of potential suspects. He was rumoured to have an unhealthy liking for children but there had never been enough evidence to arrest him. He was often seen at the allotments and when he was taken in for questioning quickly confessed to having killed both youngsters. Inquiries after his arrest produced a terrible catalogue of perversion. During his childhood and adolescence Oliphant was sometimes the victim but mostly, once he reached adulthood, was the perpetrator. It was said that he lured kiddies by promising them a shilling (5p) if they would let him abuse them.

Oliphant, fat, balding and dull, was forty and worked for the city council's sewage department. He was a loner who had been diagnosed as a 'mental defective' in 1942, when he was aged eighteen, and had suffered a terrible upbringing. His stepfather got sexual thrills by tying him up and savagely beating him. While in his twenties, he had fallen in love with a young waitress only for his hopes of happiness to be shattered when, three years into their relationship, she had died. After his arrest, Oliphant had told a psychiatrist about his bleak hopeless existence:

> I never had friends. The only time I had any friends was in a pub when I had money. I was often out at nights wandering on my own. Most evenings I went to the allotment then upstairs to my room and

read the papers. There is a queer feeling that happens to me at times. It has bothered me since I was young, a cold shivery feeling especially when I see blood.

It was a sad story, but no one felt any sympathy as he stood in the dock at the High Court in Aberdeen in February 1964 and admitted the culpable homicide of Jane and George and of lewd practices against other children.

The psychiatrist said the abuse from his stepfather resulted in Oliphant deciding to make children suffer in the same way he had when he was a child but he added, 'At no time has he showed any remorse for his actions or expressed concern for the relatives of the children involved.' Doctor Andrew Wyllie of Aberdeen Royal mental hospital said he considered Oliphant to be:

> a deeply perverted man with an abnormal childhood. The killings were a form of sexual perversion known as infantosexual sadism in which sexual gratification is gained by inflicting cruelty on others. He is so mentally abnormal that he is not fully responsible for his actions and ought to be under continuous supervision in the State Hospital. He remains a potential homicidal risk. I am of the opinion that if at large he would be liable to commit such offences again.

Oliphant was sent to Carstairs without limit of time. But his was a hopeless case. The effects of the sick acts of his stepfather were as a terrible burden from which he would never be free. Morose and brooding, he found it impossible to make friends and staff could never be sure whether he was responding to their efforts at treating him. He could not be sent to another hospital because of the ever-present risk that he might kill again but the problem of what to do with Oliphant was solved early in 1988 when he died at Carstairs of natural causes.

Little Luke Gargan would never grow up to buy his mother Brenda a Mother's Day present or play computer games but his killer could shop and enjoy the latest PlayStation models. The kiddie was savagely slaughtered in 2001. He had been asleep in his home in

Saltcoats, Ayrshire, when Brenda's fiancé, John Gourlay, who lived at Foxbar, Paisley, woke him and took him to a park twenty miles away where he killed him with a tool used by gardeners to edge lawns, almost decapitating the infant. The day before, Gourlay had discharged himself from Dykebar Hospital, near Paisley, where he had been a voluntary patient. Police used sniffer dogs, divers and a helicopter and were joined by local people when Brenda realised Luke was no longer at home, but when officers questioned Gourlay he took them to the spot where he killed the child. After he was arrested he told police, 'If I hadn't done it, they would have taken him away.'

Gourlay, then aged thirty-five, was charged with murder but after hearing from psychiatrists the trial judge, Lord Prosser, told the jury to acquit him on the grounds that he was insane and he was sent to the State Hospital without limit of time. A consultant psychiatrist said Gourlay told him he had seen garden forks pointing upwards and thought these had a special importance. 'This is a classic example of a psychotic phenomenon. Some individuals are unable to stop such hallucinations,' said the doctor. Had he been jailed, Gourlay would have been held in strict security for at least a dozen years before being given any hope of freedom. Yet only five years after he was sent to Carstairs, he was spotted by reporters from the *Sun* newspaper enjoying himself during a day out at a shopping centre accompanied by three nurses. The newspaper said he 'laughed and joked with his minders' before buying a Mother's Day gift. Then he sat in an ice-cream shop as children queued for refreshments. Before leaving to return to hospital he was allowed to wander around a computer games shop. A friend of Brenda said, 'She's understandably very upset about this. She feels he gave up his right to do the same things as anyone else when he killed Luke.' And many agreed.

The instinct of a mother to protect the fruit of her own womb is said to be the strongest of the human emotions. Yet occasionally and tragically mothers kill or attempt to kill their own. Such was the case of Janice Miller. It is impossible not to mingle sympathy with the horror of what happened at her home in Kilwinning, Ayrshire, in April 1998. Distraught and miserable after her husband left her and the couple's seven-year-old twins Louise and Kevin, broke and facing being made homeless, Janice, then thirty-one, cracked and fell victim to the utter despair that is clinical depression. One night she added a lethal mix of drugs to the children's bedtime drinks and watched them drift off to sleep, never to wake. Then she started a fire in their bedroom and tried to gas herself. She told police who charged her with murder:

> I just could not take any more of the debt. I thought it was the only way out. I promised my weans I would never leave them. If I had known I would still be alive, I would not have given them it.

While Janice was being held in Carstairs so her condition could be assessed, she secretly swallowed a cocktail of drugs in the hope of joining her twins. But she was saved after being placed on a life support machine. When she appeared at the High Court in Edinburgh, her plea of guilty to culpable homicide was accepted by the Crown. A psychiatrist said, 'She misses her children and sees no point in living without them. She sees no future for herself.' She was ordered to return to Carstairs but, because the judge, Lord Kingarth, decided not to place a restriction order on her, doctors at the State Hospital, rather than the government, would be able to decide when she could be released. Few, if any, cases in this story arouse such a degree of sadness as that of Janice. The real tragedy was that it took the nightmare of a court hearing for her to receive the support that, had it been given earlier, would have saved the lives of her twins. By making a ruling giving Carstairs doctors, as opposed to a politician, total control over her future, the judge took a sympathetic and positive view. Regrettably no amount of support or encouragement will erase the terrible memory within her of what she did.

16

PLAYING TRUANT

It was a fine Wednesday morning in May 1976 as Robert Monan, aged fifteen, and his sister Margaret, two years younger, set off from their home in the town of Saltcoats, Ayrshire, for school. They never reached their classrooms. Tragically, nobody would ever know whose idea it was to play truant. Instead of heading for St Andrew's Academy, the secondary school where footballer Roy Aitken had been a star pupil, the youngsters went off in the opposite direction.

Maybe they were heading for the seaside or wanted to watch the ferries arriving at nearby Ardrossan from the Isle of Arran. Perhaps they had secretly arranged to link up with some of their closest friends. Robert and Margaret were popular with their schoolmates, well liked but prone to taking a sly day off from time to time. Whatever they had planned, their day would soon develop from one of hopeful anticipation to a terrifying nightmare.

For Margaret in particular, the heaven of escaping lessons would turn into hell. A pretty girl, who already attracted admiring glances from some of the older boys at school, she lived at home with her mother, three other sisters and Robert. Perhaps it was because he was the only male sibling that she was so devoted to her brother, even protective of him despite being younger. The two were inseparable. When they did not return home from school for their tea their family became concerned but then youngsters often went to play and eat with friends without first telling their parents. However it was not Robert and Margaret who would eventually come through the door that night but police officers, nervous and gentle because of the terrible news they were about to impart.

That evening, two local brothers had spotted a couple in a field not far from the Monan home. At first, because they were lying so close together they thought they were about to intrude on a courting couple. Embarrassed and not sure what to do, the brothers went home to tell their father, who decided to investigate. What he found sent him running to call police. Robert and Margaret were dead. Someone had smashed their heads in. A senior detective, appalled by what he saw, described the attacks on the children as 'brutal, violent, vicious and nonsensical'. Nobody disagreed.

It was not just the manner of the killing that terrified parents in Saltcoats and in neighbouring Ardrossan and Stevenston – the Three Towns – but the real horror came in knowing that the maniac who had snuffed out the lives of the teenage siblings was still at large and, for all anyone knew, likely to strike again. Police swarmed into the area, not just to look for the murderer but in an attempt to reassure Threetowners that they and in particular their children were being protected. Officers visited schools, quietly talking to children about the importance of going straight home when lessons ended, of always telling their parents where they were and, whenever possible, staying in groups. Nevertheless an air of fear hung over the Three Towns standing on the lip of the Bay of Brodick. As far as detectives – many of them family men and some living in that very area – were concerned there was an added need for urgency to catch the lunatic responsible. A post-mortem examination revealed the slayer had attempted to rape Margaret.

Officers were sure their quarry was a local man and, as is the case in all crimes where there is a sexual element, concentrated inquiries on persons who had been convicted of sexual offences. As a result the spotlight fell on an oddball named Alan Albert Eastham, aged thirty-two, whose criminal record included a series of previous convictions. Until 1973, he had been living in north west England, mainly in the Preston, Lancashire area. That year he had travelled to Ayrshire where he decided to settle. But what was of special interest was that shortly before he moved north he had appeared in court in

Lancashire charged with indecently assaulting a young girl. For that he had been given a six-month suspended sentence. Later some in Scotland would wonder whether had he been given a stretch in prison instead the Monan children would still be alive.

In Ardrossan, the nearest town to Saltcoats, he was regarded as a queer fish. When he had first arrived, he stayed with a family who were friends, supporting himself by knocking on doors and offering to carry out general labouring jobs or working as a gardener. Few wanted to get to know him. He was weedy, wore dirty, badly fitting clothes, was usually unkempt and unwashed and he had a reputation as a peeping tom but in the town's bars boasted about his exploits as a hardman in England. With a drink in his hand, he could be argumentative and even violent. To some he was a Walter Mitty, a lonely fantasist living in a world in which he would carry out great deeds that would make him famous. Others laughed at his stories while Eastham was too backward to realise he was simply the butt of jokes. Sometimes he did not return to his bed until the early hours, wakening the household in the process. The kindly couple who had offered to take him in eventually decided there was no longer room in their home for him. When he wanted to know what was to become of him, they suggested he could live in their garden shed; Eastham agreed.

One by one, suspects were eliminated until finally only Eastham remained and, when he was taken in for questioning eight days after Robert and Margaret died, he admitted almost immediately that he had attacked them after chasing them across the field where their corpses were discovered but he said he had never meant the youngsters to die. By the time he appeared at the High Court in Ayr in September 1976, Eastham had been examined by psychiatrists who arrived at worrying conclusions. He was charged with striking Robert repeatedly on the head with a stone, kicking him repeatedly about the head and body, stabbing him repeatedly with a knife and striking him about the head and body with a piece of wood. When it came to the deadly assault on Margaret, he was accused of striking her repeatedly on the head with a stone, removing parts of her clothing and attempting to ravish her, compressing her throat, stabbing her repeatedly with a knife, kicking her repeatedly on the head and body and striking her about the head and body with a piece of wood. Although he denied murdering the children, he pleaded guilty to culpable homicide.

The psychiatrists said they could find no motive for what Eastham had done, apart from his trying to have sex with dark-haired Margaret. Dr George Swinney said the killer was suffering from a personality disorder that impaired his ability to relate to other people. It would be in the best interests of the public as a whole and Eastham himself if he was held at Carstairs because there was a danger of his carrying out more attacks. A colleague, Dr William McQuaker, said Eastham suffered from an 'uncommon genetic abnormality which led to his having a character deficiency in relation to his sexual development. He gave the impression of being eccentric and was vulnerable and inadequate.' Eastham was sent to the State Hospital, without limit of time but he was not there for long. The following year he died.

Just as some wondered why Eastham had not been locked up when a court had the chance to do so, the decision to set at large Andrew Johnston from a mental hospital cost the life of innocent Julie Ann Gilfeather who was just three years old. The story of the little girl was every mother and father's nightmare. In 1973 two teenage girls offered to take the tot for a walk, promising her mum Catherine to take good care of her daughter. Not long afterwards they burst into the home of a relative, blurting out the terrible news that a strange man had approached and simply taken the child from them, hurtling stones at them to force them to run off before disappearing. The relative raced to the spot where the man had been seen. There was no sign of man or child but then the body of a baby was spotted lying face down in a shallow pool. Frantic efforts to revive Julie Ann were to no avail.

Within minutes, police were on the scene, searching the area for the stranger and they quickly discovered Johnston, aged thirty-five. He was arrested and charged with seizing Julie Ann and pushing her into the pool where she drowned. What officers learned about the balding, podgy figure in their custody caused shock and downright anger in the community around Bathgate, West Lothian where the baby lived with Catherine and her husband William.

Johnston had spent ten years as a patient at Gogarburn Hospital near Edinburgh. Doctors there had decided in February 1972 that he could be released. He could neither read nor write and had the mental age of a child of six. He was allowed to live with his parents, but fourteen months later tiny fair-haired Julie Ann was dead and her parents, like thousands of others in the community, wanted to know why Johnston was at large and who had taken the decision to release him. Yet again, in a case where the public had a right to be answered, the response was silence. Nobody was willing to step forward and accept responsibility.

The nearest anyone was given to an explanation came when Johnston appeared in the High Court at Edinburgh in July 1973, where he was found unfit to plead to an accusation of culpable homicide and sent to Carstairs without limit of time. During the hearing a psychiatrist from Gogarburn Hospital said their monitoring of Johnston, an imbecile, showed no indication that he might be violent and he was thought to be harmless:

> If a person is violent in hospital, you can predict violence from violence. But there is always a limit to what you can predict. One would like to follow up every patient who is discharged but at that time this was impossible. Once a patient is discharged from hospital, technically the responsibility falls on the social work department. But I am not trying to shift any blame, if blame there is.

Julie's heartbroken parents insisted there should be an inquiry into the procedure for the release of mental patients. A friend of the family summed up the feelings of most when she said:

> There is something wrong with a system that frees somebody as dangerous as Johnston. People have a right to know when these individuals are released. We still don't know who was responsible for letting him out. If that had not happened Julie Ann would still be alive.

PLAYING TRUANT

Sadly this was not the first time that a patient released from a mental hospital had killed. Nor would it be the last. Examples of what the taxpaying public see as blunders abound, some more tragic than others, but what is invariably missing from these incidents is an explanation from the individual responsible for making the decision to let a patient go. The question has to be asked whether those running mental hospitals, including Carstairs, ever learn from their mistakes.

What happened in the case of James Rodgers, nine years before that involving Johnston, sent out a message that was clearly not heeded. At the beginning of 1964, while carrying out a series of housebreakings, Rodgers came across a seven-year-old boy who we shall call Liam. He said he would push the youngster out of a window and the boy was so petrified that in order to escape his tormentor he jumped out despite being fifteen feet up and was badly injured in the fall. When Rogers, aged twenty-one, appeared in court at Linlithgow, West Lothian, to admit a number of offences of housebreaking and one of assaulting the little boy, he was told that if he agreed to become a voluntary patient at a mental hospital, sentence on him would be deferred. Had the court committed him to hospital, it would have meant his being kept under much stricter control and his movements drastically limited.

He was therefore able to register at the Royal Edinburgh hospital as a voluntary patient. A report said doctors felt he was responding well to their treatment and showing no signs of aggression. The result of that was that just two months after his court hearing a doctor signed a pass allowing him to spend a Saturday afternoon on his own in Edinburgh. It was a decision that would have a terrible ending. That same afternoon Rodgers strangled another boy of seven, likeable James Anderson, after taking him to a corner shop to buy sweets. He was quickly arrested and, questioned by police about the senseless crime, he admitted, 'He was screaming and shouting and I put the rope round his neck to frighten him. I thought he was asleep and I tried to wake him.'

By the time Rodgers appeared at the city's High Court, the families of both boys were demanding to know why he had been allowed out. Little James' father, also James, told reporters, 'It is a disgrace. He should have been under much stricter supervision. The authorities knew he had already attacked another little boy.'

The judge, Lord Johnstone, told Rodgers he was ordering him to be detained in Carstairs without limit of time. 'You have pleaded guilty to a terrible crime,' he said, adding:

> As a result of your actions a young, innocent boy has been killed. His family has suffered grievously and you have brought tragedy on yourself. I am satisfied it is in the interests of the public and in your own interest that you are detained as a person having dangerous, violent and criminal propensities.

Clearly the judge had the same thoughts as the families of James and the others killed in similar circumstances when he added, 'The security regulations which you will be subject to will be at least as good as those in prison.' Or at least they ought to be. The fact is, though, that we simply don't know how secure Carstairs is. A request to the NHS for a breakdown of the various categories of occupation of those employed at the State Hospital produced only vague generalisations – no specific numbers, for instance, of security staff. And yet Carstairs exists because successive governments have ordained that the community must be kept safe from dangerous criminal lunatics. Refusing to be open about security is yet one more reason why some members of the public feel that Carstairs cannot be trusted. The public has no guarantee that events in 1976 that follow in chapters 19 to 25 cannot be repeated.

17

TILL DEATH US DO PART

In her virginal white outfit the bride looked radiant, smiling happily beneath her veil as she and the man she idolised pledged they would have, hold, love and cherish one another whether rich or poor, in sickness and in health, until death parted them. Moments later Francis Joseph Smith slipped a golden ring on to the finger of the woman he had promised to take care of forever and kissed his bride, Mary Kennedy. It was Saturday, 27 March 1976. Six days later, on 2 April, still on her honeymoon, Mary was dead, killed by her husband. This sad, sordid tragedy would enter legal records not because of the short duration of the marriage but because Frank Smith would effectively be tried twice for the murder of his bride.

Yet on 27 March, the world seemed a wonderful place to pretty Mary, who worked in a bakery alongside her mother Annie. She and Frank had applied for a house of their own and had been offered their own door. On the Friday following her wedding, Mary had gone to work early. She wanted to show her workmates her wedding ring and couldn't wait to get back to her new home to help her husband decorate. At times she must have wondered if it was all too good to be true but were the omens lined up against twenty-nine-year-old Mary?

The house in Uddingston, Lanarkshire, had only become available because the previous occupant had died. It stood at 13 Crofthead Street – a number widely believed to be unlucky because thirteen men had attended the last supper, the thirteenth to take his place being Judas Iscariot. What's more, Mary had wed during the thirteenth week of the year. Had these odd circumstances combined to throw an air of ill luck over the marriage? One thing was sure. After she finished her shift that day, Mary's mother and her workmates never again saw her alive.

After Mary died, her thirty-three-year-old husband, a building worker, was accused of killing her. She had been brutally battered to death and it was alleged he had struck her repeatedly on the head and face with a hammer. When he appeared in court a few weeks later, a psychiatrist said the circumstances of the murder, the way she had been beaten and then the worry of what had happened and the consequences of it had driven Smith out of his mind. The doctor declared him to be insane and unfit to plead with the result that he was sent to Carstairs.

The nightmare might have ended there had it not been decided that the widower had responded so remarkably to treatment that by mid January the following year it was decided he was well enough to leave the State Hospital. Not all experts agreed with this diagnosis, especially those helping his defence team. Police and the Crown had asked to be kept informed of his progress. He might not have been well enough to be tried first time around but if he was better and well enough to leave hospital then he was well enough to stand trial. And so as he was leaving Carstairs waiting police re-arrested him and once again charged him with killing his young wife. He was taken off to the less palatial surroundings of Barlinnie prison.

When he faced a jury at the High Court in Glasgow in February 1977, almost a year after the day he had exchanged vows with Mary, the charge against Smith had been reduced to one of culpable homicide. He denied killing his wife, lodging a special defence that he was insane at the time of her death. A pathologist who carried out a post-mortem examination on the body of the dead woman said she had been the victim of a 'brutal and frenzied' attack. He described nineteen separate wounds on her head and face and said her skull and jaw had been broken.

It was the evidence of Mary's sixty-year-old mother, however, that left some in the public gallery reaching for their handkerchiefs to dry their eyes. Annie Kennedy told how she and Mary were especially close because working together at the bakery meant they were with one another every day. She said the wedding was the outcome of a courtship lasting seven months. 'Everything seemed fine between them, especially after they got the keys to their new home,' she said. 'On the day she died Mary went to work early to show everybody her wedding ring. She said she was going to the house to help Frank scrape wallpaper. I never saw her alive again.' Her words were heart-breaking. She was asked if she believed Smith had any psychiatric problems. 'No, but he did silly things like carrying bags of shopping around with him,' she said. Before she left the witness box Annie had a question for her son-in-law. 'What did you do that for, Frank?' she asked. It was said in a near whisper and while Smith made as though he did not hear it most others did. All the same the question went unanswered.

A woman neighbour of the newly-weds told how she had heard a knock at her door and when she opened it saw Smith looking through the keyhole into the house opposite. 'He was agitated and garbled and said he and his wife had moved in that day, but he had lost his keys,' she said. 'He had gone out for a few pints and said his wife had promised to be at home by the time he got back.' The neighbour loaned Smith a hammer that he used to break a back window so he could get inside and very soon after she heard him screaming, 'She's dead, she's dead.' When she looked in she saw a woman lying face down in a pool of blood and Smith moaning and trying to lift her, cradling her lifeless body in his arms and crying, 'Mary, Mary.' Police who went to number 13 said at first Smith was able to tell them his name but an officer said that once they arrived at a police station he clasped his fists, shouted, 'Bang, bang' and wouldn't speak.

A consultant psychiatrist said that on the night of the killing Smith, who had swallowed a dangerous cocktail of tranquilisers and beer, was sane. Yet when he was examined six days later, the stress of his wife's death and of his being accused of her murder had sent him into such a deep depression that it drove him temporarily insane. He was recovered from the illness, though. And so the bridegroom who had escaped prison first time around was found guilty by the jury of culpable homicide and jailed for ten years, although this was later reduced on appeal to eight.

At present, the law decrees that discovery of new evidence means that, under what is termed 'double jeopardy', an accused person can be retried for the same crime. In Smith's case his remarkable recovery from insanity left him vulnerable, but even had he spent several years in Carstairs, once doctors there reckoned he was better he would still have been liable to face a court over the original allegation. It was an unusual, although not unique, situation. In fact, it mirrored a remarkable case half a century earlier.

Alexander Bickerstaff was a pedlar in his early thirties who travelled about Scotland and the north of England. He was well known to the police and used aliases including 'Alexander Hannah' but among other travellers was known as 'Noble Dan'. There was nothing very noble, however, about the brutal murder in November 1924 at Stirling of four-year-old Nessie Reid. The child's death had all the hallmarks of being the work of a maniac. Bickerstaff, who had a number of previous convictions, including one for indecently assaulting a child, and who had spent time in four different asylums, became the chief suspect. He was arrested and charged with Nessie's murder and with indecently assaulting another little girl, aged seven.

At his trial in March 1925, four psychiatrists said Bickerstaff was so insane and unfit to plead that he could not even give proper instructions to his defence counsel. Two other doctors, however, argued he was sane. The judge said he sympathised with Bickerstaff, and accepted he might well be innocent, but still sent him to the criminal lunatic department at Perth prison on grounds of insanity even though it meant he might be there for years and never have the chance to prove he was not Nessie's killer. 'I hope some of the ladies and gentlemen here will look into my case. I'm as sane as any man here,' shouted an angry Bickerstaff as he was led off to the lunatic unit. There were immediate calls for a retrial amidst a feeling he had escaped hanging and should be tried again, while his supporters argued he had not been given a fair chance to prove his innocence and called on the government to step in.

Unfortunately for them, and for Bickerstaff, he did not help his cause by escaping in August 1925. He thumbed a lift from a passing lorry but was spotted by a policeman who called in a police car which chased after the lorry and recaptured him at Auchterarder. He was sent back to the lunatic unit but in October he was freed on the grounds that he was sane. However, that meant he could now be re-arrested and charged again with murder. Police were waiting outside Perth jail as he left. He was charged and taken to Barlinnie and kept there. By December he had still not been tried but claims by his lawyer that he should be released because he had been kept in custody for more than a hundred days, were ignored. He was eventually tried in January 1926, found guilty of indecent assault and jailed for four years. The debate over whether he was sane or mad would rage on for many years, some arguing he had wrongly escaped the hangman, others that it was his reputation as a madman that had led to his being jailed.

On the other hand, the case of James Henderson left no room for doubt. It was not just the fact that his victim was Dawn, his own wife, that made him such a hated figure; what marked him down as a target in prison for other inmates was that she suffered from multiple sclerosis. Even worse was that he latched on to this helpless young woman, whose illness had forced her to give up nursing, after kindly workmates raised money to send her on a pilgrimage to Lourdes in the hope she there might find relief from her suffering. Henderson's is a story of violence intertwined with sick deception.

A native of Dundee and married with a child of his own, he had killed his father James, aged fifty-two, in the city in 1973, stabbing him in the neck. However, psychiatrists said he was so mentally ill that he was unfit to plead at his trial and was sent to Carstairs. Only eight months later, doctors announced he had recovered and was now sane. If he believed he might walk to freedom, however, his hopes were dashed.

Just as Frank Smith would discover in the not too distant future, police were waiting to arrest him as he was discharged and he faced a court for the second time, on this occasion charged with murdering his father. He was subsequently jailed for four years after the charge was reduced to one of culpable homicide on grounds that his responsibility was diminished. He served just over two years before being freed on parole by which time his marriage had disintegrated. He found work as a butcher and was glancing through a magazine when he spotted a photograph of a pretty girl being hugged by comedian Ken Dodd. Reading the caption he discovered she was named Dawn Gillanders from Huyton near Liverpool and suffered from multiple sclerosis. Forced by the illness to give up nursing, Dawn prayed for help from the healing airs of Lourdes. After reading her moving story, Henderson wrote offering sympathy. Dawn replied and the pair became first pen friends and, after he travelled to meet her, decided to marry.

Dawn learned of her fiancé's grim past, but asked Henderson's mother not to tell her own parents. She feared that if they knew she was planning to wed a killer they would somehow contrive to stop the marriage. And she would have been right. Tragically, her determination to hide his secret would cost Dawn her life. Just three months after they wed Henderson launched a ferocious attack on the bride who, according to everyone who knew her, didn't have an enemy in the world. A pathologist who examined her body said he counted 128 wounds made with a hypodermic needle. When he was charged with murder, Henderson claimed Dawn had begged for an end to her suffering and the couple agreed on a suicide pact. They swallowed what they believed would be a lethal mixture of drink and drugs and he also cut his wrists and throat. However, both survived. He said that since Dawn would have been distressed at his still being alive he spared her unhappiness by stabbing her.

In 1977, Henderson, aged twenty-nine, still on parole for slaying his father, was jailed for life for the manslaughter of his wife after the prosecution accepted his plea of not guilty to murder because his responsibility was diminished. Yet again, Carstairs had released a man who went on to take an innocent life, although Dawn's family and her many friends wondered why he had not been kept in prison for longer. Yet again a family had been ripped apart.

That was the situation, too, in another tragic case in 1977 when two children, then aged eleven and eight, saw their world destroyed in a moment literally of madness which left their beloved mother dead and their father in a lunatic asylum. James Alexander Low was a well-respected civil servant, a field officer with the then department of agriculture. He seemed the epitome of a happily married man, adoring his children and his gentle, pretty, blonde-haired wife Moira, who was nine years his junior. However, dark thoughts were raging in the deep and private recesses of his mind, developing into an increasingly severe psychotic depression that gave birth to strange and terrible fantasies.

One weekend, he had accompanied Moira to the home of her parents to play bridge, but became convinced the drink these kindly people offered was laced with poison. The next night, certain she was determined to be rid of him to be with another man, he told himself Moira had unscrewed the top of their hot water bottle in order to let out a deadly gas meant to drug and kill him. There was no one else, but soon imagination was to turn into terrible reality. One morning he took the children to school then went back to discuss a planned holiday with his wife. He would later say she had refused to go with him and so, picking up a fireside poker, he repeatedly smashed her over the head and then tried to strangle her before dumping her into the bath and drowning her. Leaving her body he went to his lawyer and confessed, 'I have killed my wife.'

At the High Court in Aberdeen, a jury decided that, although forty-three-year-old Low had killed his wife, he was not guilty of murder because he was insane at the time and he was sent to the State Hospital, a condition being that should he make a recovery he would, like Bickerstaff, Smith and Henderson be arrested and tried again. But if he was ever discharged, would the public be confident doctors at Carstairs had got it right?

Deep concerns had been felt over a case in 1971 in which a man was accused of twice attacking his wife after being released from the hospital where a court had sent him the previous year without limit of time following his conviction for theft and assaulting police. Doctors then said he 'required care and custody for the protection of the public and himself'. Only five months later, they decided that although he was of 'dull intelligence' he could not be classed as mentally defective and was not mentally ill and so he was freed. Ten days later, he forced his way into his wife's Glasgow home and threatened to throw her out of a window while two weeks further on he hit her over the head with a bottle. The man, who cannot be named for legal reasons, was jailed for six months. Fortunately his wife escaped the terror of going through the window.

Sadly, Ellen McGregor, aged twenty-four, was not so lucky. Her naked body was found by neighbours lying beneath the third floor window of her home in Dennistoun, Glasgow, in 1968. Her lover John Murray Swan, aged twenty-nine, denied killing Ellen by pushing her out of the window, assaulting her by throwing a cleaver at her and striking her. Was she pushed or, as Swan claimed, had she committed suicide by jumping? What was unusual about the case were the experiments carried out by police following her death to discover the most likely explanation.

Detective Chief Inspector Robert Brown said officers made a dummy resembling the height and weight of the dead woman from rubber and rags with sections of hose piping inserted to roughly replicate human bones. The dummy was dropped in a series of positions, sometimes face-up, sometimes head first until it landed in a similar position to that in which Ellen was found. The officer said that when tests were concluded he took the view she had not jumped.

Swan's account was that he and Ellen had argued in a cinema earlier that night: 'I thought she was making up to another man. When we went home I heard a shout and saw her jumping out of the window. I just saw her legs disappearing.' A psychiatrist told the High Court in Glasgow, 'Swan is a danger to the public. He has no sense of shame, remorse or understanding of his shortcomings.' Swan was convicted of culpable homicide and ordered to be detained in Carstairs without limit of time.

18

VOICES IN MY HEAD

What makes a man want to murder his mother or father? Tragically cases of matricide – the killing of a mother – tend to be among the most brutal and bloody. The instruction to kill may come from a strange voice purporting to be the Devil. Perhaps a son imagines he is acting on the orders of Christ. Sometimes the motive is so trifling, it is hard to believe it leads to the murder of a dearly loved one.

Norah Robinson had been so proud of her son Nicholas. He studied prodigiously and was awarded a prized place at Cambridge University where the brilliance of his work won him awards. When his retired headmistress mother gave him a telling off for leaving open the door of her home in Bathgate, West Lothian, he somehow believed her to be a witch and in 1983 launched an attack so terrible and bloody that her body was unrecognisable. Her forty-three-year-old son had been schizophrenic for more than twenty years, a condition which can leave victims suffering from weird fantasies and delusions. Norah had worried about her boy, but nothing could have prepared her for his reaction to her mild reprimand.

Picking up a knife from her kitchen, he went towards the elderly woman who, fearing the worst, begged, 'No, Nicholas, don't.' Her pleading was in vain and he began stabbing her. The knife broke, but that did not end her agony. He simply fetched another and continued his butchery. By the time the stabbing stopped, five blood-stained knives littered the room. Yet there was more. Hearing her gurgling her own blood, he broke off a call to the police and smashed her head with an Indian club and a fruit dish. Telephone operators were able to trace the source of the emergency call and arrived at sixty-one-year-old Norah's home to be told by her killer, 'Thank you for being so quick. I have just murdered my mother.' He was charged with murder but after psychiatrists examined the scale of his schizophrenia, his plea of guilty to culpable homicide was accepted and he was sent to Carstairs.

An equally brilliant university career was not enough to guarantee Alex O'Hara a job and when his mother Freda chided him for being out of work he killed her. The weapon he used was a knife he had borrowed from a neighbour to cut wood. Minutes later, he knocked at the neighbour's door in Mastrick, Aberdeen, and politely informed him he had just killed his mother. 'Would you call the police please?' he asked. Then the twenty-nine-year-old, schizophrenic, unemployed industrial chemist O'Hara went back next door to sit with his dead mother. Fortunately for his dad Anthony, aged sixty-five, he had been out at his part-time work. His son told a psychiatrist he had thought of killing him too, knowing how heartbroken he would be at the prospect of spending the rest of his life without fifty-five-year-old Freda and wanting to spare him that ordeal. He had also told the doctor he saw people on the streets as 'not real, just merely puppets' and that he killed his mum because she had nagged him about not having a career.

Yet loving Anthony bore his only child no grudges, supporting him throughout the nightmare that followed Freda's death and sitting in the High Court in Aberdeen in November 1976 to hear a jury acquit Alex of murder on the grounds of insanity. 'I bear my son no bitterness,' he said after a judge sent the young killer to the State Hospital. 'This wasn't the boy we raised. I'm heartbroken for him because this was so out of character.'

A similar sentiment was expressed by friends of David McNeil. In June 2010 he went up to a man delivering groceries near the family home at Rothesay, Bute, and told him, 'I killed my mother, but it's not me, it's the voices in my head that made me do it.' A few moments after that he called at the flat of a neighbour and said, 'I've killed my mother, but the Egyptians made me do it.' The full horror of what had taken place in the home he shared with seventy-three-year-old Mary-Rose McNeil that day was only discovered when police investigated. After her son killed her with a metal pole and a knife, he tried to hack out her brains.

What caused the tragedy? Earlier on that fatal day McNeil had not taken the medication doctors prescribed to curb the effects of his schizophrenia. He had made an emergency call asking police to come to the house but Mary-Rose insisted there was nothing to worry about. It was a mistake that cost her life. When he was arrested, her son told police, 'I heard voices in my head telling me they were all gods and that there was no God in heaven. They said my mother hadn't lived a good life and it was time for her to go. I'm still hearing those voices.' McNeil was put in the care of doctors at Carstairs.

Months after being released from a mental hospital where he received treatment for schizophrenia, Paul Black called to see his mum Ruth at his parents' home in St Andrews, Fife. He was twenty-four and a troubled young man who had been booted out of the Royal Air Force for hitting an officer and who occasionally broke into the family home to steal food. Now he believed himself to be a member of the Swedish royal family. The fatal day he visited his mother would leave many questioning whether he ought to have been allowed to leave the psychiatric hospital. After an argument, he began a horrific attack on forty-eight-year-old Ruth, first trying to strangle her, then break her neck and finally stabbing her eighteen times with a meat knife. He denied a charge of murder, claiming he only decided to kill his mother after she first tried to strangle him and he was terrified he was about to die. But he was convicted of killing her while the balance of his mind was disturbed and, after a doctor said he could be a 'menace to society', he was sent to the State Hospital.

Black had originally been treated in a mental hospital because his mother had pleaded with doctors to help him. Helen Gunn-Russell tried for three years to get help for her schizophrenic son Jason, who had developed an obsession with religion. Her efforts failed and the result could have been mortal because one night Jason, nineteen, smashed a hammer over the head of a fourteen-year-old friend.

Fortunately the victim survived but months afterwards he was still unable to walk because of his injuries. Gunn-Russell told a psychiatrist, 'I attacked him because he did not respect God.' The doctor told a court in Edinburgh in 1998, 'He thought if he killed him his problems would be solved.' Jason was found not guilty of attempted murder because of insanity and he was ordered to be detained without limit of time at Carstairs. Afterwards a family friend said, 'Helen did everything a mother could to get her boy proper treatment in hospital but seemed to permanently come up against a brick wall.'

The voices that spoke to Charles Burns were sometimes those of saints, sometimes of sinners; he was never sure which. Regardless, they convinced him to kill his seventy-nine-year-old mother Agnes. Burns had been treated in mental hospitals for practically the whole of his thirty-six years of life. He had a personality disorder and suffered from alcoholic hallucinations, a combination that made a cure near impossible. In 1967 he carried out the orders of the mysterious voices, hitting helpless Agnes with a bottle at the home he shared with her in Dennistoun, Glasgow, then strangling her. After her body was found, police made another dramatic discovery. Around the dead woman's waist was a hidden money belt and in it was almost £100. Burns, who had denied murdering his mother, was found not guilty because of insanity and sent to the State Hospital.

An ambulance driver taking a patient to her home in a remote Highland glen after a routine hospital check-up stumbled across a horror that would become a major emergency. Passing a former schoolhouse into which shepherd's widow Catherine Urquhart had recently moved with her son Kenneth, the driver spotted smoke coming from the building. He called in firemen who discovered the blood-stained figure of seventy-eight-year-old Catherine lying moaning at her back door. She had terrible head injuries and was rushed off to hospital. But where was her son? Firemen searched the cottage but there was no sign of him. Then searchers saw the half naked figure of a man in a nearby stream. Blood ran from a cut on his throat and another on a wrist. He was befuddled and helpless, and had to be led to safety, but was recognised as Kenneth, better known as Callum. Over the years a handful of those who knew him would cruelly shout after him, 'Limpalong', because he had been born with a dislocated hip that caused him to drag one of his legs. It was an ailment that depressed and sometimes angered him.

The next day, his mother died in hospital. She had been battered about the head with an axe. Her son was charged with her murder and when he was interviewed by a psychiatrist told the doctor, 'I am too wicked to live.' When Urquhart appeared at the High Court in Aberdeen in 1965, the psychiatrist said the killer was suffering from melancholia. 'He is of unsound mind and unfit to plead,' he said, adding that it would be difficult to know whether as time passed Urquhart would develop into a dangerous individual. As a result the judge, Lord Milligan, turned down a request for him to be held at Inverness's Craig Dunain. 'It is a terrible responsibility for an ordinary mental hospital to take charge of a man like this,' said the judge, ordering Urquhart to be sent to Carstairs where he died in 2006, aged eighty-two.

Eileen Howie was a woman of many talents. After her husband died in a car accident, she worked tirelessly to carry on the farm where four generations of his family had lived, to raise their son Ewen and to run dancing classes in Aberdeenshire. Despite her own many achievements, it was forty-six-year-old Ewen who was her life and soul, and mother and son seemed to get on so well together, each the best friend of the other. He encouraged her, despite being seventy-three years old, to continue her classes, passing on to others the skills she had learned when she had been a student at the Royal Academy of Dance in London and later winning a hatful of awards. Then, one night in February 2001, something went wrong.

Eileen knew her son hadn't been himself. He was nervy and unable to sleep and she persuaded him to see the family doctor who gave him a course of sedatives. In a few hours that would destroy many lives, Ewen's character underwent a terrible change. A psychiatrist would later reveal, 'He realised that everything he held dear was evil. He felt his mother had changed from his best friend to being against him.' That remarkable and awful transformation even included his developing a dread of red, his favourite colour. It reached a stage where he went through the farmhouse trying to destroy everything red. His mum had gone off to hold one of her classes and while she was away her son convinced himself she was part of a plot to kill him – that she would steal the prescribed sedatives and poison him with them.

That night when she returned home to her loving son near Cults he battered her senseless with a chair. Then, using paper, towels and a solid fuel cooker, he set the farmhouse ablaze. Firemen rescued him from the fierce flames but found Eileen, loved by everyone who knew her, dead. The psychiatrist to whom Ewen had told of his fears diagnosed him as suffering from an 'alienation of reason' and as insane when he killed his mother. Ewen was sent to Carstairs but despite their heartbreak and loss, other family members rallied from the tragedy to make it plain he still had their love and support.

Eileen died because her son thought she meant him harm. Graeme Morris slew his mother and viciously attacked his dad because he believed they had hurt him when he was a child. 'I didn't have any intention of murdering either of my parents or killing them or for them to die,' he told detectives who investigated the attack on Fred Morris, aged sixty-four, and his wife Anne, sixty-three, in 2012. Their son was thirty-eight and a former student at Glasgow School of Art who developed an obsession with the idea that he was a genius whose talent would have been even greater but for ill treatment by the couple when he was a youngster.

His brooding over the past led to bizarre behaviour and worried a girlfriend who persuaded him to seek help. Unfortunately he was told he would have to join on the end of a waiting list for a consultation with a psychiatrist. Before the appointment, however, he turned up at his parents' home in Troon, Ayrshire, and, without warning, began a terrifying attack on them. When he grabbed his mother by her hair and started slapping her, she suffered a fatal heart attack. As she was dying, he ripped the clothes from his father, and then bludgeoned the quivering, naked man before fleeing. He was arrested at Euston Station in London. Doctors diagnosed him as being a paranoid schizophrenic and said that unless he was kept in strict security he would be a danger to the public. He was at first charged with murdering his mother but later he admitted her culpable homicide and assault on his father to the danger of his life. He was sent to the State Hospital and told he could only be released with the approval of the government.

Occasionally, psychiatric hospitals in Scotland would be asked to accommodate patients from Northern Ireland, but the case of John Robertson Brackenbridge would prove a headache for doctors on both sides of the Irish Sea. The Glaswegian had a history of severe mental illness. He had been a patient in a series of mental hospitals from the age of twenty-four and was diagnosed an acute schizophrenic, who suffered from delusions, hallucinations and the belief he was a victim of persecution. Tests revealed he was unable to distinguish between fantasy and reality. Experts did their best for him but faced the age-old problem of a patient who did not follow their advice. When he was discharged from hospital, he would be given a course of medicine, which, he was promised, would calm him if he followed it. Brackenbridge didn't take the course of medicine, with the result that no sooner had he left one hospital, his condition deteriorated and he was taken into another.

During a fortnight's stay in hospital in Glasgow in 1974 doctors gave him electric shock treatment together with tranquiliser tablets and injections. The blitz seemed to be effective and Brackenbridge was allowed to leave. He went to Belfast in search of work but then his mind began playing tricks on him, with tragic consequences for one of his neighbours in Adelaide Park. Mehmet Ali Misirlizade was a twenty-seven-year-old Turkish Cypriot civil engineer, working for a Belfast company who exchanged an occasional word with Brackenbridge, although the two men were relative strangers. The Scot began hearing voices, telling him he was Jesus Christ or at least one of his disciples while his neighbour was the Devil in disguise and it was his duty to kill him.

One day he plunged a ten-inch knife into the heart of the Cypriot, killing him instantly. When he was arrested and questioned, police said Brackenbridge seemed unaware of what had happened. He was detached and remote from the reality of the tragedy. Psychiatrists said he should be kept in conditions of high security and a Belfast court ordered him to be detained in Carstairs. In Brackenbridge's case, doctors could hardly be blamed because a man refused to do as he had been told. It emphasised how difficult their job could at times be. In fact, psychiatrists have a huge responsibility when deciding just how ill a patient might be or if, indeed, he or she is sick at all or just feigning a condition in order to avoid prison or, until capital punishment was abolished in the UK in 1965, hanging.

Records showed that as far back as the 1800s doctors were being called in to make what were literally life or death decisions. In April 1887 the *Aberdeen Weekly Journal* reported on such a case. Donald Mackenzie was charged with murdering his mother Jessie at their home in Kilmallie near Fort William by smashing her over the head with a pair of fireside tongs. He faced the noose until doctors said he was suffering a severe mental derangement and was insane, citing several attempts by him to commit suicide as evidence to back up their diagnosis. Fortunately for Mackenzie the doctors were able to persuade the judge they knew what they were talking about and he was sent to an asylum.

Just how difficult it can be to judge how to treat mental illness was illustrated in a tragic case in 1999 in which doctors decided to change the medication of former Carstairs inmate John Leverage and give him a test dose of a different drug. At the time Leverage, aged forty from Glasgow, was in another psychiatric hospital where he had complained about hearing voices. He told a staff nurse, 'Men in hoods are going to come into my room and get me. The IRA are going to do things to me.' His doctors hoped an injection from another anti-psychotic drug would help calm him down. Sadly a few hours later he wandered into the bedroom of fellow patient John Dillon carrying a knife he had picked up from the hospital kitchen and stabbed the seventy-one-year-old fourteen times in the chest. Blood pouring from deep wounds, John staggered about seeking help, staff at first thinking he was drunk. Despite frantic efforts to save him, he died soon after. Psychiatrists said the killer was a paranoid schizophrenic who had been insane at the time of the tragedy and was unfit to stand trial and he was ordered to be detained in Carstairs without limit of time.

19

A MEETING OF DEVILS

Bible-punching Iain Simpson had been a patient at Carstairs since August 1962 after murdering George Green and Hans Gimmi (see chapter 4). He soon settled into the hospital routine, being a willing, even likeable, patient with evidently no thoughts of committing further violence. Reports by staff labelled him a conscientious worker who had developed such an interest in music that he taught himself not just to play a variety of musical instruments but to make them too. Six years later, on 23 January 1968, he was joined by a slim, frail, pale-faced, blue-eyed, young man with long, fair hair whose name was Robert Francis Mone, aged twenty. Born in Dundee in June 1948, his sallow complexion hid a lively, intelligent mind. The two had little or nothing in common and would come into only sporadic contact. But future events would leave them inextricably linked.

Mone made friends easily, despite being a lonely young man whose family background hid tragedy and a hint of mental illness. His aunt Doreen Gallagher had spent a series of short periods as an in-patient at Rampton in Nottinghamshire. That troubled history meant that when her daughter Maureen, aged just six, disappeared from her home in Birkenhead, Cheshire, in 1964, accusing fingers began pointing in her direction. A huge search followed, but seven weeks later, the cruelty of groundless suspicion deepened when the little girl's body was discovered hidden under sheeting on waste ground. Her throat had been cut. A local waiter, Alfred Bailey, then aged forty-one, was charged with murdering the little girl. At his trial he accused Doreen of killing her own daughter. It was a claim the jury rejected because Bailey was found guilty and sentenced to life imprisonment.

At home, Mone remembered his father Christopher, known better as 'Sonny' Mone, occasionally mentioning the terrible murder of his son's cousin. It was a memory that would never go away. He had emerged from a troubled childhood as an unhappy teenager who, although he had girlfriends, found it impossible to maintain lasting relationships with them. On enrolling at St John's Roman Catholic Secondary School in Dundee, he was assessed as virtually unteachable and only one step away from being classified as educationally sub-normal – gradings that were all the more surprising in the light of his later academic achievements. There were even darker clouds on the horizon. For the purposes of this book, and in the interests of accuracy, the accounts of what led up to his incarceration at Carstairs and the even more sensational and deadly subsequent events there are reproduced exactly as Mone wrote them in a series of letters sent by him to the author. It should be stressed that at no time has Mone ever asked for, or been offered, remuneration. In order to understand his state of mind it is essential to delve into sequences of incidents that led to two murderous occurrences.

He was a pupil at St John's School for three years, leaving at the age of fifteen. Some teachers were members of a religious order and he retains bitter memories of one in particular:

> He was a serial abuser of adolescent boys in his charge, frequently assaulting them in full view of their classmates; of those for whom he developed a particular penchant, more extensive and serious abuse occurred within his office at the close of school day. Even as boys we were aware of the immense power and authority of the Church and those who served it; no one to the best of my recollection ever resisted the demands made upon them. Few boys doubted that the school authorities were unaware of his activities so notorious was his reputation among the pupil population.

Mone lived in London for a time but, following a spell in approved school, by the age of eighteen he was unhappy and felt that he was failing to fulfil his potential. So he turned to the Army for a new start and enlisted in the Gordon Highlanders:

> I joined the armed forces fundamentally to escape a deeply dysfunctional home life and in an attempt to find focus and commitment within my own life. While serving in Germany I became embroiled in a court-martial proceeding against two superiors and was encouraged to sign statements against the men by my company commander. The effect of the statements would almost certainly be to terminate the careers of both men. Prior to joining the regiment I had been briefly attached to the Provost Staff, and entertained hopes of a career in this branch of the service. To this end I never questioned the propriety of my actions of loyalty to my superior's actions. Young, naive and inexperienced, believing that in 'doing the right thing' I would be somehow magically protected, I was sleepwalking into a hornets' nest. Now viewed with extreme suspicion by my colleagues, other areas of my life attracted growing hostility such as my apparent preference to socialise with German civilians and soldiers attached to English regiments within the Minden area; to my colleagues I seemed to be ticking all the wrong boxes. My decision to continue co-operating with the army authorities and my refusal to explain my actions to others did much to inflame the situation and cost me the support of my few remaining friends.
>
> Gradually hostility turned to threats; on one occasion I was pointedly warned that 'an army camp can be a dangerous place', on another an attempt was made to lure me to a disused building in order to persuade me to withdraw or otherwise sabotage my evidence against the men. Realising that my situation was increasingly vulnerable the army withdrew me from normal duties and assigned me an administrative task within the company office, there to await my furlough to the UK. I was now informed that upon my return to Germany I would be prepped by SIB (Special Investigation Branch) officers in anticipation of the court-martial and upon completion of the trial I would be flown back to the UK and posted to Yorkshire to undergo additional training. I would not be travelling with the regiment to my next scheduled posting in Libya.

In the sudden change of orders I saw, rightly or wrongly, the beginnings of betrayal by the army. My usefulness was almost at an end and when it was I would be discarded. It was deeply hurtful to realise that those who had engineered my predicament were now in the process of abandoning me so casually, with no words or feelings of responsibility towards me. Damaged, disillusioned, subject to increasing bouts of a depressive illness (self-medicating the condition with large quantities of alcohol, itself a depressant) and progressively more paranoid about my personal safety I applied to Minden police HQ for permission to own and carry a personal firearm – generally a formality for members of the armed forces. I withdrew my application on finding that army rules required personal firearms to be kept within the camp's arsenal. Isolated and friendless, increasingly sensitive to personal threat and sensing betrayal and abandonment by those I had trusted and respected, I left Germany feeling more alone and desolate than I had ever felt in my entire life. Feeling besieged by forces beyond my control, the future bleak and foreboding, I began to accept that this affair would end in a violent fashion.

Back in Britain, Mone did not return to the army. He was posted Absent Without Leave (AWOL) and initially headed to London where in a store off Praed Street he bought a single barrel twelve-gauge Spanish-made shotgun. Initially he thought about sawing off part of the barrel and returning to Germany with it. Instead he took it with him and travelled to Dundee. It was late October 1967. Mone began drinking heavily, falling into a routine of drinking vodka for his breakfast, heading into the city centre, where he mooched around cafés until bars opened at lunch time, allowing him to spend a couple of hours wandering from one drinking hole to another until they closed in the early afternoon. He spent the afternoons in cinemas, then drank the evenings away until publicans rang the bells for time. As the days went by, he decided to end what seemed a futile existence and visited a number of doctors in the city, complaining of feeling depressed and collecting a number of prescriptions, which he used to accumulate a hoard of mainly pain-relief tablets. Over the years, he had visited the family's doctor saying he felt depressed, but would later tell friends that he had been told that he was merely feeling low, was suffering from growing pains or they said, 'don't worry, it'll go away'. As far as the medical profession were concerned, he was sane, had committed no crime and could not be detained under mental health legislation.

> Tormented by thoughts alternatively homicidal and suicidal, almost anything would have tipped the balance at that point. I had what I believed was a fatal dose of drugs and carrying it I booked into Mathers Hotel [Now the Malmaison in Whitehall Crescent, Dundee] and attempted to end my life. Inexperienced in the use of drugs I bungled the attempt, succeeding only in making myself violently ill. In Mathers I avoided other guests and when not drinking in city centre bars drank alone in my room. Germany and the proceedings to which I was returning dominated my thoughts; I raged at the perceived injustice of my situation and longed for a return of the optimism and energy and enthusiasm I had felt on entering the armed forces. It gnawed at me like a missing limb so desperate was I to recapture that zest for a career and a life with the forces. As the depression deepened, obviously aggravated by increasing quantities of alcohol, disillusionment turned to bitterness and a burning rage against the army. That rage needed only a focal point to explode, and tragically it found it just days later.

On 1 November, Mone found himself standing outside the White Horse Inn opposite St John's School, mulling over the way he had been abused there and let down by army officers he had respected. It was a cold, wet day and he decided it was time to get a taxi back to Mathers Hotel, return to the army and face the music. He looked around for a taxi gradually becoming more soaked, each raindrop falling like a blow that hurt his pride and increased his anger. He was a wounded animal ready to pounce on his nearest tormentors. Inside the school with its lighted windows it seemed warm and welcoming. Why should those in there, part of an establishment that had caused him such shame and hurt, now be so comfortable while he stood on the outside miserable and unwanted? He wanted to scream. The trigger that was about to set off a tragedy was the fact that no taxi was to be found.

> Everything I had left I'd invested in a future with the armed services and now I was seeing it disintegrate. I simply hadn't the energy or the will to begin again. Drinking and brooding I increasingly perceived myself as an outsider, a failure, someone predestined to be irrelevant to myself and the world around me and that perception angered and humiliated me as I instinctively tried to reject it. Self-pitying and self-absorbed I was blind to the worth of other people. You can't esteem others if you can't first esteem yourself. By placing no value on my life or my future, I placed none on others. In ostracising myself from other people, seeing in them only hurtful persecutors, I lost all empathy for them and by diminishing myself I inevitably diminished them.

In an uncontrollable rage, he walked back to Mathers Hotel and then returned to stand opposite the school carrying his shotgun. Inside the building youngsters were listening to their teachers. In the needlework room on the top floor of an annexe, pretty Nanette Hanson, aged twenty-six, was with her class of thirteen girls. She and her husband Guy, a designer in a local carpet factory, had married only six months earlier in Yorkshire and moved to Scotland primarily to further Guy's career. Suddenly, Mone crossed the road and burst into the school.

> During my school years I had only ever attended one class on that floor – geography. The first room I burst into turned out to be empty. Mrs Hanson's room was the second room I entered. I had no association with Mrs Hanson or that classroom. Stranger violence is often like that, it's random, chaotic, arbitrary and unsystematic. When suddenly faced with the unpredictable – violence, death, horror, tragedy – the human mind instinctively reaches for a rational pattern, a reason, something to explain the inexplicable and sometimes there isn't one. That is what renders it so senseless.

A MEETING OF DEVILS

The stranger walked into the classroom with the shotgun under his arm. Nanette turned, open-mouthed. The room went silent and then someone laughed thinking the stranger was playing a bizarre game. That only fired up his fury and he immediately fired into a glass door, the shards tearing open the face of another female teacher as she tried to intervene. The shot was answered by the screams of children; Nanette smiled, trying to calm the intruder but that gesture simply increased his anger and as if in revenge for her coolness he sat on her desk and deliberately swiped her spectacles to the floor. Mone would later admit:

> I waited to see her reaction. She lowered her eyes, the smile disappeared and she suddenly looked so sad. She bent down and picked up her glasses and suddenly I hated myself and felt ashamed. I had behaved like a bully to someone who had done me no harm.

Petrified girls cried while their teacher, cool and brave, determined to protect her young charges. During the next two hours, while police surrounded the school evacuating other children and imploring Mone to give up, he sexually assaulted two children. Gradually he was being drained of the adrenalin that had fuelled the invasion: 'I had desperately wanted an excuse to end it but I'd lost the initiative and did not know how to stop it all. I needed something to happen. And at that point it did.' Marion Young, then a nurse, aged eighteen and a former girlfriend of the gunman, volunteered to try to end the ordeal by talking Mone into giving up. She was brought to the school and he allowed her into the classroom.

> Marion looked at me and said, 'You won't do anything anyway.' Her tone and words seemed to sum up the utter failure and futility of my life. I was an irrelevant fraud living a lie. But it was the final provocation and the response was immediate and fatal as I think I always knew it would be if that moment ever came. I knew I could never fire if I had to look Nanette in the eye. So I asked her to turn away. And as she did I raised my shotgun and fired.

As the teacher collapsed with blood spurting from a terrible body wound, police sent in dogs that leapt on Mone. Teachers and police officers piled on top and he was handcuffed. Guy Hanson had rushed from his workplace and waited outside the school desperate for news. He was ushered by a policeman to an ambulance and inside lay his unconscious wife, her face deathly pale. The blast had shattered her spinal cord, severing her nervous system from the chest down. If she recovered, she would spend the rest of her life in a wheelchair. At hospital, doctors and nurses desperately fought to stem the bleeding, but from the second Mone pulled the trigger, Nanette had been doomed and she died without being able to respond to her husband's tearful words of comfort and goodbye.

Mone was dragged off and charged with murder. He made it clear to psychiatrists who examined him in prison that he no longer cared what became of him. Doctors reported him unfit to plead, and on 23 January 1968, he was ordered to be detained in the State Hospital. He was never tried for killing Nanette.

Two and a half years later, a new face appeared at Carstairs. Thomas Neil McCulloch, a painter and decorator, was a troubled young man. During adolescence he had developed an addiction to alcohol and drugs and was so unsure of his sexuality that, fearing homosexual tendencies, he had arranged consultations with a psychiatrist. In mid May 1970, when he was twenty, he had been diagnosed as having a psychopathic personality and told he needed treatment. What doctors could not know when they made their diagnosis was that at the home he shared with his parents in Parkhall, Clydebank, McCulloch had amassed a vast private arsenal that included high-powered rifles, handguns and swords. He spent much of his spare time poring over magazines specialising in weaponry and shooting. It was a frightening array, especially in the hands of a madman.

On the night of 16 May, McCulloch went to one of his regular drinking holes, the Erskine Bridge Motel at Clydebank, where he asked for a sandwich. The formal version of what happened next was later given in court. According to that account when the sandwich was served, McCulloch lifted one of the slices, peered inside and slammed it down, loudly moaning that the butter had been spread too thinly. Told it was a normal sandwich and there had been no complaints in the past, McCulloch stormed off and staff, scarcely able to believe what they had heard, thought that was the end of the matter. But it was not. The disgruntled customer went home and collected two shotguns, a revolver and ammunition belts, but, before leaving, made a chilling tape recording in which he announced his intent to return to the hotel and embark on a killing spree. Then he returned.

At the motel, McCulloch stormed into the kitchen demanding to see chef John Thomson, blaming him for the lack of butter. Customers told him not to be stupid, but his response when the chef appeared was to shoot at him, badly injuring him in the face. Then he ran about the motel shooting through doors, one blast hitting manager Lillias Rodger. The gunfire had alarmed members of a local Round Table, who were sitting at dinner with their wives when the gunman burst in, threatening to take them hostage. During half an hour of mayhem, McCulloch took refuge behind a table in the motel lounge. Police knew they had a major emergency on their hands and the motel was surrounded. Plain-clothes detectives Chief Superintendent David Hutchin and Superintendent Allan McKinlay took command, the former distracting the gunman before both literally dived at McCulloch, all three crashing into a wall. This allowed McKinlay to disarm the madman who was handcuffed and arrested. When he appeared before a sheriff to admit attempted murder and contravention of firearms laws, McCulloch's mental state resulted in his being ordered to be detained without limit of time in Carstairs.

Even according to this account it had been a terrifying incident, but Mone says he is in a unique position to throw light on what he claims was a plot by McCulloch to commit mass murder. He gives graphic details in the next chapter. Meanwhile, incredibly at Carstairs where security was intended to be the finest possible, the sandwich man would be able to develop his fascination with guns and swords. That passion for weapons, coupled with bewilderment over his sexuality and proximity to vulnerable Robert Mone, had cast the die for a terrible tragedy in 1976, when Mone and McCulloch escaped and, in the process, murdered Iain Simpson, nursing officer Neil McLellan and Police Constable George Taylor.

20

THE SANDWICH MAN

In Carstairs, McCulloch was looked on as a near perfect patient who showed no signs of the violent behaviour that had led him there. He ingratiated himself with staff, worked hard and well in the paint shop and gained consistently good reports indicating he was maturing. In reality, McCulloch was pulling off a gigantic trick and the ease with which he did so would bring stinging criticism in an official report into his escape with Mone.

In his younger days, Robert Mone had displayed an indifference to schooling. In Carstairs, he settled down and studied diligently, gaining three A-levels, coming within a whisker of being awarded a university law degree and gaining top marks in a playwriting course. At the same time, the doctor in charge of his treatment, John Gotea-Loweg, recorded him as arrogant, supercilious and argumentative with a sadistic, schizoid psychopathic personality.

Official reports record McCulloch and Mone beginning a friendship in 1973, but what was the reality of their relationship? Only two people know the truth. One is Robert Mone. This is his story:

> Most questions about life in Carstairs relate to the normal routine of incarceration like the mechanics of life in any institution. This routine is mind-numbingly boring to read and to write. On the other hand, the more specialist areas at Carstairs including sexual abuse were predicated upon elements such as fear, secrecy, shame and particularly a brand of helplessness, low self-esteem and vulnerability peculiar to the nature of incarceration within a State Hospital where

everyone, irrespective of offence or condition, shares precisely the same sentence i.e. 'Without limit of time', be it breach of the peace, criminal damage, rape or murder, or even the transfer of a patient from a local hospital. The nature of the sentence alone breeds a crushing sense of utter helplessness from which the patient knows no relief will come from family, friends, lawyers or MPs.

None of the normal agencies within society to which one normally turns for relief are of any avail whatsoever in the case of a State Hospital where the patient has absolutely no legal capacity. He or she is a non-person to a greater extent than almost anyone in society, even the most serious convicted offender. The predominant emotions are a sense of uncertainty (reinforcing one's sense of vulnerability) and fear of the power that staff hold over patients, and the absolute certainty that any offence to a nurse would bring that power crashing down in its entirely even unto death.

According to Mone's version of events, he was aware of the sexual abuse in Carstairs of young male and female patients – incidents he reported to the police in 1973 and also to the Reid inquiry that followed his and McCulloch's escape three years later. He has also said he repeated these allegations in 2013 and Police Scotland have confirmed his account that an investigation into complaints of sexual abuse at Carstairs in the late 1960s and early 1970s was carried out by a team of detectives based at Wishaw in 2013. Police say that, following a 'very thorough and searching investigation', a report was submitted to the authorities, but after consideration it was decided to take no further action. Mone claims that, after contacting police originally in 1973, he was threatened by a senior member of staff:

The power exercised over patients was total and irresistible, even when police sought in the early 1970s to question a young man at Carstairs in connection with the 'Bible John' slayings [Bible John was the nickname given to an unknown killer blamed for the murder of three women in Glasgow in 1968 and 1969], they had to seek a psychiatrist's approval to visit the hospital and question the suspect. [The man was subsequently cleared.] When a patient had been beaten by staff so badly that he could not be seen, a nursing officer was stationed outside his door every evening in order to stop anyone observing his condition through the Judas Hole in the man's door. When his elderly mother arrived on visiting days, she was refused admission and told that her son was too mentally ill to be seen.

Mone also gives details alleging collusion in the escape of Reid and MacDougall (see chapter 12) and tells how patients were able to buy hard-core pornography:

> For my part, however, the vilest 'corruption' of all was that designed to impart negligence and culpability to Nursing Officer Neil McLellan for his failure to secure the area from where the escape in 1976 occurred while it was under his charge.

Mone says that, shortly before he gave evidence to the formal inquiry into the escape, the well-known criminal lawyer Joe Beltrami was sent to visit him in prison. Beltrami advised Mone that the position of a well-known politician was at risk:

> And to avoid further hazard stemming from embarrassing testimony, the inquiry would hear my evidence behind closed doors. The media would be told that for 'security reasons' I could not testify in Lanark in public. By this means, according to Beltrami, it would be easier to contain further damage to the politician's career. At that meeting, I was also encouraged to present my evidence with emphasis on Neil McLellan's decision to 'lose the keys' to the area from which the escape occurred i.e. to discontinue the need to lock all the exit points. It was even felt this would attach significant negligence to Mr McLellan's judgement, and during my evidence I was asked to repeat this element of my testimony to emphasise this importance. To my enduring shame, I allowed myself to be manipulated into a sickening ploy that was fundamentally immoral and deeply unjust to a man murdered at his post. My culpability was the greater because I understood the motives behind the instruction and the motives were despicable.

During the inquiry about the escape, evidence was presented by representatives of the Church of Scientology who were known to have visited patients in Carstairs: 'The Church of Scientology was highly critical of traditional psychiatry. The feeling was mutual and the UK Government was suspicious of the movement.' According to Mone, Scientologists relied on patient Leslie Johnston (see chapter 10) to publicise church activities. Mone has named another man who, he claims, preyed on young Carstairs patients but, unknown to this abuser, Johnston surreptitiously recorded conversations amounting to confessions from this individual with the intention of passing the material to Scientology representatives.

Mone has named another young inmate who we are calling 'H' and who, he says, fell under the influence of a middle-aged patient, ultimately becoming this man's catamite. Following the older man's release, the two retained contact, the older man arranging for H to organise 'porn shoots of young male and female patients'. H was suspected of the multiple rape of another young inmate and of getting a teenage female patient pregnant with the connivance of a member of staff notorious for brutality. H, Mone says, 'was a classic case of someone who began as a victim but became a perpetrator: the abused becomes the abuser'. He has also supplied details of other older patients who perpetrated the sick domination of younger detainees:

> Contraband, in the absence then of searches or CCTV, was easily introduced to the State Hospital via visitors and corrupt staff, while serious pornography was supplied and sold to patients by an employee with a reputation as something of a sex pest to the younger female patients using sleazy talk, suggestive glances and inappropriate touching. Most simply saw him as a dirty old man.

Another patient had persuaded family members to pose for pornographic images that were circulated on a hire basis in Carstairs in the mid 1970s. 'The same individual was seeking to recruit his younger siblings to produce specifically paedophiliac material, again for profit.' In the mid 1970s, the then celebrity entertainer Jimmy Savile visited Carstairs. The television star was widely praised for the work he did raising money and the profile of institutions and hospitals throughout Britain. He has since been denounced as a serial sex abuser. Mone says that, in Carstairs, he was regularly abused by another patient, who he has named, telling police in 1973 about these attacks. He was interviewed by detectives at Carstairs and made a full statement, but heard nothing more, as a result of which he repeated his claims in 2013 leading to the further inquiry when he named McCulloch as having committed sex attacks in the mid 1970s and supplied details of victims and witnesses, including staff members. Following the revelations about Savile's paedophiliac activities, a report on checks into historic abuse in Scottish institutions that were visited by him, including Carstairs, was sent to the then Scottish health minister Nicola Sturgeon. This report also covered the allegations of sexual abuse made by Mone. However, his early attempts to force a police investigation did not go down well with the Carstairs management:

> Criminal offences, even serious sexual offences, committed at Carstairs were not, as a matter of policy, ever reported to the police and victims were too terrified to report offences. When I challenged this practice and talked to Strathclyde police, I was immediately downgraded and threatened with the direst consequences if I ever again involved the police in State Hospital matters.

Following their initial 1973 meeting, over the course of the next three years, McCulloch and Mone graduated from being friends, to lovers and then killers. Theirs became a homosexual version of Bonnie and Clyde, with dire consequences. (Bonnie Parker and her lover Clyde Barrow were a young couple who committed robberies and murders across central America in the mid 1930s before being ambushed and slaughtered by police in 1934.) As they got to know one another, McCulloch opened up about his background to Mone, who says this is what the younger man told him:

> McCulloch was born to working-class parents, though he liked to portray his background as middle class. His father John was a

middle-aged minor clerk, authoritarian in nature. He had an older brother but, beyond detesting their father, neither brother had anything in common. McCulloch always demonstrated a complete disinterest in his brother. By contrast, however, his attachment to his deeply religious mother Robina was all consuming – so much so that his hatred of his father intensified at the thought of being forced to share her with his father. He would often speak of his childhood with her and beyond me she was the only human being I ever heard McCulloch profess an utter devotion to.

One of McCulloch's most influential memories, about which he often spoke to me, was of accompanying his mother to a Billy Graham rally in Glasgow at which he was overwhelmed by the sheer effect on the audience of a powerful orator. Later in adolescence, McCulloch would translate this memory into a passion for images, the sort of powerful atmosphere engendered by the Hitlerite Nuremburg rallies of 1930s Germany, a passion he would indulge by adopting a penchant for wearing dark clothing, mimicking the black uniforms of Hitler's SS and his search for items, such as flags, etc, of Nazi memorabilia.

During his teens, McCulloch developed an interest in and later a passion for firearms, a passion he shared with a small group of friends in Clydebank, two of whom visited him regularly at the State Hospital. He developed a sound working knowledge of guns to the extent of adapting and modifying them, once converting a .410 shotgun into a handgun and manufacturing rudimentary silencers. An apprentice painter and decorator, he once boasted that his first task when he went to a job at a customer's house was to search the house for evidence of guns or ammunition. He recollected on one occasion discovering a First World War Lewis machine gun. Whilst I had briefly been in the army, McCulloch's knowledge and apparent expertise and confidence around firearms vastly outstripped my own.

Moving on to the motel incident that resulted in McCulloch being detained in Carstairs, Mone says:

Sometime prior to his arrest for the shooting, McCulloch and a friend

THE SANDWICH MAN

[we are calling him 'J'] had begun experimenting with LSD and, on one occasion, it led to a homosexual exchange, which seemed to awaken a latent sexual interest in young males, but an interest the young McCulloch was too buttoned-up emotionally to pursue. His previous heterosexual experiences had been limited and of little note. It was timid and tedious and lacked the thrill and edginess that he later sought and fantasised over at Carstairs.

Of course, McCulloch's stated motive for his armed attack on the Clydebank motel was a lie. It had nothing to do with a badly prepared sandwich. On the day of the attack someone at the motel [Mone has named this man] had made a homosexual advance to McCulloch. Unable to cope with his latent homosexuality, he returned to the motel heavily armed and with a stock of ammunition. His intention was to kill the man, turn his guns on as many staff and guests as possible, finally dying in a shoot out with the police. He had planned for an Anders Breivik style wipeout [Breivik was a young Norwegian who massacred seventy-seven people during a shooting and explosives rampage in 2011]. His attack was in essence a flop and not the big glamorous spectacle that McCulloch had hoped for when he attacked. For someone utterly incapable of laughing at himself, this flop burned deeply. The unspeakable humiliation of it was a source of shame, as he saw it and rancour throughout his years at Carstairs. In his eyes, he was a failure because he hadn't killed anyone. His devotion to the sinister image he had crafted of himself – Hitlerite, SS-loving, Book of Revelations tub-thumper – had crashed and burned and he himself had become a joke.

21

ANGEL OF DEATH

As a young man Mone had been very much a loner, often preferring his own company. But as is so often the case with introverts such as himself, he was often tongue-tied when meeting others and naive, with the result that he was largely friendless and vulnerable. Academically he had previously never shown potential but at Carstairs, frequently left alone to his own devices, he found satisfaction in books and study. The law became one of his special interests and, with an eye to what he might make of himself when he was ultimately allowed to leave Carstairs and re-enter the community, he enlisted upon a law degree correspondence course with London University. Mone spent hours poring over his law books in his room in Tweed Ward, a section of Carstairs holding patients felt worthy of being trusted, and showed little or no interest in other inmates. But, as Mone now relates, that was about to change:

> I didn't meet McCulloch until about 1973, after I was downgraded from Tweed to Kelvin Ward, my punishment for reporting my own sexual abuse to the police, and naming my attacker. The downgrading destroyed my chance to continue my course aimed at securing a law degree with London University. It was especially unfair since my entire studies had been self-funded, first with matriculation and later enrolment for an LL.B. In anticipation of ultimate success, I had even applied for and received permission from the Bar Council to begin studying for the Bar Part 1 exams. I arrived at Kelvin Ward to begin my downgrade distraught at a future turned to ashes.

ANGEL OF DEATH

I was alone and friendless, ostracised by 'authority' at Carstairs for having the temerity to embarrass them by reporting sex abuse to the police. I didn't blame the police; I attached blame to the proper quarter, the State Hospital. It was at this juncture that McCulloch decided to move in and, as he often put it, take me under his wing. Only much later did it become apparent that his wings were the wings of the Angel of Death.

The most striking quality displayed by McCulloch was his absolute genius to charm all around him and increase his personal popularity. It was a quality, a skill, which made him unique among the patient population. Only later was I to discover it to be an assiduously crafted mask that concealed an utter contempt and occasional loathing of almost everyone he came into contact with. For some unaccountable reason I was to emerge as the single exception – a quirk or perhaps indulgence of McCulloch's bizarre personality, which even to this day mystifies me in a slightly alarming way. Or maybe he just judged me too pathetic to be contemptuous of.

Whatever he divined my qualities to be, his growing attention to me rapidly saw me benefit from those he held in thrall to his charm and what seemed his effervescent personality. The fact that some of McCulloch's cachet now rubbed off on me did little to console me for the years of endeavour I had devoted single-mindedly to turning my life around. It served only to convince me more deeply of just how superficial and tawdry was the good opinion of the 'crowd'.

My ambition and hard work so unfairly thwarted, as it seemed to me, my prevailing mood was one of deep despondency, only alleviated to some extent by McCulloch's constant ministrations to my battered morale. And his support of me within the wider patient community where his charm and manipulation had secured him cachet. For someone who had never been 'part of the crowd', it was a novel experience. Feeling cast adrift and without purpose, I found myself being instructed by McCulloch in one of his hobbies – soft toy making. It was a striking difference to studying law. Practical skills had never been my forte. Despite this, the hobby became an activity that occupied most of my evenings with McCulloch. Consciously or otherwise, it may have been his initial bid to absorb me into his own sphere. Later there would be many more such strategies.

With a bent for practical skills and a vague ambition to one day run his own business, McCulloch began pestering me to teach him the rudiments of law, the legal pitfalls of running and operating a small business. As time went by, I found these twin activities seemed to occupy every waking hour with almost all my time spent in McCulloch's company. Like everyone else, I wasn't immune to his charm, but gradually it became clear that McCulloch was singling me out for his special confidences, often at the expense of those who were turning to him for help, even developing a way of looking at me to signal that he was laughing or sneering at the person who was appealing to him.

Initially I was taken aback at the sheer breadth of his icy cold cynicism and utter contempt for everyone he came into contact with. I began to wonder at the sheer brilliance of his ability to 'play' people and, though taken aback, I also felt a small glow of pride that he had chosen me to open his true feelings to. In his way, McCulloch was telling me that I was special and that among all those who vied for his company or his attention, I came first. For someone who had never been first or even a hundred and first in any personality poll, it gave me a warm feeling of belonging and it was good.

That feeling of specialness was cemented early one morning when McCulloch came into my cell in Kelvin Ward and, standing directly in front of me, quietly and gently slipped his hand inside my pyjamas and sexually fondled me. I felt a sudden rush of panic at the action, understandable given the circumstances that had occasioned my downgrade to Kelvin Ward. Momentarily trapped like a rabbit in the headlights, I think I must have scarcely breathed. McCulloch never took his eyes from my face; his look was quietly confident but not at all threatening. His look was saying, 'I am big enough to take on the biggest taboos, and break them, and protect you. You now have my biggest secret, and I trust you with it.' To all who knew him, McCulloch was young, handsome, reliable, a popular hail-fellow-well-met heterosexual. By exposing to me his real sexuality, a sexuality he had sought to conceal at the point of a gun when he attacked the motel in Clydebank with the intention of gunning down everyone in sight, McCulloch had decided to elevate the relationship to a whole new level and somehow I knew it would never be the same again.

From time to time, I would speculate about trying to rekindle the dying embers of my law studies in time for the examination season, as if I could not quite let go of the one-time dream. McCulloch would listen patiently almost like an indulgent parent, and then quietly explain why I should forget the past and abandon my previous ambitions. And the force of his reasoning was often persuasive. At no expense to anyone I had set about remedying the deficiencies of a rubbish state education plagued by indolent bullying or paedophiliac teachers and then, when I was on the brink of achieving success, having it snatched away by the State Hospital, when my only sin had been to report sex abuse to the police. It was a hard pill to swallow and one that lent credence to McCulloch's negative and hostile outlook on society.

Consistent with his jaundiced view of mankind, McCulloch embraced and displayed a child-like passion for animals and nature – well, even Adolf Hitler is said to have loved his dog. When a pet mouse he had reared suddenly died, McCulloch crafted a casket for its 'internment', furnishing its interior with a soft fabric and enclosed two Polaroids, one of each of us. He then entombed the casket in the loft space above his workshop. Astonishing as it may seem, I increasingly witnessed these bizarre elements of his personality without drawing any conclusions or making any judgement. It seemed to me that, for better or for worse, this was what I had, and I should just accept it. As time went by, McCulloch's attachment grew to extreme possessiveness. Using his soft toy skills he fashioned an effigy doll of me with pale, long yellow hair and placed it in his bed every evening. And he developed the habit of always buying two of everything – clothing, jewellery and so on, identical of course. For a time, some nursing staff would refer to us as the Terrible Twins.

Over the term of the relationship, it seemed as if he was engaged in the manufacture of some kind of doppelganger or twin as my dress, musical tastes and interests began to morph into his own. McCulloch began to display an avid interest in my family history and relationships, even encouraging his mother to form an acquaintance with my family at visits and posting unsolicited gifts to my sister in England. When these gifts were returned, I had the unenviable task of trying to explain to McCulloch why my sister felt unable to accept unsolicited gifts from a complete stranger, particularly a stranger housed in a mental hospital.

His response stunned me. He flew into an angry and embittered rage at what he regarded as an unjustifiable snub, believing that his friendship with me entitled him an entree into my sister's affections. His reasoning was bizarre and outlandish, almost as outlandish as his increasing tendency to refer to me as his 'brother' and he and I as 'brothers'. I had become his replacement for the brother he rejected. I found myself so intimidated by his bitterness, his expressions of hurt incomprehension at my sister's seeming rebuff, that I could make no defence of her decision to return his gifts. I was embarrassed by his apparent naivety over the matter, or was his rejection of reality an attempt to create an alternative reality for himself with me at the centre of it as the brother he wanted?

As time passed McCulloch and I became constant companions. Though I was never one of the crowd, I knew that any attention I received was reflected from McCulloch, but strangely it didn't seem to matter. Perhaps it should have or perhaps the novelty of receiving any attention was reassurance enough and the fact that it was second-hand didn't really matter. I watched him charm, manipulate and finesse everyone around him with the skill and virtuosity of a maestro, never for an instant betraying his true feelings or losing control of events. A man for all seasons, someone who could be whatever you wanted him to be, but someone who would never be your 'tool' because ultimately you were his and he was hunting you down like a wolf. Perhaps men like him always need someone – a quiet, unassuming, non-judgemental bystander – who effectively becomes a deep well into which they can pour their true feelings and through whom they can explain or justify themselves to themselves.

With McCulloch's transfer to another ward, Tweed Ward, and the appointment of another doctor to my case, John Gotea-Loweg, I seemed to briefly flourish and find new purpose and drive for myself, diminishing the stature McCulloch had assumed in my life. I was invited to assist as a 'peer tutor' within the hospital's education centre, bringing educationally disadvantaged patients up to O-level standard, before they were passed to the hospital's only qualified teacher to be 'prepped' for their 'mocks'.

Shortly after this, John Gotea-Loweg secured my appointment as a regular features writer on the hospital magazine, *The State Observer*, preparatory to being made its editor with a remit to restructure the entire project and repackage it to read less like a school magazine and more like a professional publication. The work was challenging and absorbing and I began to enjoy being my own master again. However, I had barely commenced my new life when McCulloch started bombarding me with billets-doux, many graphic in the extreme. They were delivered on behalf of McCulloch by another patient. [We shall call this man 'K'.] This individual was a hospital source for pornography, including paedophile porn, and alcohol that were smuggled to him via hospital visits.

The evening outdoor recreation occasioned yet another opportunity for McCulloch to cajole me into meeting with him when he would indulge his bizarre fantasies and outline his increasing interest in urban terrorism as a vehicle through which the disaffected and maladjusted might vent their spleen on society as a whole. He would constantly quiz me about army bases on which I had served and about the typical security measures for arms stores. Ever since the pathetic debacle at the motel in Clydebank when all his Ramboesque fantasies of dying in a hail of police bullets collapsed into farce and he found himself overpowered and ignominiously disarmed, McCulloch's obsession with a 'Big' violent statement remained a more or less permanent preoccupation. It wasn't surprising that he would talk big and want to impress. After all, that is generally symptomatic of the 'little man' when his objectives and inventions are frustrated.

McCulloch had, in his mind, failed. All his inadequacies, his sexual ambivalences, his predisposition towards dark sinister forces such as Nazism, the Book of Revelations, and in fact anything which injected more drama into his middle-of-the-road pathetic existence – all of these elements were battling to create an explosive, dangerous and unstable fury. I recall him once attempting to prise open an altar stone in the church centre in the hall with the intention of securing a Saints relic, which he then planned to sacrifice in some bizarre satanic ceremony.

All his behaviours and outpourings became increasingly extreme and outlandish, including psychosexual fantasies such as strangling his partner at the point of sexual climax. I found myself conflicted between embarrassment and an inexplicable urge to protect him from the forces operating within him, which admittedly he himself was generating. Tragically, I wanted to believe he was the victim of his own fantasies and that as long as these forces could be contained they would be unrealised and hopefully diminish or disappear with the passage of time. It was entirely the wrong approach because it failed to acknowledge the need for boundaries and the near certainty that in the absence of boundaries these dark forces could only escalate.

22

MURDERBALL

Mone was encouraged by John Gotea-Loweg to contribute to an arts and crafts festival to be covered by BBC Scotland. He wrote a one-act play, a political statement on apartheid in the South African justice system:

> Its favourable reaction resulted in John instituting a drama group and asking me to direct it. Almost immediately, McCulloch persuaded me to appoint him the set designer which, given his practical skills, he was amply qualified for.
> The nature of the work and the parolee status of most patients involved resulted in greater levels of self-policing and a reduction in supervision staff, even when the sexes met within the hospital's recreation centre. I would often attend, either as head of drama or as editor of the magazine, reporting on the progress of the project. And McCulloch would invariably attend as my companion. Using his connections with me and the drama group, in the summer of 1976, he began to elicit a growing interest in sexually exploitative liaisons with the young, male patients at the State Hospital.
> His first victim was a young male [we'll call him 'A'] who worked on the magazine staff. McCulloch seduced him in a changing room. Later I was taken aback and angered when he suggested that it would lend piquancy to proceedings if I could participate. Was I his friend or his whore? It suddenly occurred to me that he could have a voyeuristic streak, which I found slightly gross, pathetic and humorous all at the same time. By this stage, however, there seemed few depths

that he was not prepared to plumb. He had sought to use his connection with me to entrap young males into sexual assaults. When he developed an interest in a young male, he would pester me to cast him in a production and then use drama rehearsals as a cover to assault the youth. A young male, based in Forth Ward, and who looked about fifteen years of age, became his obsession. But, conscious that any incident would compromise the integrity of the drama project and embarrass John Gotea-Loweg, I would often interview a young candidate and then find a reason to discount the application. It was an effective way of keeping them out of his clutches.

During the summer of 1976, it became evident to many at Carstairs that I was responding favourably to the new management of Dr Gotea-Loweg, and that, despite the sex abuse I had endured and the stress of reporting it to the police in 1973, the probability was that I would be transferred to a less secure facility, possibly the Royal Dundee Liff Hospital. Despite the fact that I still tried to remain loyal to McCulloch, his constant companionship and its increasing abuse became recurringly stressful as he carelessly bemoaned his own lack of progression within the Carstairs environment. It appeared he had reached the acme of his success.

But subtly interwoven into his peevish whining tone was an unspoken but implied suggestion that I owed him a debt of gratitude. After all, when I was friendless and alone he had supported me, lending me his personal imprimatur within the community and among his companions. Did that not in itself demand loyalty? McCulloch almost instinctively knew the buttons to press with me from long spells of quiet, tragic silences to the tear-filled, whipped puppy eyes. Whatever the occasion, he could be relied upon for a truly stellar performance.

One beautiful summer's day in 1976, while walking in the grounds with McCulloch, I was approached by John Gotea-Loweg. He was accompanied by a young woman. It was the first time I met Erica Robb. She was applying for the post of clinical psychologist at Carstairs. John introduced us and we stood in the sun, probably exchanging inconsequentials. Many years later, as my therapist in prison, Erica recollected our first meeting. In particular, she recalled

McCulloch and how he never uttered a word throughout the brief meeting but seemed to focus his entire attention on the way Erica and I interacted. She recalled him as silent and sinister. That's the sort of appellation McCulloch would have taken pride in. He was motivated by having an effect on people. How little she knew of the nature of our relationship that day as we chatted amiably in the sun. But later in our lives she helped me exorcise the myriad ghosts I inherited from him during three years of the most destructive relationship that it was my misfortune to enter into while at Carstairs.

In contrast, my relationship with John Gotea-Loweg was that of a wayward child to a kindly and indulgent grandparent and the object of my every working day was to inspire in him the quiet satisfaction of a job well done. As each project he handed me attained a successful outcome my sense of pride in bringing him success was boundless and here was the nub of my dilemma. I found myself trapped between two relationships, one deceitful and worthless, and the other representing everything that was decent and humane and worthwhile. How could I have allowed the one to predominate over the other? In the 1980s, John tried to visit me in prison, and whilst I was wracked by the deep sense of shame I felt regarding my terrible betrayal of his trust, I instinctively knew John would not accuse and berate me as other men would, because to do so would not have matched the man. The visit did not take place, however, because Erica stepped in and rejected his request on the grounds that it would have been too emotionally fraught for me to cope with. I regret now, however, that the meeting did not take place.

It was around this time that McCulloch first mooted the notion of escaping from Carstairs. He was aware that I would strongly resist any attempt to return me to the influence of my family, which a transfer to a less secure facility would entail. In retrospect it is clear to me that McCulloch allied this to his own increasing disenchantment with his absence of progression. He saw my star rising, while all the while the evidence was that his own was in a state of terminal decline. As the indications and projections increased that I would be a serious candidate for transfer within possibly a year or so, for the first time I began to see evidence of McCulloch's self-control beginning to slip.

He frequently talked about the hopelessness of my early dreams of rehabilitating my life. Our lives, he said, were inextricably linked and so was our fate.

I had been planning a production of *Loot*, a 1965 play by tragic playwright Joe Orton [murdered in 1967 by Kenneth Halliwell, his mentally unstable lover who subsequently died by his own hand]. I had become a passionate admirer of Orton's work after corresponding with his agent and his biographer, John Lahr. McCulloch had also developed an interest in Orton. His, however, was not a literary interest, but almost exclusively centred on the author's relationship with Halliwell and their reputed forays to North Africa for sex with underage boys. That his self-control was slipping was evident from another incident in which McCulloch attacked a young, female patient in the recreation hall where he tried to force her to have sex. I knew nothing about it until she took her distress to two young male friends who both approached me, knowing I was friendly with McCulloch. They outlined what had happened to the girl and told me to stay out of it because they planned to attack McCulloch. However, I confronted him that he had attacked her, and he dismissed her as an irrelevance.

As the summer of 1976 progressed, McCulloch amassed a store of Plasticine key impressions from staff keys in the woodwork unit. Even I didn't know exactly how many had been taken, since he took them at every opportunity. There was an array of lethal weapons including a deadly looking hatchet, about four or five lengthy daggers, at least two garrottes and the blade of a sword that he was making. A lengthy, well-made rope ladder completed his basic escape tool kit. He would obtain his supply of metals from the (secure) scrap metal storage area and manufacture the wood handles within the woodwork area. The blades would be sharpened in the area above the wood store and done within the hearing of the staff.

The seemingly unending accumulation of weaponry sparked several violent disagreements between us. I repeatedly warned that he was taking insane risks that would end in his capture, but, whenever I remonstrated, McCulloch would simply ignore my arguments and then patiently explain that his credibility with the work-shed staff was so high that he was at no risk. In the end, he was right. His various caches of weapons were extremely well concealed in cupboards fitted with false walls. He always appeared totally dedicated to this work and calmly single-minded. So confident was he of his influence over the staff that he would often take weapons, including the rope ladder, inside a black and white wooden carrying box, between the woodwork unit and the residential ward, passing through nursing staff at both points and never once was he asked to open the carrying box. His ability to charm and fool everyone stood him in good stead and I have no doubt that he retains that ability even to this day.

McCulloch's final sex attack occurred just shortly before our escape. The victim was a young male patient [we are calling 'C'] transferred to Carstairs. The scene of the assault was the same changing room in which he had sexually assaulted another youngster. C was later found wandering, confused and disorientated, in a security sensitive area and unable to even identify the ward he was based in. A senior hospital staff member later admitted to me that the hospital had been obliged to send for a doctor to examine the patient that night.

This staff member telephoned me at Clyde Ward to ask if I could explain C's condition. I had inadvertently seen McCulloch sexually interfering with the patient following a game of murderball [the original name for wheelchair rugby, owing to its highly aggressive and dangerous nature] in which I had participated in the recreation centre shortly after lunchtime. Immediately surmising another incident similar to that which provoked the ire of her two male friends, I instinctively sought to cover up for McCulloch and suggested that C's injuries might have occurred during murderball. But this suggestion was known to be untrue, because C hadn't been in the game, I'd seen him watching from the stage area with friends. Carstairs had actually banned murderball because it was considered dangerous and reckless to participants.

The staff member made it clear he was unconvinced by my suggestion and arranged to talk to me the following day. I knew, from my own earlier experience, that Carstairs would prefer to deal in-house with any sexual offences. Following murderball, I had spent the day with other staff in the magazine office doing last-minute write-ups for the monthly edition and so I had no opportunity to quiz McCulloch about his contact with C after the game. C was a parolee and, under the prevailing culture, 'off limits' for any kind of sexploitation by anyone, including other parolees, as this could damage his chances of release from the State Hospital.

When I did eventually ask McCulloch about C, as in the case of the girl, he was initially angered by my questions and then dismissed the incident as unimportant – unimportant while his immediate working area in the woodwork unit was stuffed with all manner of lethal weapons! I thought that either McCulloch had lost the plot or I was the world's worst drama queen. When I met with the staffer en route to work the following day, he seemed absolutely relaxed about our earlier phone call and indicated no further interest in the matter. Clearly C had been spoken to, code for 'shut your mouth or beware the consequences'. It was the same message given to me when I had been sexually abused in 1973.

As the long summer days of 1976 wore on into the autumn, the mood around McCulloch became darker and darker. Gone were the days of almost easy juvenile fun and laughter. Now his attention was focused on the subject of escaping with me to some ill-defined and cursed haven far away from a world that he rejected and loathed. More and more, he returned to the Orton-Halliwell theme and the notion that their violent demise was the logical outcome for two young men, outcasts, in search of an eternal peace where they could find happiness unencumbered by other people. Increasingly, McCulloch's world had shrunk to two people, with all the rest dismissed as 'futiles' – an expression that became his favourite word and adjective.

At the very time I craved John Gotea-Loweg's attention, reassurance and support, he was less and less in my life as so many other demands crowded in upon me, leaving me exposed and vulnerable to McCulloch's gloom-laden and murderous philosophies. He talked more and more about death and him and me in the same breath. It was becoming difficult to distinguish one from the other and the notion that all roads would lead to the same destination. McCulloch had often told me that he had no objection if I took a partner for amusement, despite the fact that I had no desire to do so, but if I ever became emotionally entangled with anyone he would not hesitate to kill them. It was his way of telling me that my world was also shrinking and that my options were limited. The increasing darkness of his mood during this period told me that not for a moment should I doubt his resolve, because he had already been discussing my death as though it were an accomplished fact. It was always outlined in a calm, matter-of-fact way. Having accomplished his personal objectives and no doubt wreaked havoc among the 'futiles', I would go to sleep one night and simply not wake up. Once he had safely placed me beyond the reach or temptation of anyone, there would be no purpose to his continued existence and nothing left to which he could link, and at that point he would end his own life. I was wedded to someone who already saw me as a corpse. And to some degree it seemed an almost natural outcome, or at least it didn't seem to shock me.

Meanwhile, fearful that McCulloch's increasing indiscretions in his workplace would result in his capture, I offered to keep an alert for him while he was manufacturing his weaponry. One incident was memorable. McCulloch was seated in a deep armchair while I stood drinking a cup of coffee several feet away. In the course of our conversation, he grotesquely mispronounced a word upon which I instinctively laughed. McCulloch had an absolute horror of being mocked and lacked any capacity whatsoever to laugh at himself. Though standing at a distance, I swear I never saw McCulloch leave that chair, so lightning-quick was his response. In a fraction of a second, his face a mask of cold fury, one hand clamped around my wrist while the other sent the coffee cup spinning across the room to shatter against the wall. The speed at which he had moved completely unnerved me. I blustered and faked fury, as one does to regain the initiative. McCulloch released my wrist and then quietly and patiently explained he had grabbed my wrist to stop me being scalded by the coffee as he smacked the cup away from me. Despite the lightning speed of his response, his actions had been surgical in their precision. Now, for the first time in my life, I realised I was afraid of

McCulloch. If he could respond with that speed and exactitude in anger, what could he do if calm and deliberate? I didn't want to find out.

Two years ago, I discovered that I almost did. Someone in a position of authority confided to me that McCulloch systematically planned one further murder the night of the escape from Carstairs. This individual told me, 'You were next.' It was a chilling announcement. According to what I was told, official records revealed McCulloch planned to murder me as soon as he had evaded the police pursuit. In the event, of course, he did not evade capture and I didn't get murdered.

Returning to the coffee cup incident, to cover my nervousness I snapped that it was over and I didn't want to see him again. As I spoke, the man seemed to crumple in front of me, and silent tears coursed down his face. He stood like a broken reed and, as I watched, I felt the resolve within me collapse. He had lifted me up at my lowest ebb and now when he was disintegrating before my eyes, this was no time to abandon him. As I watched those tears course down his face, I could feel a steel trap snapping shut around me.

23

THE BIRTH OF HELL

According to the report by Sheriff Robert Reid on the findings of his official inquiry in 1977 into the escape, McCulloch and Mone spent six months making and collecting equipment for their getaway. It was astonishing how their preparations for the birth of hell were able to move on unnoticed.

The sheriff reported how visitors naively provided maps, money and a flashlight. But he said McCulloch went to extraordinary lengths to manufacture an array of deadly weapons, often using the excuse that he was making props for a Christmas production by the hospital drama group.

He created a rope ladder from stolen cord with wooden rungs secretly made in the woodworking department and weighted with a lump of lead taken from a discarded floor polisher. The ladder was hidden for a time in a loudspeaker cabinet. Machinery used in the paint shop helped turn out fake identity cards, their apparent authenticity improved with photographs of the pair taken with a Polaroid camera given to Mone for use in his job as editor of the hospital magazine. The drama group prop box provided Mone and McCulloch with nurses caps and false moustaches.

McCulloch showed himself to be a skilled weapon maker. He produced three knives from steel stolen from supplies in the woodworking shop intended to manufacture runners for sledges, while a sharpened piece of metal stolen from the occupational therapy department was turned into the head of an axe. Reid described it as 'very light and small enough to be hidden easily but its blade was very sharp and it proved a frighteningly effective weapon'. One of two garrottes was made from a violin string. He made belts and sheaths to carry the weapons, painted wooden replicas of pistols used as stage props so they appeared totally realistic, started making a sword and succeeded in producing a crossbow, but broke it up because there was nowhere to hide it.

Anyone attempting to stop their escape was to have ammonia thrown in their face, but, unable to get this, McCulloch stole Nitromors, the caustic paint stripper, for this purpose instead. All the equipment was made or stolen under the very noses of staff who were supposed to be ultra-vigilant. For much of the time, McCulloch hid some weapons in a box he openly carried around the hospital. It was never searched. Nor was he or Mone.

The escape was planned for Tuesday, 23 November 1976 – they had studied the volume of traffic passing the hospital on different days and at different times, and discovered it was at its heaviest on Tuesday evenings, meaning that it would be easiest to hijack a passing vehicle. At the last minute, however, they aborted the attempt. According to Sheriff Reid's version of events, the decision not to go ahead that night was due to the discovery that nurse Neil McLellan was expecting a telephone call and his absence would raise concern. Reid states that a week later, the unexpected appearance of nurse Mary Hamilton worried McCulloch and Mone until she moved on to another part of the hospital.

Once the escape got under way with attacks on Neil McLellan and Iain Simpson – the patient jailed in 1962 for double murder (see chapter 4) – in the former's office in the hospital social club, Mone cut the internal and Post Office telephone wires. After climbing over the wire fence, they were confronted by a police van carrying two officers on routine patrol, Constables George Taylor and John Gillies. McCulloch fatally stabbed PC Taylor, a father of four.

The two inmates drove off in the police vehicle with McCulloch at the wheel. But it had been many years since he'd last driven and conditions were icy. Almost inevitably, he skidded off the road, down an embankment and into a field. William Lennon and Jack McAlroy, who were passing in their works van, stopped to help but one was stabbed, the other hit with an axe and their van stolen. This took the escapers further south before the vehicle left the road and became bogged down. They waded over the River Clyde and found a farmhouse with a family watching television. Threatened, the farmer handed over the keys to his car, but his twelve-year-old daughter bravely crept to a back room and telephoned police. Mone and McCulloch drove south but, nearing Carlisle, McCulloch once more lost control and crashed. Four youngsters in a Mini car stopped to help. The runaways ordered the driver and passenger out and clambered in, but, before they could move, they were surrounded by armed police and recaptured.

24

PERDITION

Twenty-five patients were interviewed in private by Sheriff Reid in his attempt to discover precisely what had happened, what had gone wrong and what was needed to prevent any repetition. With their evidence and that of many other witnesses, including hospital staff, officials and police, Reid built up his account of the escape and its repercussions. It was official and formal. But now, in his own words, Mone has recounted his version of the glaring horror of the three terrible hours that dominate the history of the State Hospital. Parts of his testimony are at odds with evidence given later at the trial of the two men.

On 23 November 1976, McCulloch moved all his weaponry and escape equipment to the chosen site, Neil McLellan's office in the single storey administration block. McCulloch had scheduled the escape for that evening. In the event, it did not take place. It did not take place because I refused to go ahead. I refused because, unexpectedly, Mary Hamilton, Neil's deputy, arrived and settled in for the evening. Mary Hamilton was Ian Hamilton's wife. Some years previously Ian Hamilton was Charge Nurse in Kelvin Ward during a period when my morale was very low and Ian had supported me; I never forgot his kindness. I knew that McCulloch loathed Mary Hamilton. She was never 'taken in' by his 'act' and remained sceptical of him to the last. I knew that if things went wrong, Mary Hamilton would be McCulloch's principal target, simply because he hated her.

PERDITION

As McCulloch began unloading his weaponry in an adjoining room, I told him that I would not go ahead with Mary present. McCulloch, his face furious, tried to change my mind but I was unmovable on the issue of Mary Hamilton, and McCulloch had no choice but to dismantle his plan. Do I believe that my decision on that night saved Mary Hamilton's life? I believe that without a shadow of a doubt. There is no evidence that she ever knew of the original date of the break-out, or how closely she came to death. Ian Hamilton's kindness and support to me during a stressful time in my sojourn in Carstairs saved his wife's life that night.

In the intervening seven days, leading up to 30 November, McCulloch piled on the emotional pressure designed to break down any remaining resistance and render me more pliable to his will, a will which was indomitable. There were long periods of hurt silence, looks and accusatory signs that screamed 'betrayal' at me. In his every step and movement he carried all the poignancy of an abandoned puppy left out in the cold and destined to starve in a cruel, heartless world.

I was never allowed to escape the guilt of condemning him to an unjust fate after all the goodness he had shown to me. I felt that I had snatched away what was left of this demented man's tortured life. Unaccountably, I felt that I had acted rashly and with a sense of supreme selfishness. Through the summer and the autumn, the sense of gloom that accompanied McCulloch's obsession with the Orton–Halliwell relationship and the utter inevitability of its bloody climax lingered like a curse. McCulloch's psychosexual fantasies and repressed rage against the Carstairs system and the 'futiles' – that great, amorphous mass that he never clearly defined – seeped into my bones like a cancer and sapped me of the will to resist his plunging madness.

Exactly one week later, on the evening of 30 November 1976, no imperatives acted on me as they had done seven days previously. As a consequence, in no way can I claim to have restrained McCulloch's hatchet-wielding fury as he finally got the opportunity to make his big, violent statement, and innocent blood flowed and a terrifying night ensued.

CARSTAIRS

That evening, I had scheduled a reading of Steinbeck's *Of Mice and Men* to ascertain how to keep the essential storyline but reduce the number of scene changes. Steinbeck was a follow-up to *Loot*, still in production. Throughout McCulloch's insane preoccupation with escaping from Carstairs, my own punishing schedule of activities had continued, in the forlorn hope that his insanity could be staved off until I was transferred far away from his corrosive influence and atmosphere.

Neil McLellan collected me from Clyde Ward at close to seven o'clock in the evening. He was already accompanied by Iain Simpson and together we collected McCulloch from Tweed Ward. McCulloch emerged, passing a nurse at the door and holding his ever-present carrying box, the box containing his rope ladder and beloved weaponry. Anyone carrying out the most cursory search would have uncovered everything. Ahead I could hear him chatting unconcernedly to Neil. Within the hour, he would hack Neil to death and leave him in a pool of blood. But right now he was the very image of your average hail-fellow-well-met. He really did fool everyone.

On entering the administration block, Neil and Iain relaxed in Neil's small office. McCulloch steered me into a larger room across the corridor and busied himself unpacking the carrying box with its rope ladder, hatchet and several knives, handing me a container filled with diluted paint thinner. I had suggested ammonia. When it proved unattainable, I insisted the thinner was diluted to avoid scarring and tested the solution on myself. It created a burning sensation but no scarring, more like an irritant.

He told me to disable Neil. From the carrying box, he lifted two army-style belts, each fitted with two sheaths and two daggers, the buckles of the belts emblazoned with 'Gott Mit Uns' (God With Us) insignia. McCulloch was obsessed with German militaria. I'm convinced that if he had access to them, McCulloch would've decked us both out in Waffen-SS uniforms.

I entered the office and immediately took out the disabling spray and squirted it in Neil's face. He leapt to his feet and, as I grappled with him, we both stumbled into the corner, where I tried to pin him.

PERDITION

My most vivid memory, as we struggled, was looking into his face and not understanding why he wasn't looking at me. He was staring over my head beyond me, almost transfixed by something behind me, his eyes bulging, his jaw dropped and his face a mask of fear and horror. What was transfixing Neil was McCulloch, hatchet in hand, raining savage head blows to Iain Simpson, still seated and defenceless. Shards of Iain's skull were later found embedded in McCulloch's clothing.

Despite my effort to pinion Neil in the corner, he broke my hold and raced for the open door. Startled and already depressed by the shambolic affair, I turned but saw no one. I walked towards the door and immediately fell over Iain's legs, his upper body concealed by the desk. I fell heavily into a collection of gardening tools. As I attempted to rise, Iain turned and slashed out with a knife. Grabbing the blade, I felt it cut me. There ensued a violent struggle, with Iain repeatedly trying to slash my hands. Reaching blindly behind me, I grabbed a garden fork and twice struck him, the blows catching him in the back as we twisted and turned on the floor, our legs entangled. Iain was bleeding heavily from hatchet blows and a thumb was almost severed.

After the blows to the back, he fell forward and lay still. During the fight with Iain, I glimpsed McCulloch kneeling astride Neil in the darkened corridor and heard him scream, 'Help me with this one.' I ignored his call, still recovering from the exchange with Iain Simpson. At one point, I saw McCulloch rain down vertical blows on the figure beneath him.

Struggling to rise and disentangle my legs from Iain's form, I felt a sharp blow to the head and immediately thought it was the door edge. Later in custody, a police escort said McCulloch had lashed out at me for ignoring his cry to help him with Neil. I walked shakily away from Iain's prone form, only to trip over Neil lying still in the unlit corridor. McCulloch led me through a heavy wooden door into an adjoining corridor saying, 'Stand there.'

The hatchet still dangling in his hand he re-entered the unlit corridor and office area, closing the heavy door behind him. Shaken and bleeding from the head injury, I can't be sure how long I stood there.

The heavy wooden door opened and McCulloch reappeared carrying Neil's keys and an axe, three to four feet long, the sort used in fires. There was no sign of the hatchet. When I left the venue of the escape, both Iain and Neil were down and seriously injured, but alive. I believe McCulloch re-entered the corridor/office area to finish both men off. He didn't need keys, as all the exits were open. He didn't need a fire axe because he already had an array of weapons. He entered that area purposely, to kill both witnesses.

When McCulloch emerged, he led me from the administration block, passed the hospital garage and on to the fence area. He calmly and patiently secured the rope ladder, covered the barbed wire with sacking and sent me over, passing the fire axe to me through the bars. He then scaled the fence himself, unaided.

Dropping onto a railway track, we reached the nearby road across fields. On the road I was told to lie prone, a victim of an accident. After some minutes, a large, dark Volvo came down the incline at speed. McCulloch, in a fake uniform, signalled the vehicle to stop. The driver, possibly not seeing me on the unlit road, ignored the signal and raced to within inches of hitting me. I smelled the smoke from its exhaust and felt grit thrown up by its tyres strike me in the face as it sped on. Badly shaken by the experience, I rose, only to be told to lie down again because another vehicle was approaching – a small, mustard-coloured car.

This time, the ruse worked and the driver slowed and stopped. But almost immediately, a police vehicle with two officers aboard arrived, stopping about sixty yards away. As one officer approached me, I saw McCulloch suddenly attack the second officer with what could have been a dagger or a truncheon. My intention had been to drop the fire axe by the roadside and claim I was an accident victim. But seeing McCulloch launch an immediate attack, I abandoned that strategy, simply raising the fire axe as a warning gesture to the oncoming officer. PC George Taylor did not hesitate and ignored the warning, immediately launching himself at me and grabbing the axe handle. With his superior size and strength, he literally swung me from side to side like a rag doll, trying to shake me free of my hold on the remaining length of the axe handle.

PERDITION

I was suddenly aware of McCulloch's presence as he leapt at George Taylor. Glad to be free of the fray, I relinquished my hold on the axe and raced to secure the police vehicle where I was confronted by PC Gillies who was frantically radioing for assistance. I drew a dagger and, keeping about six feet between us, not wanting to invite another close quarter struggle, I repeatedly ordered him to stop radioing his position. After some moments, when he appeared to be in a state of panic, he ceased calling, turned and raced down the road. I made no effort to stop him; a getaway vehicle was secure.

Turning back to the fight between McCulloch and George Taylor, it appeared to have ceased and I last saw PC Taylor lurch, drunkenly, in the direction of Carstairs Junction. At that point I did not know that he had been fatally stabbed. McCulloch took over the vehicle and raced it away and passed the State Hospital, while I attempted to transmit broken fragments of calls, hoping to confuse police communications.

At some point distant to the hospital, McCulloch lost control of the vehicle. It swayed wildly from side to side and then leapt off the road, nose diving into what looked like a deep irrigation ditch. I was immediately catapulted through the shattered windscreen and over the bonnet, landing a few yards from the crashed vehicle. I may have been semi-conscious for some minutes but, as I tried to stand, I immediately fell down. This occurred a number of times. I seemed to lack any sense of balance. From the roadway above, I could hear McCulloch shouting, 'Help me with the prisoner,' trying to pass himself off as a policeman. Still bleeding from the head wound, now showered with smashed windscreen splinters and my sense of balance worryingly impaired, I tried to think rationally. Still on hands and knees, I drew the dagger and plunged it into the earth ahead of me time after time, dragging myself to it until I had escaped from the ditch and made my way to the road above.

Emerging onto the road, my first sight was of a thick-set young man – Mr Lennon – bearing down upon me. Believing myself to be incapable of offering meaningful resistance and in the circumstances oblivious to the fact that I was still clutching a dagger, a fight did ensue with Mr Lennon. To my continuing regret and shame, he suffered incredibly severe chest injuries, which would have proved fatal but for his stamina and the skill of the surgeons who treated him. I have only fragments of memory of the confrontation but recollect screaming at him to 'Stay down' as he tried to rise. The occupants of two vehicles witnessed the affray, though I have no recollection of their presence. Ahead of me, I saw McCulloch assault another man (Jack McAlroy), who was clearly terrified.

As I collapsed on to the seat of yet another hijacked vehicle, the enormity of that awful night of needless and insane violence welled up inside me and I was violently sick, retching again and again. It felt as though my very soul was in revolt against the sheer horror of what must have occurred. Nothing was ever meant to end like this. The long, lazy halcyon summer days of 1976 had turned into a Wagneresque nightmare of shattered dreams and grotesque, maniacal butchery. Outside, the night looked black and dreich and depressing, as McCulloch engaged upon yet another reckless drive southwards.

Suddenly, the vehicle slowed to the roadside and I was told to get out because a roadblock was ahead. McCulloch led me down a steep banking to a stretch of water – the Clyde? – and then on into the icy cold water. A short distance from the opposite bank, with McCulloch already ashore, I lost my footing on the gravel bed and floundered, immersed in the cold. Unable to regain my footing, I screamed for McCulloch to get me out. For what seemed an interminable time, he just stood there, not moving, casually and almost speculatively assessing whether or not to rescue me from the water. Finally, almost leisurely, he reversed the fire axe and held out the helve for me to grasp. Did he at any point contemplate raising it and simply burying the axe head in me? It's possible – by his lights, I was already dead anyway.

From the very outset, McCulloch had claimed that anyone faced with a knife threat would not resist and would immediately cooperate. Well, the events of that night had demonstrated how utterly fallacious that notion was because at every turn there was resistance, and people had been injured. As McCulloch led the way to a random farmhouse, I resolved to overcome that notion by adopting a more rational, if extreme, deterrent. McCulloch forced his entry into a kitchen area where he struggled with the home owner, while I entered a living room and in retrospect must have presented an appalling sight: my head and hands bloodied and me half-drowned from the nearby river. A collection of children were gathered fearfully around their mother, television blaring a St Andrew's Day Scottish music programme, a peaceful family evening's television rudely disturbed.

I demanded the farmer's gun on the rationale that only a suicidal madman would resist a gun threat whereas most people during the night's horrific drive seemed utterly impervious to a knife threat and had suffered injury as a consequence. Fortunately, however, probably realising that the net was closing, McCulloch decided to abandon the farmhouse without further violence, only demanding the keys to the farmer's car, the third vehicle hijacked.

As the car sped down the motorway I glanced nervously at McCulloch several times. His features were absolutely rigid, deathly white and set in stone. He had been almost silent all night, never a word wasted and at times almost oblivious to my existence in the seat beside him. I had never known fear or nervousness in the relationship and this was a new experience. At one utterly mad moment, watching the tarmac on the road race by outside, I contemplated opening the car door and simply throwing myself from the vehicle. I was trying to gauge the chances of escaping death and/or serious injury were I to adopt such a ridiculous strategy, desperate as it was. As the concrete bases of succeeding flyovers hurtled towards me, I became increasingly convinced that at some point McCulloch, without word or warning, would simply aim the car at one of them, killing us both instantaneously and, oddly, there was a quiet feeling of equanimity when I considered the possibility, a sense of fatalism. And then suddenly, as if waking from the seductive peace of fatalism or rebelling against it, I became desperate to arrive at Carlisle, for I had determined to leave the car. I just wanted to get away from McCulloch and his roadmap to mayhem.

The journey ended when we came to a large roundabout on the outskirts of Carlisle. Attempting to take it at high speed, McCulloch lost control of the car and it skidded crazily off the main drag and shot up the side of a grass banking, stopping momentarily before plunging into a meadow below it. As he raced from the vehicle, he screamed at me to get into the car, having identified his fourth getaway vehicle. The young driver was ordered out but had the presence of mind to grab the ignition keys as he went. The car contained the driver's friend and a couple in the rear. McCulloch sat there staring stupidly at the dashboard, realising that the vital ignition keys were missing. His getaway had gone away and now he was trapped. His big event, his big, violent statement, was now only a whimper of surrender.

Later in the car returning me to Lanark police office, I heard them laughing that while in custody at Carlisle, McCulloch had evacuated his bowels while being questioned. He had literally shat himself. So much for the SS nut and Hitler fan!

Suddenly, the crowded roundabout was descended upon by uniformed policemen and cars with blue flashing lights while lethal looking guns were levelled at the interior of the car and its occupants. Good sense prevailed and no one fired; had they done so, it is almost certain bullets would have passed through McCulloch and myself and killed the couple sitting, trapped, in the rear. Almost with a sense of relief, I felt hands grasp my arm and I was pulled from the front passenger seat and surrounded by other officers, before being led to a police car and driven directly to Carlisle police office to await collection by Scottish police.

25

AFTERMATH

While the escapers sped south, big, brave George Taylor, the Carstairs village bobby, was being rushed to the Law Hospital at Carluke, but doctors were unable to save him. He had suffered severe head and chest injuries. Back in the State Hospital, Neil McLellan and Iain Simpson were already dead. Three months later at the High Court in Edinburgh, McCulloch admitted murdering all three victims and Mone pleaded guilty to the murder of Constable Taylor. The judge, Lord Dunpark, made history by ordering them to remain in prison until they died – the first time natural life sentences had been handed down in Scotland. Courts would much later amend the judge's rulings and fix the length of the sentences.

The prison terms raised questions as to why Mone and McCulloch had been in Carstairs. According to psychiatric reports given to the judge, both were sane at the time of the attacks and, significantly, neither would ever be returned to the State Hospital or any other psychiatric facility. In the midst of widespread fury over apparent security failings at Carstairs, a new voice entered the fray. From his Dundee home, Sonny Mone claimed he had told management that the relationship between McCulloch and his son was unhealthy. However, he said his warnings that the pair were too close had been dismissed. Had Mone senior been genuinely concerned about the influence of McCulloch, or was he a mere publicity seeker? Time would tell in a terrible and dramatic way, because the aftermath of the escape would drag on.

Meanwhile, most wondered the real reason behind the escape. It is a question that has never been answered until now. According to Mone, he was being considered for a move away from Carstairs. McCulloch, a control freak, became paranoid at the prospect of losing his paramour and concluded the only way he could be sure of retaining his hold was to escape and take Mone with him. Mone, vulnerable, weak and easily led, went along with the plan, never sure up until the final week whether it would actually go ahead. As with Reid and MacDougall four and a half years earlier, the runaways had carefully organised how to get out of Carstairs, but failed to make detailed plans of where to go once they were over the hospital fence.

McCulloch, the younger of the two but leader of the pair, had headed south knowing most police reinforcements would probably arrive from the north and from the Glasgow area. He knew Mone had family in the English Midlands, in London and in Ireland, and having already had his gift rebuffed by a relative in England may have decided to try crossing the Irish Sea. Mone says McCulloch had not discussed any likely destination: 'His chief priority, I'd say, was putting distance between himself and Carstairs, getting his five minutes of notoriety and taking me down with him.'

And if McCulloch had, as Mone states, intended making up for not getting himself headlines through the dramatic shooting at the Clydebank motel, he surely succeeded as a result of the escape. Newspapers throughout Britain used splash headlines to portray the dreadful murders. 'Carstairs: 3 Murdered' screamed the *Daily Express*. The *Daily Record* was equally blunt with 'Mad Axemen Kill Three'. In Carstairs itself, nurses protested they had lost faith in some doctors; staff actually locked out John Gotea-Loweg for a short time and workers angrily pointed out that security had been neglected. There were strike calls, the situation being calmed when the government promised a full and deep-reaching public inquiry, appointing Robert Reid to the job. When his report was eventually published, it contained some scathing criticisms of the way Carstairs hospital was run. He had questioned the escapers and concluded:

AFTERMATH

Mone presented himself as the planner of the escape but it was McCulloch's energy, his ability to make weapons and escape equipment and his skill in concealing them that made the escape possible and by making escape possible drove them to attempt it. McCulloch achieved so much so easily that they must have been tempted to think that there was nothing in which they could not succeed.

Reid drew attention to failures in search procedures that, had they been carried out, would have uncovered the escape equipment and weapons, praised the 'great courage' of Neil McLellan, revealed that at one stage there had been suggestions Iain Simpson had been in on the escape plot – something quickly dismissed – and pointed out it was more than an hour after the escape before the State Hospital alarm siren was sounded.

On the security issue, and the absence at Carstairs of an experienced and dedicated security chief, the sheriff said this:

McCulloch and Mone more than once in the course of their evidence stated that any means of detention could be subverted and that the best method of maintaining security was to search for the individual who was a security risk and not for breaches of security precautions. There is much truth in that advice but it is not easy to carry into effect. There are no patients more quick than psychopaths to complain of unfairness and inequality of treatment and nothing is more difficult to justify publicly than special restrictive measures applicable only to long term patients in an institution whose avowed purpose is therapeutic. Security must be the concern of every member of staff. It was this consideration which led the management committee to refuse to appoint a security officer. They feared that if the responsibility for security was seen to be vested in one person, many others might feel less responsible for maintaining it. This reasonable apprehension does not sufficiently take into account the fact that an important – perhaps the most important – duty of a security officer is to encourage in members of staff a feeling of personal responsibility for security.

The sheriff also revealed that two separate groups of Scientologists had offered evidence. 'The two Scientology organisations have not behaved responsibly,' he stated. 'One member posed as a patient's cousin to visit him and was given pornographic literature which he took out of the State Hospital.' Even more remarkable than an inmate acting as a pornography dealer was that the Scientologists had asked the patient to hand over money.

Among a series of proposals the sheriff put forward were: more random searches of patients and any boxes carried by them; better supervision in the woodworking department; the erection of more fencing; the installation of alarms that would go off if anyone tried climbing or cutting fencing; more checks of visitors; the removal of patients' radios that could be tuned to police and internal hospital frequencies; and the appointment of a security officer. The fact remained, though, that yet again the stable door was being closed too late.

While he was in Perth prison, Mone was visited by his father and he would later tell the *News of the World* what transpired at the meeting. He said Sonny asked him to use prison contacts to supply him with a gun because he wanted to shoot dead eight family members including his second wife Mary, to whom he'd been married for twenty years at the time, their daughters and his own mother. Sonny had become so jealous at the infamy of his son following the escape that he craved even greater notoriety. He would never descend to those depths but he came near in December 1978, when he sadistically murdered three women in a Dundee flat. Jailed for life he was fatally stabbed at Craiginches prison, Aberdeen in January 1983.

In jail, Mone became skilled in producing braille books for the blind. He has been allowed an occasional, escorted day out, but there are presently no plans for his release. Previous hopes that he might be freed on licence have been dashed. Prisoner number 7406, he now goes by the name James Smith. To the surprise of many and anger of even more, McCulloch was released on life licence in 2013 and set up home with a divorced mother-of-three in Mone's former hometown, Dundee.

AFTERMATH

Since the escape, Carstairs has undergone a major revamp, costing close to £90 million, reducing the number of patient places to a maximum of 140 and seeing all women inmates transferred to other psychiatric establishments. In effect, a brand new hospital has been constructed with many of the original buildings demolished. The new set-up provides a remarkable range of luxury facilities for both patients and staff including sparkling new wards, outside gymnasiums, a pet therapy centre and an aviary. Visitors to Carstairs say the new institution is the envy of the rest of the NHS and the prison service, both of which frequently have to operate in antiquated buildings with failing equipment. But whether the security lessons of the 1976 escape have finally been learned remains to be seen.

26

A GENTLE MAN

All murder is wicked. The very act is a breach of God's Commandments. But can there be any killing more dreadful than one committed in any of God's houses? On 29 December 1170, the Archbishop of Canterbury, Thomas Becket, was slaughtered in his Cathedral by four knights who believed, probably wrongly, that they were carrying out the wishes of Becket's one-time friend King Henry II. After his death, Becket became a saint, his name venerated throughout Europe, and even today the spot where he died is regarded with great reverence.

Few, apart from his family and friends, remember the name of Alexander McGraw who was slaughtered just over 800 years later. But this gentle man, aged eighty-eight, holds much in common with the Archbishop. Both were devout, each prayed daily to God for others and both were foully struck down in church. Just as it did for Thomas Becket, heaven holds a place for Alexander McGraw. Just as hell beckoned for Reginald Fitzurse, Hugh de Morville, William de Tracy and Richard le Breton, who carried out Becket's murder, so it does for Lawson Imrie, killer of kindly old Alexander. The needless deaths of these two men, left lying in their own blood, shocked and horrified. However, while the murder of Becket was inevitable once the four knights believed they had been given encouragement by King Henry, that of the pensioner in an Edinburgh church could have been avoided. His killer had been freed from a mental hospital and allowed to walk the streets of the capital city.

There was one more similarity between the two slayings. The

foursome achieved notoriety for the remainder of their lives. Imrie too wanted fame. After he was arrested, he told stunned detectives, 'I wanted to get myself in the papers.'

Alexander McGraw – 'Sandy' to friends – had been a pillar of St Andrew's Roman Catholic Church in Belford Road, Edinburgh, since the end of the First World War, when he was in his late twenties. There was rarely a day when he was not to be seen pottering about, carrying out odd jobs or simply sitting quietly at the rear of the church deep in prayer. His was a familiar face to a succession of parish priests, including Father Kiernan, who was in charge of the church one morning in September 1977 when Sandy had made his way along Belford Road to join other worshippers at Mass. That afternoon, the priest went back into the church expecting to find it empty, but what he saw horrified him. Sprawled half in the aisle and half in a pew lay Sandy McGraw. Blood was running from his mouth and he had curled himself around a floor kneeler. He was unconscious but breathing and Father Kiernan ran to phone for help, telling an operator at ambulance control, 'I think he's had a heart attack.' Paramedics raced to the scene and were worried by the condition of the old man. He was rushed to hospital where nurses began removing his clothing and discovered their patient had been stabbed in the stomach.

Sandy was in a bad way. While hospital staff fought to save him, Father Kiernan led daily prayers for him. But neither the priest's devotion nor the skill of doctors and nurses could prevent his death four days later. Now the attack in the church had become a murder investigation. Detectives knew their task would be difficult. The victim hadn't spoken before he died and, although a handful of other parishioners had popped in and out of the church, some of them noticing Sandy, none confessed to seeing anything suspicious. Furthermore, no one could think of a solitary reason why someone so harmless and well-liked as Sandy should have been targeted.

Then came an odd development. Three days after Sandy's death, a journalist received a telephone call from a man who refused to give his name but said he had information about a serious matter. Asked what he was talking about, the caller would only disclose that it concerned an incident in Edinburgh and he was responsible. 'You want to tell me about it?' asked the journalist, who was told, 'I want £500.' The reporter said, 'I'll need to know more,' but the stranger at the other end of the line was refusing to say more, other than promising to ring again.

Police were told and arrangements made for any further calls from the same man to be recorded. When he did ring, his price had been upped to £2,500 but he was quick to claim, 'The money's not for me, I want it for my mother. But I've got a real story for you.' The journalist pressed for details of the matter for which the payment was being demanded and, when the caller hesitated, asked him outright, 'Is this about the murder of the old gentleman in the church?' The reply was, 'The man is dead. Stabbed in the stomach. I felt it going in.'

A check by telephone engineers of all calls made to the journalist's office revealed the caller had been ringing from an area of Edinburgh with a '556' code. Further examination of telephone records narrowed the search down to a hostel in Northumberland Street run by a social work department for men suffering from mental illnesses. When detectives called, the door was opened by Imrie, who then disappeared but was later arrested in a nearby street. 'We know it's you who made phone calls to the newspaper,' said an officer.

Imrie told a detective inspector he had been to St Andrew's Church previously and had seen Sandy there, praying. On the day he attacked the pensioner he had bought a sheath knife in Edinburgh and, after walking around, decided to visit the church again. His victim was there, praying in a rear pew.

> He looked pathetic. I was looking for somebody to rob. I just grabbed him. He stood up and I stuck the knife in his stomach. He said, 'Oh God, he has killed me.' He was still standing and leaning on a chair. I never meant to kill him. It was an unfortunate accident. I only meant to wound him to get myself in the papers.

Then he asked, 'How did you know it was me that made the phone calls?' Imrie accompanied detectives to the church. It was closed, but he was able to point through a window to the very spot where he had seen Sandy half-kneeling and half-sitting in the back row. He was charged with murder and also with starting fires in another Edinburgh church.

But it emerged that Imrie had been held at the Edinburgh Royal Hospital as an inpatient in 1973 after he was diagnosed as suffering from mental illness and questions began to be asked as to why he was allowed to stay in the hostel, where he had total freedom to wander the crowded Edinburgh streets whenever he wanted. In 1975, security on him had been relaxed, even though hospital staff had complained he was aggressive and sometimes threatening. He was discharged and told he could stay with his family on condition he turned up at the hospital each day for treatment. Then doctors approved his move to the hostel, where there were no restrictions on his movements.

In December, at the High Court in Edinburgh, Imrie denied murder. A social worker said Imrie had asked him how much a newspaper might pay for his life story and wondered if he might get as much as £2,000. Another social worker said, 'Imrie's desire to be famous was a constant thing. The idea of being famous was very attractive to him.' The jury convicted him of culpable homicide. A psychiatrist said although he suffered from a psychotic illness, he was sane and fit to plead, but he added, 'He should be detained in the special security wing at the State Hospital because he has dangerous, violent and criminal tendencies.' And the judge agreed. After the case, questions were asked about the wisdom of Imrie being allowed to live at the hostel and whether psychiatrists responsible for him had got it wrong because, had he been ordered to remain in the Edinburgh Royal, then old-age pensioner Sandy McGraw would not have had his long life ended by a lunatic's knife.

Eleven years later, innocent blood would once again stain the floor of a hallowed place. This time the victim was pious, caring, middle-aged nun Sister Josephine Ogilvie. It is difficult to portray the disgust, anger and revulsion her death provoked because, not content with simply taking her life, her twisted killer mutilated her body in a manner that is difficult to comprehend. If any consolation could be got from the slaughter of Sister Josephine in May 1988, it was the fact that she mercifully died from a heart attack before some of the sordid desecration of her body was committed. This delightful lady had chosen to offer her life to God, but it was a sick drug addict who took it. The name of this reviled and loathsome creature was Mark Reynolds, another of the horrors to be sent to reside in the plush, comfortable surroundings of Carstairs State Hospital.

Thirty-five years before she died, Sister Josie had become a member of the Sacred Heart, a religious Roman Catholic Order dedicated to teaching. She was loved by the girls she taught, their parents, her fellow nuns and everyone lucky enough to come into her company. When most other woman of fifty-nine were thinking of retirement, she had no desire to call it a day. She loved her work and she loved her church.

She had been in the pastoral care centre at St Mary's Roman Catholic Cathedral in Aberdeen when a scruffy, stinking, shaven-headed stranger, high on LSD, arrived asking to see one of her colleagues. Politely, bespectacled Sister Josephine told the stranger the nun he had asked for was not there. His response was to launch a totally unprovoked, terrible assault. Using his fists and feet, he pummelled the grey-haired nun and she screamed, tried to protect herself begging him to stop. When she fell, he stamped on her body, then slashed her with scissors and tried to throttle her. By then she was dead, although that did not stop the blitz on her lifeless body as blows continued to rain down. The maniacal assault only stopped when the cowardly attacker heard the sounds of approaching feet.

Father Colin Stewart was returning to his office in the cathedral. He was about to open the door when it was pushed shut from the inside. The priest instantly concluded a burglar was inside and ran for help from a caretaker. The men looked outside and saw a young man, naked to the waist and covered in blood, fleeing down a fire escape. Father Stewart ran back and discovered the dead remains of Sister Josie. Police arrested her killer within hours. They found Reynolds, aged twenty-five, the nun's blood still on his face and hands, sitting in lodgings, enjoying the leftovers of a takeaway curry. 'I have done a terrible thing and I don't want to talk about it,' he said. He was hauled away, charged with murder and remanded to the city's Craiginches jail where he told a prison officer, 'I woke up this morning and realised I was a killer and had strangled someone.' Many features of the tragedy were hard to understand, the most obvious being why anybody would want to kill and defile the body of a nun.

What was baffling, too, was that Reynolds came from a staunch Catholic family, decent law-abiding people. Yet something had snapped. He had turned against all the teachings of the Church, wearing a reversed crucifix around his neck to symbolise his devotion to Satan and his works and even believing during lengthy sessions on LSD that he was the Devil. He became a devotee of the ninja, vicious mercenaries who carried out assassinations centuries ago in feudal Japan from the fifteenth to the seventeenth century. The secretive ninja, sometimes called Shinobi, were the equivalent of modern-day contract killers. The services they offered ranged from espionage and sabotage to infiltrating organisations and wealthy families in order to root out secrets and ultimately commit murder. The ninja were largely confined to one small area of Japan but have in modern times been popularised in films and television shows. Reynolds' obsession with the ninja extended to buying books and video films about their exploits and even taking to wearing the baggy, black trousers and blouses that were their trademark. Acquaintances of Reynolds told how he would sometimes sit for hours in the black garb, mumbling what he believed were ninja oaths of allegiance.

When Reynolds appeared at the High Court in Aberdeen, he pleaded guilty to the reduced charge of culpable homicide on the grounds of diminished responsibility. Psychiatrists said he had been diagnosed as schizophrenic six years earlier and was suffering from mental illness. Members of the public, who included Reynolds' mother Stella, listened appalled as the advocate depute described the injuries suffered by Sister Josie. He said she had fought fiercely for her life and suffered eight fractured ribs and a fractured spine: 'She was in a condition expected to be found in a motor traffic accident. The actual cause of death, perhaps mercifully, was by cardiac arrest caused by injuries to the front of her neck which fractured her larynx,' he said. Reynolds was ordered to be detained in Carstairs without limit of time.

A church might occasionally be the setting for brutal, even deadly, crime. But who could expect police scenes of crime officers to be concentrating on a funeral parlour? In 1968, John Prentice from Glasgow was sent to the State Hospital without limit of time for the culpable homicide of a woman aged forty-nine who was the victim of his sexually motivated attack. He spent sixteen years in Carstairs before being released. But was that too early? Within two months, he attacked another woman, this time in the funeral parlour where she worked.

At the High Court in Edinburgh, it was said he turned up at the parlour claiming he wanted to arrange a funeral for his dead sister, but then he leapt on the sixty-year-old victim who suffered a head injury when he pushed her to the floor. As she lay helpless and pleading for help, he ordered her to take her clothes off and indecently assaulted her. Before running off, he took £100 from the safe. Prentice, thirty-four, was jailed for six years.

27

THE FAMILY MAN

David Anderson doted on his family. But, for him, it was not enough to provide them with only the best. He wanted neighbours and friends to see the pride he felt at being able to give them the comfort and happiness he was convinced they deserved. It all meant that, to those around him, he was the man who had everything, a gentle, kind, caring husband and father whose family was his entire world. What made him all the more remarkable was that behind his mask of satisfaction lay a deeply troubled and tragic past, one that might have driven others to despair. But the face of the forty-five-year-old driving instructor gave no hint of the demons that lurked deep within his mind – devils that struggled to emerge to wreak havoc and desolation.

Throughout his life, he had fought depression and illness. His father and sister had taken their own lives in separate incidents; his mother, who he worshipped, had died after being struck down with cancer and one of his own sons had been diagnosed with leukaemia, succumbing to the disease in 1965. David himself had tried to commit suicide when he was just twelve years old. It was an episode from which he had never fully recovered, its memory mingling with those of the other tragedies to leave him more vulnerable than most to anxiety and the fear of being unable to cope with the simple day-to-day problems that beset any average family.

Yet as he calmly guided his pupils about the streets of Edinburgh, there were many who envied what David Anderson had achieved. Were his success and the apparent ease with which he faced life due to his passionately held belief in God and the teachings of Jesus Christ? Certainly religion was important and he owed God thanks for presenting him with his wife Dorothy. The couple had met at a Christian mission and in the twenty years they had been together had produced three children. Although one son had sadly died, their daughter, Elaine Dorothy, and a second son, Scott Robert, survived. As the calendar turned over into January 1972, however, time was running out for the Anderson family.

There were no signs of clouds on the horizon for bubbly, pretty Elaine, aged sixteen and attracting the glances of young men passing the family home in Edinburgh's Portobello district. Estate agents would describe the house as 'desirable' and 'sought after'. It had set David Anderson back around £5,000, and he and Dorothy had thought long and hard about moving from the comparatively modest council house in another part of the city where they had raised their children.

Shifting to the new home meant forking out for fresh furnishings, decoration, taking on a mortgage. Then there were the inevitable bills for making sure their children were happy. Both were at good schools. Elaine was a pupil at James Gillespie's High School for Girls, founded with a legacy from a leading city tobacco merchant and famous for one of its former pupils, Muriel Spark, who based the lead character in her sensationally successful novel *The Prime of Miss Jean Brodie* on one of her teachers.

Although Elaine had taken a leading part in the annual school pantomime and was a keen member of the hockey team, her real aspiration was to follow the author into a writing career. One of her pieces for the school magazine had been well received and it reflected the importance of religion and family life to the Andersons and the growing awareness of a teenage girl embracing adolescent independence. Entitled 'Let's Love One Another', her article, in the form of a letter to her mother and father, read:

> Dear parents, I have noticed recently that there is some unfairness in our treatment of each other and I as a future enfranchised citizen of the world would like to air my grievances. Firstly I would like to

point out that though the Bible does say 'Honour Thy Father and Thy Mother' it also includes 'And parents rouse not your children into anger'. I think the meaning is quite clear. Secondly, I appreciate having a room to myself. I think it is good to have somewhere that belongs to me, a place where I can be private. But that's half the trouble – I'm not. You see the notice on my door means what it says, 'Leave Me In Peace'. Still on the subject of my room, Mum I'm sorry about the mess. But when you tidy it I can never find anything. And Dad please, letters that have my name written on the envelope are meant for me not for general entertainment. After all I don't read the gas bill do I? To sum up, what I would like to say is 'Finally my brethren let us love one another and I'm sure that way we'll have a nice, happy family.' Your loving daughter, Elaine.

There were high hopes, too, for Scott, who his parents had enrolled at Edinburgh's prestigious Royal High School, founded in 1128 and the first in Britain to be designated a high school. Likeable and good-looking, the boy had everything to look forward to.

With David, Dorothy, Elaine and Robert lived Dorothy's mother, eighty-six-year-old Sarah Smith, who, in the twilight of her life, found joy in her hopes for her grandchildren. Despite her age, she remained alert and intelligent. So here was a family that was an image of middle-class contentment and ease, the picture completed by a new car and now there was a further addition to be parked in the driveway. As a sixteenth birthday gift, David had taken out a loan and bought the daughter he so loved a motor scooter. It was her pride and joy. But there was a cost for all of this and it was a price no family man could ever expect to have to pay.

As the bills began to mount, the old banshees once again surfaced to torment David Anderson and wail their song of melancholy. As if to plunge him even further down the ladder of despair, he was hit by a bout of influenza, weakening his resistance to attacks of despondency. Night after night, he lay awake, unable to sleep as he desperately tried to work out a solution to his troubles. When one came, it had a sting in the tail. He decided to follow the example of his father and sister by committing suicide. It seemed an easy way out, but as he pondered over the consequences he came to the terrible realisation that by killing himself he would leave his wife and children open to awful embarrassment. The fact that he could not pay his way was bound to emerge. There was every likelihood Dorothy would be left destitute and, unable to afford the mortgage, his family would be forced to quit their home and his children their schools.

Then something in the mind of David Anderson snapped. His grotesque solution came in the early hours one morning and, with it, an insane belief that he could not afford to delay carrying it out. He decided to kill himself. However he was sure his suicide would heap shame on the family he so loved. How could he spare them that humiliation? The answer was to kill them first. And so, soundlessly he rose from his bed, crept downstairs, disconnected the telephone and then, taking a hammer, set about his terrible task.

Scott was battered into oblivion as he lay in bed. Elaine was smashed about the head and body more than a dozen times. Dorothy somehow survived a hail of blows before blessed unconsciousness took her from the nightmare of pain, terror and bewilderment. Aged sleeping Sarah literally never knew what hit her. The bloodlust was not yet over. The killer then slashed his wrists in what was intended to be the final act of his appalling plot.

Help eventually came in time to save Dorothy and her husband, although many months later she was still helpless and paralysed in an Edinburgh hospital, struggling to understand how, in a few dreadful moments, her world had collapsed at the hands of the man who had both fathered her children and then taken their lives and that of their grandmother. The same doctors who fought to save her, now battled to preserve the life of the killer and when he recovered he was sent to Saughton prison, Edinburgh, to await his trial while psychiatrists tried to work out what had triggered the triple tragedy.

By the time he appeared before Lord Leechman at the city High Court, Anderson had calmly described to relatives who visited him in jail and to other inmates why he had destroyed three lives and almost a fourth. He told family members, 'I just couldn't leave Dorothy and the children to face the disgrace that would follow when I killed myself.' And a fellow remand prisoner said Anderson had revealed to him:

> I loved my family, they were everything to me and I could not bear the thought of what would be said behind their backs about the husband and father who committed suicide. They would have to move home, the kids give up their schools and there just wouldn't be enough money to go round. I often wish we'd stayed in our council house, because it was only after we moved that the money problems started. God will judge me for what I have done.

The prisoner added: 'What's really scary is that it is just impossible to believe when you talk to this man that he was accused of killing his family. He is such a nice, quiet guy who trusts God to see him through all of this.'

Anderson remained in prison for just over three months. He was formally examined by consultant psychiatrists whose task was to report what they believed his state of mind to have been on that terrible night. They needed to discover whether he was a cold, calculating, uncaring murderer or a man stricken by a mental illness that left him unable to differentiate between right and wrong. He faced three charges of murder and one of attempting to murder Dorothy, but, while agreeing he had carried out the attacks, he denied the charges, claiming instead that at the time he was insane and not responsible for his actions. Some believe that anyone who kills is insane, and the jury had little doubt that this was the case as far as Anderson was concerned. Acting on an instruction from the judge, they acquitted him of murder and attempted murder and decided he was insane. One of the doctors who investigated his case said Anderson's mental illness could be treated if he was in hospital, and Lord Leechman sent him to Carstairs without limit of time. And so the man once cocooned in love would fight his greatest battle to regain his sanity surrounded by strangers.

Fear of his children becoming the victims of humiliation had led Anderson to take their lives. It was a similar thought that caused Michael John Bagot to slay the little daughters he loved with an all-consuming passion. In his case, he became convinced a family member was having an adulterous affair and their promiscuity would rub off on his children. Desperate to protect their innocence, he killed them. What began as a routine police inquiry turned into a horror story. Motorists travelling along the spectacular road between Fort William and Mallaig in the north west of Scotland – the world famous Road to the Isles – noticed a man behaving oddly. He seemed confused and bewildered, according to what a caller told the police who, in the interests of the stranger's safety, decided to find him and talk to him. It was early January 1977, cold and dark, and officers worried in case the stranger was ill and needed help. They began their search, but did not have far to go, discovering him in the early hours at Achdalieu, just outside Fort William and scene of a famous battle in 1654. 'My car broke down and I'm looking for it,' said the wanderer, who told them he was Michael John Bagot from Brentwood, Essex. He was more than 500 miles from home and seemed distraught and upset so police took him to their station at Fort William.

Officers based in that remote area were used to dealing with strangers who for one reason or another had lost their way. But none were prepared for what came next. 'I have murdered my two daughters,' said the small, neatly dressed visitor. Police raced back to where they had found Bagot and soon traced his car, fifty yards from the roadside. A plastic hose had been taped to the exhaust pipe. It led inside the motor and on the back seat lay the dead bodies of eight-year-old Tina Louise and her sister Lisa Victoria, aged just six.

A search uncovered a briefcase and inside was a lengthy document in which Bagot had written of his torment. It said he had intended to kill himself and amounted to a confession to be found after he was dead. 'I have committed the most terrible crime that any man can commit and for which there can never be a justifiable excuse,' his story began. 'I love my two daughters with all my heart yet I have been frightened to show that love because of the fear that one day they would be taken away from me.'

Bagot, aged thirty-three, was separated from his wife Karen, who looked after the children at her home in Lancashire. He said he was worried that the girls might be affected as a result of knowing about the affair the relative was having and think this was normal behaviour. He lived in Essex, where he held a senior position in the family nautical instruments business. A fortnight after Christmas, he collected Tina Louise and Lisa Victoria, promising to take them to Scotland to see the snow. Just outside Fort William, he linked the hose to the exhaust pipe and the youngsters died from breathing in the carbon monoxide fumes. 'How does a man write about what I have to write about, when he is not sure whether he is sane or insane?' he had written in the document in the briefcase.

He was charged with murder. While he waited for his trial, two psychiatrists examined him and, although both said he was fit to plead, they added that they believed he had not been sane when he killed the children and that he had tried to kill himself twice. One said:

> He was obsessed with the idea that his daughters might grow up to be promiscuous. He intended to die with the children. He was in such a state of despair for his children and himself he tried to commit suicide and take his daughters with him, but, as often happens, the homicidal element succeeded and the suicidal one failed.

The jury went along with a recommendation of the judge, Lord Macdonald, by finding him not guilty of murder through insanity, but that he had killed the girls. By a strange quirk of fate, at almost the same moment in March 1977 as the judge at the High Court in Inverness was ordering Bagot to be detained at Carstairs without limit of time, another judge in Lancashire was granting Karen a divorce on the grounds that the marriage had irretrievably broken down.

And so, as one wife had decided she could no longer live with her husband, there were many outsiders and even friends who had been taken aback by the support shown a year earlier by Carol Coston for her husband Sidney. She told friends she loved and longed to be with him, even though he had picked up their baby son by his feet and smashed the child's head on the floor. It was an act so callous that it horrified and shocked anyone who knew the family because Sid, devoutly religious and a one-time corporal in the Royal Army Veterinary Corps, was a loving and totally devoted husband and dad. When Carol had given birth prematurely to twins Jonathan and David eight months earlier at their home in Mosstodloch, Morayshire, Sid had skilfully and tenderly delivered the babies himself. Yet now he found himself in the dock in the High Court at Inverness accused of murdering little David. The manner of the death of the baby was all the more tragic for Sid and Carol because the couple had battled desperately to overcome money problems as they raised their five children.

They had moved to Scotland from the north of England and started a fruit and vegetable venture, the former soldier knocking on the doors of houses in Highland villages offering his wares, only for the business to crash, leaving them heavily in debt. Not one to leave others out of pocket, Sid took on work as a milkman, each week setting aside money to pay those he owed. It appeared there was nothing with which the big man could not cope. When his daughter Sian, aged six, was in danger of choking to death after swallowing a coin which lodged in her throat, the quick-thinking dad upended her to dislodge the disc before dashing off with her to hospital, where doctors and nurses had nothing but praise for him. Yet within gentle Sid, all was not well. Just a few days after saving Sian's life, the worry of that incident, of repaying creditors and of overworking suddenly led to him snapping and, in a terrible moment, killing David as the infant cried.

In the community around the family's home, there was considerable sympathy for him, an emotion that even softened the hearts of staff at Porterfield prison, Inverness, where he was held on remand to await his court appearance. Another of the children, Charles, conscious that his father was no longer at home, became convinced that the coffin holding tiny David was in fact for his dad who had died. Jail officials took the unusual step of arranging a special meeting at which Charles could see for himself his father was still alive.

At court in January 1976, Sid was found insane and unfit to plead to the charge that he murdered David. A psychiatrist said he was suffering from a mental illness for which he could not reasonably be held in a regular mental hospital. As a result he was sent 205 miles south to Carstairs without limit of time, dashing the hopes of Carol and the surviving children that they might be able to make regular visits to see him at Craig Dunain Hospital in Inverness. A friend of the family said: 'Despite what has happened, Carol and the children are absolutely resolute in that they are standing by Sid. They want him well and back home. His entire life was wound up around Carol and the kids.'

28

FREED TO KILL

Standing on the banks of glorious Loch Fyne in Argyll is one of the most spectacular and desirable hotels in Scotland. But the beautiful sixty acres of woodlands that surround nineteenth-century baronial manor Stonefield Castle were the scene of a vile and terrible murder. And the killer was a twisted sadist who had been released from Carstairs because he was thought to have been cured. Even the judge who dealt with the case demanded an investigation into why the maniac was allowed to walk free.

Lynda-Jayne Walters was a lovely, gentle fourteen-year-old schoolgirl and the apple of her mother June's eye. This kind, popular child had everything to live for. She was good-looking and bright, and her reports from Rushcliffe School told of her 'excellent attitude to life and its problems'. Lynda-Jayne would also never want for money. Dad Michael had worked hard to build up a supermarket business and was a millionaire as a result. In July 1978, he drove his wife, Lynda-Jayne and her eight-year-old brother Richard from their Nottingham home to Tarbert on the Kintyre peninsula where the family had made reservations at Stonefield Castle Hotel. They planned to walk, see local sights and relax, enjoying the luxury of the converted castle and its surrounds, and most importantly take pleasure in the company of one another.

Early in their stay, Michael and June asked the children if they wanted to join their parents on a visit to an ancient nearby crypt. It didn't interest the youngsters, who announced they would stay behind, Lynda-Jayne telling her parents she intended going for a walk in the castle grounds. The family waved her goodbye. They would never see her alive again.

When Michael and June returned from their outing in time for lunch, they found Richard in the hotel, but there was no sign of their daughter. They wondered if she had become so engrossed in her walk that she had forgotten time or if she had maybe joined up with another party of holidaymakers exploring the loch. Their concern turned to real worry when she was not back with them by early afternoon and so they began searching the hotel and surrounding area. Failing to discover any sign of her, they were joined that evening by other helpful guests and hotel staff. Meanwhile police were told that the girl was missing. Among the workers who offered to take part in the hunt for Lynda-Jayne was gardener Robert Bone Gemmill, aged thirty-one, who had originally been taken on as a part-time general handyman and kitchen porter, but his attitude so impressed management that he was offered full-time work helping to look after the grounds and even promoted to assistant gardener.

He seemed happy enough, having been married a few months earlier to a local woman who had also been on the hotel staff. However, neither she nor anyone else at the hotel knew Gemmill had a past that he wanted to keep secret. Earlier that day, he had approached his immediate boss and asked for a knife. When asked why he wanted it, his explanation seemed straightforward. 'I've lost mine,' he claimed. The man had no reason to suspect anything was wrong. He had occasionally seen Gemmill using a sheath knife to cut vegetables and Gemmill was a reliable worker who gave no cause for complaint. Soon after joining in the search he asked a senior member of the hotel management, 'If I find anything, what do you want me to do?' and was told, 'Go straight to the police and tell them.'

As the Walters family vainly waited for news, their hearts increasingly heavy with pessimism and despondency, the darkness of summer fell with still no sign of Lynda-Jayne. There was little point in stumbling around in woodland in pitch blackness and so the searchers were stood down. Next morning at first light, the hunt was resumed and when senior officers knocked at the door of June and Michael Walters' room, the couple instinctively knew the worst. The body of a girl had been discovered partially hidden beneath leaves and bushes. Michael had the wretched task of identifying the clothing and confirmed it belonged to his daughter.

Lynda-Jayne had been the victim of a terrible and frenzied attack, stabbed with a heavy knife at least a dozen times in the back and groin, at times the weapon penetrating four inches into her flesh. Now the search for a missing teenager became a murder hunt. Police checked the hotel register to see whether any guests had a criminal record but all were quickly cleared. However, when it came to investigating staff, detectives soon discovered a fact that seemed potentially highly significant. Before coming to work at Stonefield Castle, Robert Bone Gemmill had been a psychiatric in-patient at Argyll and Bute Hospital in Lochgilphead, Argyll, and was released first to work at the hotel on a day-to-day basis until his final discharge in September 1977, when he became a full-time member of staff. There was something else that made the police wonder if Gemmill knew something. As he wandered along a path through the woods surrounding the hotel accompanying two officers, his eyes darting from side to side, evidently searching for signs of the missing youngster, one policeman noticed he suddenly switched from one side of the path to the other. The officer whispered in Gaelic to a colleague that the gardener was upset about something, and later when they went back to the same spot they found Lynda-Jayne's corpse. As the hours passed, there would be even more to disturb officers.

When he was interrogated by Detective Chief Inspector Angus McLeod, a shrewd veteran of many murder inquiries, Gemmill shifted uneasily in his seat, fidgeting and excitable before blurting out, 'All right. I know you suspect me because I was at Carstairs. But I did not do it.' The officer would later say, although his assertion was disputed by lawyers acting for Gemmill, that, until that point, he had no idea Gemmill had been a patient at the State Hospital. 'I was amazed to learn this. Why was a man who had been so long in Carstairs now working at a hotel?' said the Detective Chief Inspector, who died in 2013, aged eighty-six.

The gardener was held overnight to allow more inquiries to be made into his background and when questioned early next day promptly brought the hunt for Lynda-Jayne's killer to a close. Sitting in an interview room he confessed to the Chief Inspector, 'It was me that stabbed the girl. I will tell you everything about it if you don't send me to Carstairs.' The significance of what Gemmill said was that, up until then, police had not said how the girl had died and news-papers, although aware she had been stabbed, had gone along with a police request for them not to publish this fact. They were words that condemned Gemmill, who was distressed and at one point seemed on the verge of bursting into tears. He slouched forward, his head in his hands, but suddenly, after being given a glass of water, appeared to regain control of himself and told of the last terrible moments of Lynda-Jayne:

She was walking in front of me in the drive and I did it on impulse. I stabbed her in the back with my sheath knife and pushed her into the bushes. She screamed twice. I lost my head and stabbed her all over. My clothes were dirty and I went home and changed. I admit killing the girl, but I don't want to go to Carstairs. Don't do anything to my wife for washing the clothes. She did not know anything about it. I don't know what came over me. It was all over before I realised what I had done.

After his confession – which he would later deny making – Gemmill was charged with murder. At his trial at the High Court in Oban in December that year, Gemmill pleaded not guilty. Following psychiatric evidence, the charge was reduced to one of culpable homicide on the grounds that his responsibility was diminished. During the hearing, he had a very different version of his activities. He said he was in his flat next to the hotel when he heard a scream and thought someone had been knocked down by a car:

I went out and heard another scream. I ran towards some bushes where I thought the scream came from and found a body. It was covered in leaves and grass and I cleared them away and saw it was a girl. I put my arm beneath her head to support her then turned her over and saw she was in a hell of a mess. I did not know for certain if she was alive or dead. I was physically and mentally not in a state to go for help. I was deeply shocked and horrified. I dropped the body in a fright.

My state of mind at that time was that I could not accept what had happened so I turned coward and ran. I went home to change my clothes because they were wet and muddy. I wanted to explain to my wife what I had seen but just couldn't. I couldn't bring myself to tell anyone.

What about his confession to the police? And what about another confession he made to his mother when she visited him in Barlinnie prison while he was on remand awaiting trial? They were untrue, said Gemmill – both the police and his mother had made them up.

The description of Lynda-Jayne's brutal murder was shocking, but there was worse to come when Gemmill's past was revealed: many were astounded that he had been allowed not only to be free but to work among children and young women at a hotel. Born in Drumchapel in Glasgow's east end in 1947, his parents James and Marion despaired of him, even as a youngster. He was unruly and moody and when they asked doctors to assess the extent of his intellectual disabilities, the outcome was uncertain but he was nevertheless sent to a special school. In 1962, he assaulted a girl and stole her handbag, spending a month in a remand home before being put on probation. But the experience did nothing to deter an apparent pleasure in ill-treating the opposite sex and in violence against females. The following year, after assaulting another girl as well as a mature woman, psychiatrists decided he was feeble-minded and he was sent to Lennox Castle, a mental hospital in Dunbartonshire where he appeared to respond to treatment, doctors reporting that he was a 'progressive patient'. Behind the evident improvement in his conduct, however, lay the fact that all was not well.

By 1966 while still at Lennox Castle, it was clear something was seriously wrong with the teenager because he attacked another woman. This time his victim was a young pregnant social worker who was seized and battered in the hospital grounds where Gemmill was working as a gardener. The incident would chillingly and tragically be repeated twelve years later. There seemed only one outcome if women were to be protected and that was for him to be sent to Carstairs. He spent eight years at the State Hospital, where he was a loner, preferring his own company to that of other patients. Doctors placed him in the painting department, where he seemed to enjoy solitude.

Eventually it was agreed to free him from the tight security of Carstairs. That decision alone was astonishing. But what made it even more amazing and what drew into question the whole position of the existence of the State Hospital was that Gemmill had been diagnosed as a psychopath. Carstairs did not treat psychopaths for the simple reason that the condition was regarded as untreatable. With the state in full knowledge that he was dangerous, particularly to women, unpredictable and prone to using violence, he was transferred in 1974 to the relaxed surroundings of Argyll and Bute Hospital as an in-patient. In July 1976, it was decided he was improving and given a conditional discharge, which meant he could live outside the hospital, but continue as an outpatient. By September 1977, the then Secretary of State for Scotland, Bruce Millan, acting on advice from experts, gave permission for Gemmill to be absolutely discharged from all restrictions upon his movements specified in the original order used to detain him in Carstairs, made under the Mental Health (Scotland) Act 1960. The formal discharge meant he could marry his fellow hotel worker, who told friends, 'I've never been happier. We have so much in common and love one another's company.' Ten months later, innocent, loving, beautiful Lynda-Jayne was dead.

Consultant psychiatrist Dr Hunter Gillies examined Gemmill while he was in prison following the killing. What he told the Oban court led to outrage at the fact the madman had been set free. The expert said that while Gemmill had poor literacy skills, he was articulate, able to express himself easily:

There was nothing wrong with his memory and he had no delusions or hallucinations. I found no evidence of mental disorder. In my opinion if it is proved that he did commit the murder, his actions were brought about in order to satisfy sadistic sexual urges. He is suffering from a personality disorder but the State Hospital is unwilling to accept him and he would not be fit for a mental hospital because there was no treatment for personality disorders of this type.

Gemmill's illness began to border on insanity, said Dr Gillies. What was so staggering about the doctor's evidence was that it appeared Carstairs had taken eight years to come to the conclusion that it could do nothing for or with Gemmill. Many wanted to know why a dangerous, violent man with severe mental illness had gone on to be given total freedom. After the jury had convicted Gemmill of killing the schoolgirl, it was a question to which the judge, Lord Kincraig, also wanted an answer. He said:

> Your conviction of this horrible crime raises again the question as to whether persons like you who have exhibited vicious sadistic tendencies in the past should ever be liberated and become a potential danger to innocent people.
>
> Members of the public are well entitled to doubt the wisdom and judgement of those who make such liberation possible particularly in cases where the only treatment given to these persons is a passage of time. It may be that the decisions can be justified, but it is tragic that a young life has to be destroyed. Perhaps your case and others like it will lead to a searching inquiry into the procedures which enable potential killers to be released to menace the lives of innocent people. All that this court can do is to make recommendations and I sentence you to imprisonment for life and recommend that you be detained indefinitely.

Anxious to deflect potential blame, the Scottish Office took the unusual step of making a detailed statement about an individual case, with Mr Millan admitting he had authorised Gemmill's conditional and then absolute discharges. The politician said:

> I was satisfied that Gemmill's progress was such that no further

supervision was necessary. His doctor and my medical adviser no longer considered him to be suffering from a mental disorder. I should make it clear that since Mr Gemmill was judged to be no longer suffering from mental disorder which has since been confirmed by psychiatrists who have recently examined him for the High Court and since the evidence of his conduct over a period of twelve years had led the doctors and others concerned with his case to conclude that he was no longer dangerous, it would not have been possible for me to continue his detention.

There were other victims of the tragedy. The killer's wife, for instance. The flat where she had shared a bed with Gemmill was only a few hundred yards from the spot where he slaughtered the girl. She had helped look after the Walters family and following the finding of the body had cried and sympathised with them. She had never known her husband had been a patient in Carstairs or had committed violent acts against other women. She was left heartbroken and distraught and immediately announced she was seeking a divorce. Michael Walters, who clutched a photograph of his happy, laughing family, as his daughter's killer was led off to prison, said:

> I hope that what has happened to him will put anybody else off from doing the same thing. This has been a horrible experience for all of us and we'll try to get back to pick up the threads of our lives as soon as possible.

The family would make frequent vigils to Lynda-Jayne's grave. But while her husband had at least some small comfort from knowing the killer had been given life, nothing could ease the pain of his wife. June said:

> She was the sort of daughter every parent dreams of having, lovely, kind, caring and a joy to her mother, father and brother. You can try but the words to tell how you feel never come. We had her and we lost her.

School friends were equally distraught: 'Lynda-Jayne didn't have a bad thought in her head; everybody liked her; everybody wanted her on their team.'

The story of evil Gemmill does not end there. In order to protect him from the wrath of other inmates in the prison system, he spent most of the next twenty-four years caged among rapists and paedophiles at bleak Peterhead jail in Aberdeenshire, never giving up hope of being freed again. Eventually it was decided he was no longer a threat and he joined a lengthy programme preparing him to rejoin the rest of normal society. As part of the run-up to his freedom, he was moved to Greenock jail. But it quickly became apparent that, once again, a mistake had been made. For some reason nobody could fathom, Gemmill was allowed to leave the jail and walk to a nearby swimming pool, where he swam unsupervised alongside innocent children, including girls the same age as Lynda-Jayne when he had killed her. Other Greenock inmates watched in disbelief as Gemmill would wander off to the pool carrying his towel and trunks and, enraged by the thought of a creature who might be swimming alongside their own children, telephoned the *News of the World* to complain. In 2002, the newspaper reported the fury of pressure group Mothers Against Murder and Aggression, which said that letting Gemmill out endangered the lives of children. A spokeswoman said, 'It's absolute madness. I can't believe the authorities could be so stupid as to allow a man with this type of track record back into the community.' The publicity was responsible for the killer being sent back to Peterhead. Some speculated that if his release from Carstairs had attracted the same media fury, then Lynda-Jayne would still be alive.

Just as her life had ended prematurely, however, so did that of her slayer. In 2003, Gemmill was released from prison on compassionate grounds when he was diagnosed as suffering from cancer. He died shortly after.

29

FREED TO DIE

Carstairs, the hospital for horrors, has held men and women who have committed the most heinous crimes. The idea behind incarcerating people who have committed violent crimes at Carstairs is to keep them away from the rest of society while doctors and psychiatrists work on their minds to try to cure the mental illness that has left them warped and dangerous. Occasionally these patients are released, apparently having returned to normality. But those who decide to set them free, while acting in good faith, sometimes get it wrong. Was that the case with David Little? Was the decision to grant him freedom effectively the signing of a death sentence?

As a young man growing up in Annan, Dumfriesshire, where the Scottish writer and philosopher Thomas Carlyle went to school and later taught mathematics, Davie Little fancied his good looks might well be his passport into an acting career and from there into the beds of fawning female admirers. Probably the part he would liked to have played had his dramatic aspirations worked out would have been that of the legendary Italian lover Casanova. He had a well-rehearsed collection of chat-up lines. His conversation after an initial pleasantry, however, was limited. 'Davie had his brains in his underpants,' recalled one of his early girlfriends. 'He thought that if a girl agreed on a date with him, it was a signal that she wanted to get her knickers off for him. Too often he could never accept that "No" meant just that.'

However, by the time he came of age, many wondered if he had calmed down when a local girl, Sylvia Marie McEwan, one of his neighbours, had agreed to become his wife and the couple were wed in Annan in 1968. Some of Sylvia's friends questioned whether she was not too young to wed a man who seemed a complex character and prone to moodiness if he failed to get his own way. At first, the couple appeared to be happy enough, especially when Sylvia gave birth to a boy and Little enjoyed helping raise his son. But his lust continued to linger. It lay dormant during the early years of married life, but then returned one night on a road near his home.

A young woman was walking home, passing a stretch of waste ground, when a maniac struck, throwing her to the ground, cruelly and harshly ordering her to take her clothes off and then savagely raping her. Sobbing and bloody, she blurted the name of her attacker to the police, David Little, and he was arrested. While he waited for his trial he was examined by doctors who found him sane but suffering from mental illness. When he appeared at the High Court in Edinburgh at the beginning of February 1971, Little pleaded guilty to charges of assault and rape and, after reading the doctors' reports, the Lord Justice Clerk, Lord Grant, decided he was sufficiently dangerous to be ordered to be detained Carstairs without limit of time. Sylvia had loyally visited her husband while he was in prison awaiting his sentence, but it was obvious to her and to friends of the couple that only misery could come from staying married to him, and so the marriage was ended. She went on to remarry.

In Carstairs, Little did his best to convince psychiatrists he was responding to treatment. He longed to be free and, while knowing there was no longer a future with Sylvia, still harboured hopes of finding another woman to share his bed. After four years in the State Hospital, he was adjudged to be no longer a menace and transferred to the more relaxed surrounds of the Crichton Royal Hospital in Dumfries. To prepare him for life back in the community, he was allowed an occasional day of freedom and it was during one of these releases – still technically on licence from Lord Grant's 'without limit of time' sentence – that he met and began chatting to a local girl who told him her name was Veronica Sharkey. Starved of a woman companion for almost five years, Little went back to his old charming ways. 'I'm in the car business,' he told Veronica, displaying all the patter of the successful second-hand car salesman. His words won her over, while he also convinced hospital staff he was cured. Little was discharged in 1976 and one of his first acts was to marry Veronica and the couple set up home in Dumfries. Marriage is a relationship in which trust is all important. Loving newlyweds should have no secrets from one another, but the bridegroom did not tell his new wife he was a convicted rapist who had spent four years locked up in Carstairs and was considered highly dangerous to women.

Was he really safe? Had the devils been banished from his head? Specialists decreed the answer to both was in the affirmative. But was that really the case? What happened next raises important questions about the Little case. There was no doubt he was a hard worker. He opened up his own garage and impressed customers with his skills. At home, however, the moodiness began to re-emerge. Then rumours began circulating that Little had a past he did not want carried the fourteen or so miles between Annan and his new home in the Lincluden area of Dumfries. It had been more than five years since the rape and, while some might have forgotten, plenty of others still remembered. Word reached Veronica who challenged her husband one day. 'Davie, have you ever been in prison?' she asked, and when he demanded to know why she wanted to know, she insisted:

'Well, have you?'

'No, I was in hospital.'

'Which one?'

'Carstairs.'

'Why were you there?'

'They said I raped somebody, now leave it.'

It was as though the questions had triggered off a jealous streak. He began resenting anyone who took an interest in Veronica. When she announced she was pregnant, he was offhand and at times violent and even brutal. His viciousness worsened after the birth of their daughter, Samantha, in 1977. At times, he bullied both mother and tiny baby, snatching his daughter from her cot and shaking her until his wife screamed for him to stop. Her reward for having tried to protect the child was for him to launch a horrific attack, kicking and punching her until she needed hospital treatment. She told doctors she had fallen, but injuries to her spine necessitated an operation and she was left with a limp.

When Veronica fell pregnant for a second time, his tempers became even more frightening. She had been carrying the baby for six months when, during yet another outburst of fury, he attacked her so violently, punching her in the stomach that she miscarried. Was his crazed mind enslaved by an insatiable lust for sex? She would later tell friends that during one of his outbursts he forced himself on her, ignoring her pleas that she was in terrible pain. Bored with the wife who had given him a child, he turned his unpredictability towards a teenage babysitter who had begun to attract him.

Soon after Samantha was born, Veronica had asked her friends if they could recommend a babysitter. One evening the daughter of a neighbour knocked at her door, offering to look after the baby. With her was attractive, dark-haired convent schoolgirl Elaine Freda Haggarty, who looked older than her then fifteen years. Elaine became a regular visitor to the Little home and as is so often the case when a budding, developing girl comes under the eye of an older, sexually experienced man, a bizarre and dangerous situation developed. Increasingly, Little turned his attentions to the girl. He arranged secret liaisons with her. At the same time, his wife was no fool, suspecting he had instigated an affair with the youngster and accusing him of cheating. Her charges enraged him to such an extent that twice he tried to throw her out and when that failed he warned her that unless she agreed to permit his blatant indiscretions he would vent his anger on little Samantha. 'Shut up or the next time you see your baby she'll be in a pine box,' he stormed.

Occasionally, during daytimes, he would disappear from his business. He began arriving home late in the evenings, coming up with lame excuses that he had been entertaining customers. At first, Elaine was flattered by his attention, flaunting her body before him even when she called at his home, unaware that her youth and naivety were leading down a sexual abyss at the bottom of which beckoned disaster and tragedy. At first she had been a willing, submissive sexual partner but as her confidence in her body grew she became more demanding, seeking to take control of the situation and of her lover. Matters came to a head when Elaine told the Littles she was pregnant and he boasted to Veronica that he was the father.

When he threatened to break off the affair, Elaine warned him she had secretly kept a diary, detailing the times and places of all their meetings. It was an attempt at emotional blackmail to which Little responded with violence, first turning his fury against her, then on his wife, breaking Veronica's nose. The outcome was that Elaine turned to Veronica for comfort and was met with open arms. The wife and mistress began a lesbian relationship that only further infuriated Little. Unable to cope with his violence any longer, Veronica demanded he leave. His response came in the form of punches to both women.

It was clear the marriage was breaking up. Little enquired about renting a local authority flat and, to strengthen his case and increase his chances of getting one, took Samantha with him and formally applied for custody of her. Veronica's response was to take her daughter home and begin divorce proceedings, while Elaine wrote to him saying, 'I'll never be happy as long as you are alive. Every night I pray that you are dead.'

While Little lived, the prospect of his violent and terrifying tantrums hung over the women. If he was out of the way, then both could continue with life together. Elaine was friendly with Territorial Army cadet William MacKenzie, eighteen, who had long made it plain he was attracted to her. More importantly, from the point of view of her and Veronica, MacKenzie had a frighteningly passionate interest in guns. She persuaded him to loan her and Veronica his .22 rifle, but when the pair practised with it, they succeeded only in accidentally pumping a bullet into the bed they had shared and it was clear they were incapable of firing it into a moving target. And so MacKenzie was seduced into the idea of killing Little by Elaine's talk of how he would earn a reputation as a contract hit man. Later he would boast that, as her contribution to his recruitment, Veronica had bedded him. Whatever the truth of that, he agreed to become a murderer. His fee would be £120, enough to pay for him to travel to the Far East to study martial arts.

On the night of 25 November 1981, Little called at the Lincluden home Elaine shared with her parents after she had asked to see him. MacKenzie was already waiting. He had made his preparations carefully, even to the extent of obtaining bullets washed in gold because he had been told these would be more effective, and as Little left the house, MacKenzie blasted him five times in the back and head. Elaine, who had followed Little, helped the gunman haul the body into a wheelbarrow that they pushed to Little's car, thrusting his corpse into the boot and driving to a lovers' lane five miles out of Dumfries. They left the body in a shallow grave beside a lay-by under a couple of sacks. The next day, a girl out riding her horse made the gruesome discovery of the dead man and galloped off to call police.

Once David Little had been identified as the victim, murder squad detectives at first wondered whether he might have been killed during a robbery because it was known that occasionally he carried large amounts of cash from his business. However, most murders have a domestic background and officers were soon knocking on Veronica's door. She feigned surprise when told her husband was dead. 'I'm shocked to hear that he died like this,' she told reporters. 'We parted five months ago and I had started divorce proceedings.' But her protestations of innocence were not to last long. Unable under the pressure of continued interrogation to stick to her story that she knew nothing, she began blaming MacKenzie who, in turn, pointed the finger of guilt at Elaine, telling officers who arrested him while he was taking part in a TA exercise, 'It was their idea and they were going to do it with my gun, but I had to do it.'

Veronica, aged thirty, Elaine, now seventeen, and MacKenzie were tried at the High Court in Dumfries in 1982. All three denied murder, MacKenzie lodging a special defence of incrimination which named Veronica. She had to be helped by court officials into the witness box when her turn came to give evidence about her husband's violence that had left her a cripple. 'It got worse after Samantha was born in October 1977,' she said. 'He seemed to resent her. Sometimes he was nasty to her. He would pick her up and shake her and once he said he would put her in a pine box.' She said that on the night she returned from hospital after suffering a miscarriage, Little had raped her.

She admitted opening a bank account in Elaine's name and that she had withdrawn £100 on the day of the killing. Asked what the money was for, she said, 'Elaine told me she wanted it for Christmas presents.' She denied asking MacKenzie to shoot her husband but agreed she wanted rid of him: 'I wanted peace from him. I was afraid of him.' She said she had been watching television on the night of the shooting and, at about 11pm, MacKenzie arrived and said, 'I have just killed David Little.' Veronica said, 'I told him not to be daft but when he came into the lobby I saw a bit of a rifle. I still didn't believe him and told him to get the gun out of here. I told Elaine to go and see because I still didn't believe him. When she came back she said, 'He's been shot, it's him' and then I believed her. MacKenzie said one of us would have to help shift the body and said if we didn't he would rope us into it.'

Their claims of innocence fell on deaf ears and all three were unanimously convicted of murder. MacKenzie was sent to a young offenders' institution for life and Elaine was ordered to be detained without limit of time. Spectators described how Veronica shook and sobbed as Lord Allanbridge jailed her for life, and as she left the dock she collapsed crying, 'God help me!' She had to be carried out of court before being driven off to Cornton Vale women's prison in Stirlingshire to begin her sentence. But this story of intrigue, deceit and horror does not end there. After Elaine was released on licence, she was unable to put the case behind her and began finding relief in drugs, so much so that she developed a serious addiction and died in 1999, aged just thirty-five. And so two people had died while the lives of two others were cocooned in a nightmare. But there are those who believe it could all have been avoided. A woman who spent time in prison alongside Veronica said:

> Many will think of her as evil, but at the end of the day this all happened because David Little was a violent man who obviously had a problem controlling his sexual urges. Rapists are usually sent to prison so for him to have been sent to Carstairs after the rape there

must have been very strong evidence that he had serious mental problems. There was a lot of sympathy for Veronica among the other women prisoners, and I wonder whether the blame for all of this lies at the door of those who decided to free David from Carstairs. If he had stayed there, he would not have been murdered and the others wouldn't have gone to prison. In Elaine's case, had she not met him she would have probably gone on to marry and have a loving family instead of a miserable death from drugs. How could any man be thought to be cured of mental illness when he then goes on to cripple his wife, beat up a girlfriend, rape his wife the day she has a miscarriage and threaten to kill his own baby daughter? After the case ended, there ought to have been an inquiry into whether the discharge of Little from Carstairs was a mistake and a very costly one at that.

30

SEX, DRUGS AND BLU-TACK

If ever a man made a mockery of Carstairs State Hospital, then that man was Noel Ruddle. He was a nasty, cowardly killer, made fools of staff and showed security to be a joke at the establishment, which had been specifically created to be the most secure in the land. The English-born menace was freed with what was effectively a licence to create fear and havoc because state lawyers simply weren't up to the job of making sure laws intended to protect the public did precisely that and because doctors weren't up to the task of finding treatments for those needing help. The Ruddle case is the story of a shambles.

On Saturday, 30 November 1991, Ruddle opened fire in the Glasgow Gorbals with a Russian-made Kalashnikov rifle that he said he had bought in a bar in the east end of the city, along with ammunition from a former Gulf War veteran. He had been drinking and would later claim voices in his head he knew as the 'evil set' ordered him to start shooting, but the terrible consequence was that when one of his neighbours, popular dad-of-three James McConville, aged thirty, called to see him, a shot rang out and James fell dead, blasted at point-blank range. It was only by sheer good luck that the death toll was not greater because Ruddle shot at a friend of the dead man, who managed to run off. The killer than started firing randomly at passers-by, cars and buildings from the balcony of his eighth-floor flat during an eight-hour siege before giving up to dozens of police officers, many of them armed. He was arrested and accused of murdering James, but, after being examined by psychiatrists, who came to the conclusion he was suffering from a mental disorder, it was decided to reduce the charge to one of culpable homicide.

When Ruddle appeared in the High Court in Glasgow the following March, he pleaded guilty to three offences under the Firearms Act, two of assault to danger of life, one of the culpable and reckless firing of a rifle to the danger of life and the culpable homicide of James. He was sent to the State Hospital without limit of time. In the outside world, memorable dramas were unfolding. A brief scene in the movie *Basic Instinct* in which knickerless Sharon Stone uncrossed and crossed her legs in front of Michael Douglas was creating a sensation. Scotland's Wet Wet Wet were storming up the music charts with 'Goodnight Girl'. Multi-talented entertainer Roy Castle was about to announce he was suffering from lung cancer. John Thaw was solving murders galore in Oxford in the *Inspector Morse* television series. Glasgow Rangers were on the verge of clinching the Scottish Premier League title. At Carstairs, staff were not to know their newest patient would make his own mark on the world. But not before some were left with red faces.

By a strange irony, Riddle's mother and father had both nursed in psychiatric hospitals. Born in late 1954, he had never been able to settle in the family's home with elder sister Bernadette and younger brother Brendan in Epsom, the Surrey town famous for its racecourse which hosts the annual Epsom Derby. In Carstairs, he boasted to other patients how, as a young man in his twenties, he had travelled abroad, through France and Spain. Some wondered if he was another Walter Mitty character, whose description of his exploits was occasionally unconvincing and might be coming from a fantasist. On the European mainland, he said he first began delving into soft drugs, chiefly LSD and cannabis, but, as is so often the case, these led him into the mad and frightening world of heroin. Drugs and booze helped him cope with spells of depression. Returning to Epsom, he was taken into hospital in 1982 after taking an overdose of an antidepressant drug, suffering from anxiety and depression and when he was released doctors reported he was suffering from 'personality disorder of the psychopathic type'.

His family hoped his problems might be solved when, at the age of thirty-one, he met a young woman named Jane and agreed to move with her to Scotland. At first, the couple lived on the Isle of Bute but then shifted their home to Glasgow. It was a volatile relationship. When he had been drinking, Ruddle tended to be violent, while Jane's depression, which arose from their not being able to have children together, resulted in her taking an overdose and needing hospital treatment. Unable to cope with his mood swings, she left him and now, living on his own, he relied even more on drink and drugs, landing minor drug-dealing convictions. It was in a booze-fuelled state that he became the killer of James McConville.

At Carstairs, he quickly became a minor 'Godfather' figure. The media had dubbed him the 'Kalashnikov Killer', a nickname in which he revelled. Ruddle was slick. Scots would say he had the 'gift of the gab', and, like some smooth-talking second-hand car salesman, he was easily able to impress not just the duller-minded patients around him but even some members of the hospital staff, and one in particular. His tales of exploits in the great cities of Europe, along with anecdotes of time spent in prison in England, left the impression that these were not the ramblings of a twisted mind, but of a big-time figure from the south of England underworld. These accounts did not go unnoticed by some among the medical staff who at one stage reported that Ruddle:

> continued to exhibit manipulative behaviour and to test the limits placed upon him. He could be dominating, abusive, intolerant and threatening to those he perceives as less capable. He threatened to attack a fellow patient if he was made to share the same dining table.

A report in 2000 by Lord Carloway on a claim by a former member of the Carstairs staff – we will simply name him 'Richard' but that is not his real name – for damages against the State Hospital went into detail about Ruddle because the claimant's dispute with the institution partly stemmed from an incident involving the Kalashnikov Killer. Describing Ruddle as a 'celebrated patient', Lord Carloway said he had originally been diagnosed as schizophrenic, but this was changed by one of the consultant psychiatrists to a psychopathic personality disorder due to alcohol and substance abuse:

> Mr Ruddle could become particularly dangerous if he secured access to drugs or alcohol. These could cause a relapse into paranoid schizophrenia. He was intelligent and a smooth talker who had to be observed very carefully because of his charming and manipulative manner. Although wearing a mask of sanity, this concealed a remorseless individual with no concern for others.

Had Richard been influenced by the Ruddle patter? During his early days at Carstairs, Ruddle had been held in Tinto Ward before being moved to Tay Ward. According to Lord Carloway's report, staff members had claimed Richard 'had secured favourable rooms for Mr Ruddle in both of these wards. In Tay Ward it was certainly the case that Mr Ruddle had managed to secure a room with private facilities.' A lot of the patients of both sexes wanted to be in Tay Ward because it held men and women. If a question mark remained over the possible influence Ruddle had over Richard, there was no doubt whatever about the hold he gradually took over a woman teacher at the hospital. We will refer to her only as 'Ms S'.

In December 1994, staff held the annual Christmas party for Tay Ward. It would lead to a scandal that rocked the State Hospital to its foundations and left taxpayers writing to newspapers demanding, yet again, 'What the hell is going on in there?' Lord Carloway stated:

> At the party, which started about 5pm, staff noticed after a while that three patients were behaving in a loud and uninhibited way. They were found to be under the influence of alcohol. The ward manager decided that the three patients should be returned to their rooms. This was achieved with two, but the third, a celebrated patient called Noel Ruddle, struck a member of staff and had to be restrained and kept in a 'safe' room. Drink is not permitted in the wards and a breach of that rule is regarded as a serious matter.
>
> The day after the episode, a ward search was carried out together

with intensive questioning of the patients. Certain items were found in Mr Ruddle's room. He was a particularly dangerous patient whose background as a dealer in illegal drugs had included homicide. In Mr Ruddle's room were found some legitimate medicines, alcohol in the form of at least two small lemonade bottles full of whisky, cans, glass bottles, batteries, tins, glue, Blu-tack and aerosols. Some of the items were on open view, but others concealed. Because of the number of items, it was clear that they had been accumulated over a period of some time. For that to have occurred, collusion with a member or members of staff was necessary . . . staff had frequent opportunities to see what was in a room since they required to attend at the rooms to open them up in the mornings and close them at night. Blu-tack was a problem because of its potential to take an imprint of a key. Glass bottles could be used as weapons. The discovery of alcohol was extremely serious especially when amphetamine sulphate (speed) was also found, this time in Mr Ruddle's paint box in the education block.

How had these highly incriminating and scary items got there? More importantly, who was smuggling them to Ruddle? Those searching the room would soon find the answers:

Letters were also found in the search disguised as lawyers' correspondence and contained in a shoebox in Mr Ruddle's locker. Access to these lockers could only be gained through a nurse who would have held the key. If the letters had been picked up by Mr Ruddle in the educational department then he would have still required the assistance of a member of staff to conceal them. If the letters had come in through the mail then they would have been read and registered by a member of staff.

The letters contained sexually explicit material and indicated that there was some form of intimate relationship formed between Mr Ruddle and Ms S. The existence of such a relationship between a patient and a member of staff was unheard of in the past and represented a considerable threat to security. The letters were from Ms S to Mr Ruddle and because of the volume involved [somewhere between

100 and 200] had accumulated over a period of between one year and eighteen months during which the relationship had been allowed to develop. Although the relationship had probably not involved sexual intercourse ... the content of the letters was such that Ms S would have 'done anything' for Mr Ruddle.

The contents of some of the love letters had been leaked to newspapers and as a consequence it was agreed they should be destroyed. Afterwards someone remembered one letter from the teacher to Ruddle included a phrase that caused special concern. One version was said to be that the teacher would need to give an unnamed member of staff 'a bung for allowing me to see your room'. Another version of the phrase was that the staff member should be thanked for 'letting us up to your room on that occasion'.

The teacher, who had been highly regarded for her work at the State Hospital, had no alternative but to resign. Richard was suspended while an investigation was carried out into whether he had encouraged and helped her and Ruddle to carry on their affair. Richard later left Carstairs and then began his legal action, winning a small amount of damages. Ruddle meantime gave psychiatrists increasing problems because his condition had undergone a remarkable improvement and they did not think they could make him any better. He was effectively untreatable, because there was no longer an illness to treat. It was decided in 1996 to transfer him to a special Personality Disorder Unit at Broadmoor Hospital.

Authorities there agreed to the move, which would take place when a bed became available in 1998 and would mean Ruddle being nearer his family in Surrey. However, a development that was to cause near panic in legal circles was about to take root. By agreeing to move him to Broadmoor because Carstairs couldn't treat him, the door was left open to his lawyer, Yvonne McKenna, to apply for him to be given his freedom. The law stated that if someone was untreatable then there were no grounds for keeping them locked up, and Ruddle, a callous killer and to many a danger, was untreatable.

Each year, patients could appeal against their continued detention in Carstairs. Usually they failed, and in 1999, despite the alteration in his condition, the government still refused to let Ruddle go. By now his attempt to go free was causing a media frenzy, much of it targeted on Yvonne McKenna, who was, after all, merely doing her job to the best of her ability. It was decided to appeal against the government refusal, a move that was so contentious it was one of the very first items to be discussed by the new Scottish Executive's cabinet.

The transfer to Broadmoor was put on hold until his appeal was heard by Sheriff Douglas Allan. Following days of evidence at Lanark, including that of five psychiatrists who agreed Ruddle was not receiving treatment at Carstairs that would change his condition, it was announced that:

> The Sheriff, having resumed consideration of the cause, and being satisfied that the applicant is not at the time of the hearing of this appeal suffering from mental disorder of a nature or degree which makes it appropriate for him to be liable to be detained in a hospital for medical treatment, directs the absolute discharge of the applicant as from this date.

Simply by using the law and exploiting a gap that government lawyers had failed to close, McKenna became an overnight target of hate. She was tagged a 'champion of child killers' but more often, 'the Devil's Advocate'. It was unfair and in an article in the *Journal of the Law Society of Scotland* in October 1999, she wrote:

> It has been suggested that I am 'cashing in' in attempting to 'win freedom for psychos'; arriving at Lanark Court in a £30,000 Mercedes. I have received hate mail. It seems the consensus of opinion is that I am to be criticised for carrying out my professional duties to the best of my ability.

As Ruddle left Carstairs, having served just seven years for killing a man and shooting at others, and headed back to his family in Surrey, the government were panicked into action as other high-profile insane murderers, among them Alexander Reid, the killer of Angela McCabe, were seeking to follow him to freedom. They rushed through new legislation designed to prevent any repetition. A change in the law – brought in with the excuse that it was meant to protect the public – would let courts rule a patient had to stay locked up even if he or she was not getting medical treatment.

Carstairs, already the target for criticism over security bungles that not only allowed Ruddle to receive contraband but also failed to spot his haul, now came under fire from the Mental Welfare Commission Scotland, which said Ruddle could have been treated and described the standard of management at Carstairs as poor. It insisted on an investigation into improving ways that security and medical experts worked together. The family of his victim asked reasonably why, if doctors could no longer do anything for Ruddle, he had not simply been transferred to prison. They pointed out, 'This makes a joke of the law,' and nobody disagreed.

Ruddle, meantime, was finding life on the outside of an institution more difficult than he thought. Just a few days after arriving in Surrey, his family made it plain to him he was not wanted and he called social workers to seek help. They placed him in a hostel while enquiries were made to find a permanent home for him. But the Kalashnikov Killer could just not stay out of trouble. In October 2000, just over a year after he was allowed to flee the confines of Carstairs, he telephoned a female social worker and told her he intended killing the local Roman Catholic priest. When she asked why, he said, 'Why not? I have done it before.' He claimed he wanted revenge for being abused by priests when he was younger. Police arrested him and he spent six months on remand before being given a three-year Community Rehabilitation Order. There was more to come.

In 2005, he was back in court after threatening to kill another man. The sentence was another Community Rehabilitation Order, this time to last eighteen months and in order to save him from prison his eighty-two-year-old mother had reluctantly agreed that he could have a room in her home. But on 19 March, only two days after the Order had come into effect, while drunk, he made an alarming telephone call to his sister. When she asked how he was, he told her:

How do you think I am? I can't cope here living with her. I would like to kill her. I seriously thought last night about killing her. It would save a lot of problems if we got the money from her property.

His sister called police and Ruddle was arrested. He was sentenced to 160 days in prison, but once again discovered there were advantages to appealing when he successfully applied to have the sentence reduced and the figure was shortened by forty days. His lawyer told the court, 'The threat was made through drink and without any intention of carrying it out. It was meant almost as a joke on his part. Unfortunately, because of his previous character, it was not taken as a joke by the police.' The Kalashnikov Killer, the man who might have led an exodus from Carstairs, was finally in a prison cell.

31

ONCE IN, NEVER OUT

Noel Ruddle was not the first inmate to want out of Carstairs. Men and women had been arguing why they ought to leave almost from the day the first patients arrived there. The excuses they gave and the methods they tried, in one case extreme and deadly, were many and varied. The escape from a psychiatric hospital in 1961 of Iain Simpson (Chapter 4), and particularly how managing to avoid recapture for twenty-eight days meant he could not be taken back, did not go unnoticed by others. Among those who read of Simpson's exploit was Dennis Garwood. He thought little of it at the time, but in 1963 was committed to Carstairs. His crime? He climbed over a wall and was trying to steal clothing from a washing line.

Normally it would have earned a mild rebuke, a fine or at worst a month or so in prison. But when he appeared in court, Garwood, who had a drink problem, threatened women witnesses. He was carted off to Carstairs at the age of thirty and remained there for nine years, regularly pleading in vain that he was sane and ought to be freed. He had never forgotten the Simpson case and when finally an opportunity to escape came he took it and after climbing to freedom vanished and kept low for more than a month in the south of England, by which time the authorities were forced to acknowledge he could not be recalled.

Garwood had made many friends among the other patients and had promised not to forget them. Once he was legally free he contacted the Scottish Council for Civil Liberties, claiming several other inmates were sane and should either be released altogether or moved to less secure psychiatric hospitals. The council arranged for a psychiatrist to examine Garwood and the doctor reported he was merely suffering from a mild personality disorder, a condition that in no way justified anyone being detained at Carstairs. At the time, the council insisted, 'What happened to Dennis Garwood must never be allowed to happen again.'

Eventually Dennis returned to Scotland and settled near Stranraer. He knew his rights. Having used them in 1972 by escaping to freedom, in 1999 he announced he was making full use of the services available on the NHS by seeking sex reassignment surgery costing £10,000. He told the *Sun* newspaper, 'It's not a waste of money. I've wanted to be a girl since I was a boy. I don't think I'm too old.' And his boyfriend revealed, 'When he gets dressed up he's pure woman. I treat him as I would a woman. He looks, thinks and acts like a woman.' Dennis's optimism wasn't shared. One politician complained, 'NHS cash is being wasted. I am aghast that while we pour money into operations for oddballs like him, we are neglecting hospital staff and the vital services needed by the majority of Scots.'

Like Dennis, James Kelly spent nine years in the Lanarkshire institution. But, unlike Garwood, he was guilty of no crime, had committed no offence. He was sent there in September 1997 after being dragged from his east end of Glasgow home by police who told him they had information that he had been associating with known criminals, which made him a danger to the public. It later emerged the information came from an anonymous telephone caller. One name thrown at him by the police was that of Paul Ferris, a leading figure in the Glasgow underworld who had been arrested in London four months earlier after a lengthy monitoring operation on his movements by MI5 and Special Branch officers. Weapons were discovered in Ferris's car and security specialists were concerned about possible connections to paramilitary organisations in Northern Ireland. Ferris was ultimately jailed for ten years, although this was reduced on appeal to seven.

Kelly's argument that knowing Ferris hardly made him a threat because many in Glasgow, including businessmen, journalists and police officers, were also friendly with him, fell on stony ground. He admitted having been jailed for two years when he was a teenager after being caught up in a drunken brawl but argued he was not a leading gangland personality. He also pointed out that most families in Glasgow knew someone with a criminal record. His detention was probably the result of his making regular trips to Ulster to support Glasgow flute bands and watch parades.

Kelly was initially taken to Leverndale Hospital in Glasgow under a section of the Mental Health (Scotland) Act 1984, and then transferred under heavy escort to Carstairs and detained under a Compulsory Treatment Order on the grounds that he had a mental illness. As soon as he entered, he began campaigning for his release, including writing to every one of Britain's MPs seeking their help. Around one third replied, sympathising. Ultimately he embarked on legal action, appealing against his continued detention and opposing regular renewals of the Compulsory Treatment Order, and was finally released in 2006, when he told the *News of the World* about his ordeal. He said:

After my arrival doctors at Carstairs said there were no grounds to justify my being kept with special security, yet nothing had been done to release me. My wife divorced me on the grounds of mental cruelty as I wasn't around to act as a husband or father to our two children. It was a living nightmare. There was a lot of violence and I was in constant fear of being killed by the psychos inside. I was attacked three times, saw men slashed and stabbed, and was forced to swallow 'treatment' pills that turned me into a zombie. Not a day passed when I didn't demand to be freed, but when I sued Carstairs over my injuries from the attacks, alleging the hospital failed to protect me, it was realised I was serious about wanting out.

Kelly lost his damages claim, but the hospital was forced to hand over reports that suggested he was not mentally ill. Shortly after this he was released.

Almost sixty years before Kelly's fight to show there was no justification for keeping him among seriously disturbed mental patients, supporters of a man named Francis Healy were demanding to know why he was being similarly detained. The case highlighted concerns over the way in which ordinary prisoners could be certified insane and sent to an asylum. Healy, a Glaswegian convict, had been treated in Gartloch Hospital to the east of Glasgow for a minor medical condition. In February 1938, a specialist there decided he had recovered and Healy, now sane and well, was moved to Perth prison to finish his sentence. Two months later, two prison doctors declared him insane and Healy was told he was being moved to Woodilee Hospital in Dunbartonshire. Realising that, once in an asylum, he might never get out, Healy was distressed and had to be dragged from the car taking him there by male nurses and warders. A number of Glasgow MPs were equally upset, pointing out that the diagnosis should have been made by an independent doctor.

Steven Wilson, too, discovered that once in an asylum, there was no guarantee of ever getting out. In his case it was argued that he had only himself to blame. His story is one of the strangest to come out of Carstairs. In 1988 Wilson, then aged twenty-three, was convicted at Knightsbridge Crown Court in London of manslaughter after he stabbed a friend to death in a drunken brawl outside a bar. He convinced psychiatrists he was insane and was ordered to be detained without limit of time in an asylum. Wilson would later claim he feigned mental illness and fooled the doctors because he believed he would have an easier time in a hospital than in prison. When he realised he might never be freed, he began insisting he should rightfully be in a jail. His demands were ignored and he found himself moving around some of the most notorious institutions in Britain.

From court he went to Broadmoor, and then to Ashworth, near Liverpool, where he rubbed shoulders with Moors murderer Ian Brady. To draw attention to his situation he went on hunger strike, but it only worsened his position because he was moved to Carstairs. There was plenty of support for him led by his childhood sweetheart Marilyn Wright and finally, in July 1999, following five months when he was allowed to stay midweek with Marilyn in their Glasgow flat, Wilson was fully released on conditional discharge from Carstairs. Marilyn was quick to point out, correctly, that had her man been sent to prison instead of an asylum, he would have been freed much sooner. She told newspapers, including the *News of the World*, 'I know Stephen is not mad. He has been in these mental institutions because of his own foolish scam. He is not a danger to society and never has been.'

During his liberty, Marilyn fell pregnant and would later give birth to a son, but the baby's father would miss his arrival. He was recalled to Carstairs for breaching the terms of his discharge. Mental health campaigners wondered why the authorities continued to hold him in the expensive high-security surroundings of the Lanarkshire institution. They pointed out that if he was ill, then he should not have been permitted day releases during which he could mingle with members of the public. Wilson himself was continuing to plead for a transfer to prison, which would then allow him to apply for parole. By 2007, he was once again being allowed day releases from the State Hospital only for him to abscond. He was at large for just a few days before police traced him and he was returned to Carstairs. At no time during his various days out had Wilson showed any signs of using violence and because he was assessed as not being a danger he was moved to the less restrictive surroundings of Leverndale Hospital. Clearly things here were considerably easier, for, unlike Carstairs, where letters and telephone calls were strictly censored and vetted, Wilson was able to call known prostitutes from Leverndale. So it was hardly surprising that when, following a long spell of day releases from Leverndale, he went missing in 2012. Police vice squad detectives searched the Glasgow red-light districts and quizzed hookers over what they knew of Wilson. Two of the women were suspected of knowing where he was lying low but refused to cooperate. Two weeks after he disappeared, Wilson was tracked down by police to an address in Ayrshire.

His spell of illicit freedom caused a major row. He had vanished on 30 March, but politicians criticised the authorities when they were appealing for information as to his whereabouts, for waiting more than two weeks to confirm he had killed a man. The government was accused of trying to hide Wilson's history. But friends of the runaway were quick to remind the critics he had not been accused of any violent acts since his conviction in London almost a quarter of a century earlier.

Steven Wilson tried escaping to highlight his argument that he should not be in an asylum, least of all Carstairs. The attempt by Charles Reid Wawrynkiewiez to win a discharge was unique indeed. In June 1970, the appeal court in Edinburgh was told that a letter written by Wawrynkiewiez from Carstairs was so well formed and articulate that it could only have been penned by someone who was sane. Wawrynkiewiez, it was said, was entitled to have doctors carry out more examinations to find out just what his mental condition was. His counsel said tests would show there was no need for his continued detention in Carstairs. Instead, the sentence that he was to be detained there should be amended to one of prison or even a fine.

Wawrynkiewiez had been convicted by a jury in Glasgow of assault with intent to ravish. Following the evidence of two psychiatrists that he was suffering from mental illness and the public had to be protected from him, he was sent to Carstairs without limit of time. Fearing he might spend the rest of his life there, Wawrynkiewiez was desperate to be allowed to leave. One of the psychiatrists had stated the offender had the mental age of a seven-year-old, the other of a boy of ten or eleven. But after arriving at Carstairs, Wawrynkiewiez had written to his solicitors asking for his sentence to be reviewed and his counsel described his letter as 'both clever and articulate'. Checks had been made to make sure Wawrynkiewiez and nobody else had been the author of the communication. Could that letter have been written by somebody suffering from such a severe mental condition that it was felt they needed to be sent to the State Hospital? He asked the appeal court to seek the opinion of a third psychiatrist on his condition. But three appeal judges turned down the plea, saying they did not think the letter, however well it was written, was enough reason to overturn the view of the two psychiatrists.

Three years later, lawyers for James Moore argued before a sheriff that, as with Wawrynkiewiez, his condition had not been fully investigated and this contradicted the rules of natural justice. The background was that in 1963, Moore had been convicted of assaulting his wife and, based on reports by psychiatrists, was sent to

Carstairs, where he stayed for three years before being released and given his freedom provided he behaved himself and stayed at an agreed address.

In August 1963 at Glasgow Sheriff Court, Moore was convicted of wife assault and detained at Carstairs under Section 35 of the Mental Health (Scotland) Act 1960. A further order was made under Section 60 of the Act whereby Moore was the subject of special restrictions. However, in 1971, Moore was recalled and sent to another psychiatric hospital. His legal team argued that his mental state had not been properly looked into and, unless this was done, it was wrong to continue to detain him. The sheriff threw out Moore's plea and, in doing so, raised the hackles of civil rights campaigners because he said Moore wasn't entitled to put forward evidence about his condition because by being sent to Carstairs under mental health legislation he had lost the rights normally due to a free man. What was even more surprising about the sheriff's ruling was that, after his recall, two doctors who examined Moore concluded there was no need to keep him in a mental hospital, yet the government had not bothered to read their report. The result, said his lawyers, was that Moore had been refused the chance to have 'a fair and equal hearing' under the rules of natural justice.

The case left many feeling that once government psychiatrists decided a man or woman was mentally ill, then the individual lost any rights to challenge their findings – that the stakes were weighed totally in favour of the state. The feeling that psychiatrists were given almost godlike status, that their word was sacrosanct and not to be challenged, was not new. It was a view that had surfaced in 1967 when George James McGerrachan, aged twenty-eight, was called into the office of a governor at Barlinnie prison and told he was being transferred to Carstairs. McGerrachan had been arrested and accused of assault. Shortly after he was detained, he was examined by doctors, who said he was not unfit to plead, and when he admitted the offence, he was sentenced to three months' imprisonment. He could have expected to be back walking the streets a free man in just a few weeks. However, in Barlinnie, two psychiatrists examined him and decided he was insane. Their report was sent to the Secretary of State for Scotland, who automatically agreed and, as a result, McGerrachan found himself waiting for a van to take him to Carstairs. It was what amounted to a potential life sentence because unless doctors said he had recovered he would never get out.

His lawyer appealed against the ruling that he should go to Carstairs, arguing that the Secretary of State had simply rubber-stamped the decision of the two psychiatrists while McGerrachan had never had the chance to have his say. 'I think this decision was unfair,' said the lawyer. 'He might be kept under sedation at Carstairs for the rest of his life like some kind of human vegetable. He had no opportunity of making any statement on his own behalf.' One of the psychiatrists had told the court, 'He is a schizophrenic and could become violent with alcohol. While awaiting his trial he attacked a warder.' But McGerrachan was not asked whether any of this was true. He lost his appeal and the sheriff who gave the ruling said:

> One of the grounds of the appeal was that McGerrachan was unable to make a statement on his own behalf after the decision to transfer him from Barlinnie to Carstairs. There is no stipulation in the Act that this opportunity should be granted by the Secretary of State. There is ample provision for appeal within the Act.

Once again, civil rights supporters were angered, arguing the government had deprived a citizen of the right of free speech. Allegations persist that Carstairs is consistently at the centre of complaints that patients are deprived of their human rights. The case in 2002 of Darren Crichton emphasised huge failings in the system created for the treatment of patients with mental illness. At the age of just seventeen, he had been sent to the State Hospital, but his condition quickly improved and doctors recommended his discharge. However, despite fervent campaigning by his parents for their son to be freed, he was still in Carstairs three years later, the argument being that he had to remain there as there was nowhere else adequate for him to go. His case was one examined by the Scottish Health Advisory Service, which said that, at any one time, up to forty patients at the State Hospital were in the same limbo-type position.

Thomas Docherty found himself in Carstairs for a similar reason, but in his case he had done nothing wrong. In February 1980, the body of Tracey Main, aged thirteen, was found at her home in the Glasgow Gorbals. While her parents were at work, a killer had stabbed her seven times in the chest and strangled the schoolgirl. Docherty, a neighbour with the mental age of eight, was accused of her murder and in June went on trial at the High Court in Glasgow. He denied the charge but the jury was directed to clear him after a detective admitted he had failed to inform Docherty of his right to say nothing once he had been cautioned. There were angry scenes outside the court and, for his own safety, Docherty, who was within his rights to return home, was advised to stay in a cell while his lawyer, Joe Beltrami, pondered what to do.

It was obvious from the chanting of the baying crowd that Docherty could not go to the Gorbals, or into a hotel or hostel. Beltrami and his staff, together with social workers, frantically telephoned throughout Scotland and the north of England searching for somewhere to accommodate forty-one-year-old Docherty but had to admit defeat. Eventually it was realised the only place he could go was to Carstairs. As a result, he was placed in the State Hospital – the only patient there not insane, potentially violent or a danger to the rest of society.

32

A LOVER OF NUDES

The young woman was smiling, happily confident she had found another customer for the paintings she sold door-to-door. The man she was visiting had shown a keen interest in seeing works depicting female nudes and had promised to have the necessary cash when she called. But what happened after he invited her into his home would be imprinted on her mind for the rest of her life, as she was terrorised and made the victim of multiple rape by a sexual deviant who, despite being classed as being a high risk to reoffend, had been released from the State Hospital and was supposed to be under close supervision by police and social workers.

His victim had gone innocently to the flat of Sean McKay, aged forty, after a chance meeting in an Edinburgh cafe when he had said he would buy a painting he was shown of a naked female. But once inside she suddenly found her customer producing not money but a knife. 'People are following me. They want to do bad things to me,' he said, pushing her into a bedroom. At his later trial in 2008, when he admitted abduction and rape, the prosecution detailed the full horror of her thirteen-hour ordeal before police rescued her. 'He told her to do as he told her, or he would cut her head and then kill himself because he had nothing to lose,' said Mr Alex Prentice, QC. 'She replied that she would do anything he wanted so long as he didn't hurt her.'

She was raped twice, then McKay let her ring her boss, who guessed something was wrong and called police. The rapist's plan was to lure officers to the flat in Edinburgh, kill one and then commit suicide. Even after the flat was surrounded by the police, McKay raped her twice more. By 10am the next morning, exhausted, he fell asleep and his victim scrawled, 'Force the door' in condensation on the window to a watching policeman and, moments later, his colleagues burst in and rescued the traumatised young woman.

Could her nightmare have been avoided? McKay was a schizophrenic and known sex terror. He had been jailed in 1991 for five years after another siege and for sexually assaulting a schoolboy. In 1996, he took a boy of sixteen prisoner in a flat and was jailed for eight years for indecency. He had been a patient at Carstairs and at another mental hospital, was a registered sex offender with a long history of mental problems and was supposed to be monitored. Like other mental patients, when he was released, he was put on a course of medication. Just a few days before he put the woman in Edinburgh through hell, he had told a psychiatrist he was hearing voices and felt stressed. And he had stopped taking tablets prescribed to calm him. But no one was there to make sure he did what doctors had ordered because police and others had no authority to force him to stick to his course of treatment. Experts said his condition could get much worse under extreme stress and in prison he had been placed on suicide watch. McKay didn't even hear what was said in court. He let his lawyer apologise on his behalf and pass on his 'shame and regret that the offences occurred'. He was given a life jail sentence and told he would stay in prison for at least nine years and, even after his release, would be supervised until the day he died.

Just what had gone wrong? Who was responsible for allowing a man to leave Carstairs and then perpetrate a despicable crime, polluting the life of a decent young woman? No one was answering these questions. Appallingly, just as of other crimes, instances of rape or sex attack by former inmates are scattered through the Carstairs story. But does anyone in authority learn from these? In 1974 the *Daily Express* newspaper wondered:

> Is it not the case that too many people are already getting out of Carstairs long before they are ready for release? Are they all cured when they are released? Evidently not. Some, even among the most

dangerous – the killers and rapists – are being released prematurely. We expect doctors to be dedicated to their patients, especially doctors with such difficult patients as those in Carstairs. But we expect doctors also to display their concern for the public. Current evidence points to a disparity in these duties.

What had prompted the newspaper to make what most saw as reasonable points was an appalling case reported in the *News of the World* in late May 1974. The article read:

William Fyfe was given a chance by a mental hospital where he had been sent after raping a girl nine years before. It meant weekend passes to stay with his parents and a gradual return to normal life. But there was nothing normal about what happened on a quiet road near Cowdenbeath, Fife, at midnight. A fifteen-year-old girl walking home alone after a dance heard footsteps behind her. She turned and saw twenty-eight-year-old Fyfe approaching. He put his hand over her mouth and dragged her across the road to a partly built house. He ripped a polythene cover from a window and pushed the girl into the house. Then he threatened her, banged her head on the ground and hit her. The sobbing girl told Dundee High Court that Fyfe forced her to make love three times. When he left her he told her not to follow him. But later she told police and identified Fyfe.

Fyfe was found guilty of assaulting and ravishing the girl and jailed for six years.

Nine years earlier, at Edinburgh, Fyfe had been found guilty of rape, robbery and attempted rape. He had been sent to Carstairs without limit of time but doctors there had eventually persuaded the Secretary of State for Scotland that, because his condition had improved, he could be released and moved to the more open Bangour Village Hospital, from where he was allowed to spend weekends with his family. After his conviction for the disgraceful attack on the youngster at Cowdenbeath, the Advocate Depute, Donald Macaulay, had told the judge, Lord Stott, 'This is a serious situation. You may feel there should have been some form of supervision.' It was a suggestion echoed in a number of newspapers, the *News of the World* commenting, 'The public must wonder if there are any more ex-Carstairs patients enjoying similar freedom and if their supervision is as loose. This is a case for a rapid and short inquiry.'

Just three months later came another case in which a psychiatric hospital had allowed a convicted sex offender freedom to commit a vile attack on another youngster. This time it wasn't Carstairs, although that was where James Sinclair would end up, but Lynebank Hospital in Dunfermline. And once more calls would come for something to be done, although now the government, becoming uneasy at the strength of public feeling over the way in which the perpetrators of vile crimes against the young were able to get freedom to cause more distress, would finally act. What made this case so dreadful was that Sinclair's victim had been forced to suffer her ordeal because of an official bungle.

Married with two children, cinema attendant Sinclair had appeared at Kirkcaldy Sherrif Court in Fife, where he pleaded guilty to raping a twelve-year-old girl from the Edinburgh area while she was on a Sunday school picnic. It was a dreadful story, but after the facts were known, there was even more that gave rise to anger. The youngster had been with her mother and was sitting alone when Sinclair approached and sat with her. When she said she wanted to rejoin her mum, he told her to stay where she was and when she jumped up and began running off he gave chase, caught her, pushed her to the ground and raped her. That was bad enough, but in July 1972 Sinclair had been committed by a court order to Lynebank for indecent exposure and assault. He already had a number of previous convictions. In June 1973, he was given a leave of absence during which he committed a sexual offence on a girl aged four. He was sent back to the same hospital under a new order, but six months later allowed to discharge himself as the result of a technical mix-up. The result was a nightmare for a little girl enjoying herself on an outing with her mother.

What had gone wrong? A Glasgow MP demanded an investigation, pointing out that, 'A young child has gone through agonies because of what happened.' The Secretary of State for Scotland at that time was William Ross and he ordered a report. Lynebank Hospital blamed the Mental Welfare Commission for Scotland, which, in turn, said it was all the fault of the hospital's carelessness. So how was Sinclair able to walk out and attack the child? According to the commission, the hospital should have gone to a sheriff to have the new order, following the June 1973 incident, confirmed within twenty-one days. But that had not been done and it meant Sinclair was technically a voluntary patient being detained illegally and nobody could stop him leaving. Why wasn't it done?

The hospital claimed the commission had said this wasn't necessary. The commission hit back, saying that wasn't the case – that it had told the hospital to have the order confirmed. In turn, the hospital said that when the commission pointed out there was no confirmation of the order it was forced to agree that Sinclair was being detained illegally. A hospital psychiatrist said Sinclair had been responding well to treatment until it was discovered he could not be detained. 'I don't think we would have discharged this man if left to our own resources,' he said. Back came the commission with a statement:

> When it was found that the legal requirements for detention had not been complied with, the hospital were advised of this and it was left to them to decide what action they proposed to take to rectify the matter. They decided to take no steps to have his compulsory detention renewed. It is incorrect to say that the Commission decided Sinclair was officially fit to be released.

What happened next to Sinclair was hardly reassuring. He was sent to Carstairs without limit of time, and the State Hospital would shortly be again in the firing line.

In July 1975, James Sharp, aged thirty-six from Clydebank, was jailed for eight years after a trial at the High Court in Glasgow for the horrific rape of an old-age pensioner. He and another younger man had attacked their female victim in her home, repeatedly violating her and then stealing from her before they fled. She was seventy-three years old and was raped three times. Sharp's protestations of innocence, during which he claimed, 'I am pure and innocent of these charges,' did not impress the jury, who convicted him. The court was told he had thirty-nine previous convictions. That was remarkable enough but what made headlines was the revelation that Sharp, who had an IQ of sixty-four, had spent seven years as a patient at the State Hospital. The circumstances under which he was allowed to leave were sensational.

He had been sent there in 1957 and reports described him as a difficult patient, a feeble-minded defective, who appeared to get no improvement from his treatment. From time to time, he was released on licence but his conduct caused trouble and he was always sent back within two months. Finally in 1964, when the State Hospital's board of management discussed his case, it was decided to give him an absolute discharge, allowing him total freedom. The decision was taken even though the board believed that while Sharp was not felt to be dangerous or violent, he would continue to get into trouble. It was left to the judge, Lord Stott, to show sympathy for the victim: 'I cannot regard this as a case where leniency is possible. An old lady's home has been invaded and she has been outraged.'

33

SMOKING MAD

So, what does go on at Carstairs? In 2004, the *News of the World* published the first part of an investigation into goings-on inside the State Hospital. Desperate to prevent more articles appearing, lawyers acting for the institution went to court to seek an interdict banning further publication on the grounds that the newspaper had been helped in its enquiries by a former State Hospital nurse. The hospital was prepared to use cash intended to treat seriously demented, highly dangerous criminals in order to stop information about its internal workings reaching the public. Challenging the action would have run up a huge legal bill for both sides and the newspaper, deciding the hospital should be spending its money on patients and not lawyers, backed down. The action taken by the institution, however, demonstrated why suspicions continue as to what goes on within its walls.

What actually does go on is clearly a touchy subject as far as those managing Carstairs are concerned. The hospital declined to discuss, for the purposes of this book, how patients are treated. Is it still smarting over a 1968 House of Commons estimates committee private hearing at the State Hospital into allegations of staff brutality? Evidence was taken from some patients and hospital workers including nurses, one of whom said that handling patients was easy, but dealing with relatives difficult. Sometimes staff were targeted by claims they trained at Belsen, the Nazi concentration camp, or were likened to Gestapo officers. Workers were cleared of wrongdoing but one former patient has told this author that some patients believed they were used as guinea pigs for experiments by doctors. There is no way of checking whether this is or has been the case.

Methods used to treat the mad have, in some instances, been little other than barbaric, including: electroconvulsive therapy, ECT, better known as shock treatment in which electric currents induce seizures; patients being dumped in scalding hot baths and then immersed in freezing cold water; black draught that involved lunatics being dosed with a saline mixture more commonly given to animals as a laxative, the theory being that the devastating results on a human being would purge an afflicted lunatic of the devils that caused their madness; sodium pentothal, better known as the truth drug; and lobotomy, involving the surgical removal of part of the brain. No one can say whether any of these devastating attempts at remedy have been or are used at Carstairs and by its refusal to discuss the treatments it has and does use, the State Hospital has naively imposed censorship upon itself.

A former patient has listed some drugs he says were induced into him and these include chlorpromazine hydrochloride, stelazine, phenelzine and modecate. The patient said, 'Most of the time I was at Carstairs I felt the world around me wasn't real, I was like a zombie and I didn't know what these drugs were supposed to be doing for me.' Some treatments now concentrate on group therapy under the guidance of psychiatrists, but the efficacy of these kind of treatments is not yet certain.

Since the first patients entered Carstairs, staff have faced accusations that inmates are ill treated. Regrettably, such complaints are a part of the job and investigations invariably show they have no substance, but the fact is that among some patients, distrust and suspicion remain, and secrecy is a breeding ground for doubt. A classic example is the death in July 1974 of Alexander Shepherd, aged thirty-eight, from Airth, Stirlingshire. He was a schizophrenic who had ended up in the State Hospital five years earlier after assaults on police officers. The patient died in a padded cell and leaks from the hospital suggested the tragedy occurred while he was being given medication. A particularly cruel feature of the man's death was that, after being given the heart-breaking news, his parents, Alex senior and mum Janet, were not allowed to see his body or to be even told where his corpse had been taken. The dead man's father was reported in the media as having said, 'We had come to accept he was a schizophrenic, but we cannot accept the secrecy over his death.'

A fellow inmate of the dead man has given a different version to that leaked from Carstairs, but for legal reasons we are prevented from giving his full account. However, it includes this: 'He had assaulted a male nurse and was placed, naked, into a padded cell . . . Male nurses then went in . . . I saw the body, draped with a bed sheet being slid into a police van.' A fatal accident inquiry later cleared anyone of wrongdoing, but the fact remained that a patient sent to hospital for his and the public's protection had died while in custody.

Arnold McCardle had a number of friends in the vibrant and dangerous Glasgow underworld. He was well liked, but clearly unwell when he appeared in the city's Sherrif Court in 2002 to face a breach of the peace and firearms charges after waving a gun and an axe at a drugs crisis centre. While in the dock, he slashed his throat. He had made allegations linking a senior police officer to drugs dealers. Arnold was sent to Carstairs. In December 2003 appeal court judges ruled he had been illegally detained and freed him. Instead he was taken back to Carstairs by staff who said an order for his continued detention had been granted the previous day. The following May, he wrote to a psychiatrist in Carstairs, saying, 'I have made it absolutely clear that I have the steadfast belief I was sent here to be silenced, perhaps murdered.' He was dead seven months later.

His family was told he had died on Boxing Day after collapsing from a heart attack. Friends who saw Arnold in his coffin were shocked by the sight of terrible facial and head injuries but the authorities refused to allow a full copy of the post-mortem report to be made available. More than a year later, a fatal accident inquiry determined he died of natural causes, but the withholding of the full contents of the report left his friends wondering about the reason for the secrecy. Like so many before him and others since, Arnold feared he would never escape the invisible shackles doctors at Carstairs placed around him by diagnosing him as mentally sick. He used the law to try re-entering normal society, a strategy to which other patients have turned for reasons that to taxpayers might appear at best frivolous. When specialists decided, in 2011, that the majority of patients were overweight largely due to visitors bringing in junk food and fizzy drinks and needed to slim down, hospital management ordered a ban on these treats and placed restrictions on the supply of takeaway meals from outside to patients.

The response from one inmate, Clifford Lyons, was to use legal aid to challenge the ruling on grounds that he needed the likes of chocolate bars and fizzy drinks such as Lucozade as part of a rigorous fitness programme. Hardly surprisingly, Lyons' move did not go down well in some quarters when it emerged he had been granted legal aid to pursue his case. The reason why he was in Carstairs only increased the controversy. In 1990, he had been accused of raping a girl aged ten, pouncing on the youngster as she crossed a field near his Drumchapel home to visit her grandmother. He was on bail, at the time, for another sex offence and was ordered to be detained in Carstairs.

Lyons complained the junk food and drinks ban infringed his human rights and, in a written judgement, Lady Dorrian came down in his favour, declaring that management had not kept patients sufficiently in the picture and casting doubt on claims by staff that a survey showed a majority of patients favoured the proposed changes. She said, 'It is highly questionable whether even such feedback as was obtained was properly put before the board. The summary of the feedback was incomplete and in some respects incorrect.' Was this another example of the hospital shooting itself in the foot through its habit of proceeding without consulting?

Management had another ban challenged that year. In common with many institutions it banned smoking and the possession of tobacco throughout the hospital and in its grounds. Schizophrenic Charles McCann, who had been detained at Carstairs for eighteen years, fought the ban, complaining it had infringed his human rights as a patient and prevented him enjoying what was said to be a forty-a-day habit. In 2013, by when he had been transferred to another psychiatric hospital, he claimed £3,000 compensation, although a judge at the Court of Session in Edinburgh, who agreed with 'a degree of reluctance' that his human rights had been breached, refused to award him any money, pointing out that by not being allowed to smoke at Carstairs, McCann had already saved £8,000. However, in 2014, McCann was forced to stub out his smokes when the hospital won an appeal, with the Lord Justice Clerk, Lord Carloway, announcing, 'The decision about whether patients, or staff and visitors, should be permitted to smoke within the boundaries of the State Hospital was, and is, one of management.'

A ban of a very different nature upset Carstairs patient John Johnstone in 2007. In 1991, he had married girlfriend Hazel McQuarrie at Kilsyth, Lanarkshire, but six years later was arrested and charged with the terrible murder of Lizzie Duffy, aged twenty-seven. Johnstone had arrived at the door of Lizzie's sixth-floor flat in Royston, Glasgow, and, after a vile sexual abuse of the young woman, threw her naked body out of the window to her death. CCTV footage showed the killer actually smirking as he was spotted walking past her crumpled body. Two psychiatrists confirmed he was a danger to the public and suffering from mental illness and at his trial in 1998, the prosecution allowed him to plead guilty to culpable homicide on the grounds that his responsibility was diminished.

The outcome was his being sent to Carstairs without a time limit, a punishment that meant he could no longer have sex with Hazel. Her visits to him were strictly supervised, with staff watching their every move. The total lack of privacy was the excuse Johnstone made for his decision to end the marriage in 2007, even though Hazel wanted it to continue. From his comfortable room in the State Hospital, Johnstone arranged a divorce and disappointed Hazel received the decree nisi, despite tearfully pleading she wanted to remain his wife. Had Johnstone an ulterior motive? In 2013, he appealed against his continued detention at Carstairs, claiming he had set out to fool the psychiatrists because he felt he would be treated less harshly if he were thought to be mad. It was a familiar claim and, like others who had used it, Johnstone found it did not impress when he went to court pleading to be allowed to transfer to a prison. His request was thrown out.

Johnstone was at least allowed a brief excursion to go shopping, but accompanied by hospital minders. These short releases, even under escort, regularly resulted in controversy when the media discovered them, with critics arguing that if psychiatrists had said patients were too dangerous to be sent to a prison where they would legally be entitled to know the maximum period they would serve before being entitled to be free, then even a few hours of liberty was putting the community at risk. These brief excursions into public places were never justified. Nobody was willing to explain what was the point of giving patients who had committed terrible acts an expensive few hours of freedom to usually wander around busy shopping centres or recreational facilities among women and children. One argument against these jaunts was that the families of victims were not given the opportunity to express a view and ensure there would never be a chance of them coming face to face with someone who had caused them such distress and pain.

One particularly disturbing case was that of Robert Robb. In 1974, he had been jailed for eighteen months for assault involving an attempted strangulation. He finished that sentence but three years later was sentenced to ten years in prison for the culpable homicide of neighbour Margaret Norman, aged seventy-one, after it was decided he had been suffering from diminished responsibility. He had tried to have sex with Miss Norman, not realising she was already dead. Just a few months after being freed early for good behaviour in 1984, he killed again. This time his victim was respectable, well-liked Frances Mould, wife of a senior local government official. She had gone berry picking near her Falkirk home when Robb pounced, raping the defenceless woman before strangling her with his tie. Sickeningly, Robb claimed Mrs Mould had consented to have sex with him, but he was convicted of her rape and murder. Was this the work of a madman? Two psychiatrists found him sane and fit to plead although one doctor believed he was suffering from severe personality disorder and warned, 'I consider him to be an extremely dangerous man, especially to women.'

Jailing him for twenty years for murder and twelve years for rape, the judge, Lord Brand, said:

> You have been convicted of two crimes, which are so appalling they defy description. All I can do is express the court's sympathy for the family of the deceased lady. It is quite clear you are a public menace and a menace in particular to women. There is not the slightest element of excuse which can be put forward for the acts of which you have been convicted.

In 1988, because of concerns over his mental state, Robb was transferred from prison to Carstairs. But only four years later, he was allowed out of the State Hospital to visit a relative and go sightseeing. Bearing in mind the comments of one of the psychiatrists and the judge, it was hardly surprising that an MP described these jaunts as 'almost incredible'.

Even more controversial has been the freedom granted to Michael Ferguson, who was ordered to be detained in the State Hospital without any time limit in 1994 for slashing a man in a doctors' surgery, scarring his victim for life. A psychiatrist warned at the time he was dangerous and prone to delusions. At Carstairs, he was a troublesome patient. In 1997, he attacked a charge nurse and a female staff nurse and a year later tried escaping from a hospital in Lanarkshire, where he had gone from Carstairs for treatment, by jumping through a window. He was recaptured and sent back to the State Hospital. In 1998, he threatened to throw acid into the face of his doctor.

The following year, Ferguson failed in a legal attempt to be moved away from Carstairs, with a report on his plea hearing stating Ferguson, 'has displayed a very unstable and deteriorated pattern of behaviour when at liberty and, associated with this behaviour pattern, has a long history of alcohol and drug abuse, including benzodiazepines, amphetamines and heroin'. Part of his claim was that he had pretended to be mentally ill to avoid going to jail. In 2001, he climbed on to a roof at the hospital and threw slates at those trying to bring him down. He said he was protesting against the refusal of management to let him move to a psychiatric hospital in Ayr so he could be nearer his fiancée.

Remarkably three years after this incident, staff at Carstairs let him go off on his own with a mobile telephone and £250 of his own money on a shopping expedition, during which he was due to meet up with his bride-to-be. He failed to return. Police had to drop other duties to hunt for him. The public was warned he could be dangerous, especially if he began drinking, which raised questions from politicians as to why, if that was the case, he had been allowed out. Three days later, he was spotted in an off-licence and returned to Carstairs.

Two more applications for his discharge, in 2005 and 2006, failed but finally, in 2011, he was released, only to be returned to the State Hospital shortly afterwards following an alleged incident outside a nightclub. Another release in 2012 proved equally short lived because as the result of a police report he was sent back. However, his discharge was not far off, as doctors said he had been cured of his mental sickness. How could they be sure? So many times in the past, patients had been given the all-clear only to commit the most terrible crimes, as our story has shown.

Perhaps those running this extraordinarily expensive NHS facility should hang in their consulting rooms and offices this extract from a talk given by Carstairs psychiatrist John Gotea-Loweg to the annual conference at Peebles of the Scottish Association for the Study of Delinquency and remind themselves of it before making decisions concerning the release of inmates. The State Hospital, he assured delegates, was 'A very peaceful place with little or no violence.' The date was 13 November 1976. Seventeen days later, Thomas McCulloch and Robert Mone escaped, brutally slaughtering three men.